**Rhetoric & Composition**
PhD Program

## PROGRAM
Pioneering program honoring the rhetorical tradition through scholarly innovation, excellent job placement record, well-endowed library, state-of-the-art New Media Writing Studio, and graduate certificates in new media and women's studies.

## TEACHING
1-1 teaching loads, small classes, extensive pedagogy and technology training, and administrative fellowships in writing program administration and new media.

## FACULTY
Nationally recognized teacher-scholars in history of rhetoric, modern rhetoric, women's rhetoric, digital rhetoric, composition studies, and writing program administration.

## FUNDING
Generous four-year graduate instructorships, competitive stipends, travel support, and several prestigious fellowship opportunities.

## EXPERIENCE
Mid-sized liberal arts university setting nestled in the vibrant, culturally-rich Dallas-Fort Worth metroplex.

### English
DEPARTMENT
Contact Dr. Mona Narain
m.narain@tcu.edu
eng.tcu.edu

# composition STUDIES

Volume 45, Number 2
Fall 2017

**Editor**
Laura R. Micciche

**Book Review Editor**
Kelly Kinney

**Editorial Assistants**
Kelly Blewett
Christiane Boehr
Ian Golding
Christina M. LaVecchia
Janine Morris

**Former Editors**
Gary Tate
Robert Mayberry
Christina Murphy
Peter Vandenberg
Ann George
Carrie Leverenz
Brad E. Lucas
Jennifer Clary-Lemon

**Advisory Board**
Sheila Carter-Tod
*Virginia Tech University*

Elías Domínguez Barajas
*University of Arkansas*

Qwo-Li Driskill
*Oregon State University*

Susan Martens
*Missouri Western State University*

Aja Y. Martinez
*Syracuse University*

Michael McCamley
*University of Delaware*

Jessica Nastal-Dema
*Prairie State College*

Annette Harris Powell
*Bellarmine University*

Melissa Berry Pearson
*Northeastern University*

Margaret Price
*The Ohio State University*

Jessica Restaino
*Montclair State University*

Donnie Sackey
*Wayne State University*

Christopher Schroeder
*Northeastern Illinois University*

Darci Thoune
*University of Wisconsin-La Crosse*

## SUBSCRIPTIONS

*Composition Studies* is published twice each year (May and November). Annual subscription rates: Individuals $25 (Domestic), $30 (International), and $15 (Students). To subsccribe online, please visit http://www.uc.edu/journals/composition-studies/subscriptions.html.

## BACK ISSUES

Back issues, five years prior to the present, are freely accessible on our website at http://www.uc.edu/journals/composition-studies/issues/archives.html. If you don't see what you're looking for, contact us. Also, recent back issues are now available through Amazon.com. To find issues, use the advanced search feature and search on "Composition Studies" (title) and "Parlor Press" (publisher).

## BOOK REVIEWS

If you are interested in writing a review, please contact our Book Review editor at kkinney@uwyo.edu.

## JOURNAL SCOPE

The oldest independent periodical in the field, *Composition Studies* publishes original articles relevant to rhetoric and composition, including those that address teaching college writing; theorizing rhetoric and composing; administering writing programs; and, among other topics, preparing the field's future teacher-scholars. All perspectives and topics of general interest to the profession are welcome. We also publish Course Designs, which contextualize, theorize, and reflect on the content and pedagogy of a course. Contributions to Composing With are invited by the editor, though queries are welcome (send to compstudies@uc.edu). Cfps, announcements, and letters to the editor are most welcome. *Composition Studies* does not consider previously published manuscripts, unrevised conference papers, or unrevised dissertation chapters.

## SUBMISSIONS

For submission information and guidelines, see http://www.uc.edu/journals/composition-studies/submissions/overview.html.

Direct all correspondence to:

> Laura Micciche, Editor
> Department of English
> University of Cincinnati
> PO Box 210069
> Cincinnati, OH 45221–0069
> compstudies@uc.edu

*Composition Studies* is grateful for the support of the University of Cincinnati.

© 2017 by Laura Micciche, Editor
Production and printing is managed by Parlor Press, www.parlorpress.com.
ISSN 1534-9322.
Cover art by Ian Golding.

http://www.uc.edu/journals/composition-studies.html

# composition STUDIES

Volume 45, Number 2
Fall 2017

## Contents

**From the Editor**   10

**Articles**   12

"Multilingualizing" Composition: A Diary Self-Study of
Learning Spanish and Chinese   12
*Carol Severino*

The Symbolic Life of the Moleskine Notebook: Material Goods as a
Tableau for Writing Identity Performance   32
*Cydney Alexis*

Writing by the Book, Writing Beyond the Book   55
*Kristine Johnson*

Bodies in Composition: Teaching Writing through Kinesthetic
Performance   73
*Janine Butler*

Valuing Writers from a Neurodiversity Perspective: Integrating New
Research on Autism Spectrum Disorder into Composition Pedagogy   91
*Elizabeth Tomlinson and Sara Newman*

Forget Formulas: Teaching Form through Function in Slow Writing
and Reading as a Writer   113
*Michelle Tremmel*

The Linguistic Memory of Composition and the Rhetoric and
Composition PhD: Forgetting (and Remembering) Language and
Language Difference in Doctoral Curricula   130
*Carrie Byars Kilfoil*

**Course Designs**   151

Taco Literacy: Public Advocacy and Mexican Food in the
U.S. Nuevo South   151
*Steven Alvarez*

Stretch and Studio Composition Practicum: Creating a Culture of
Support and Success for Developing Writers at a Hispanic-Serving
Institution     167
    *Cristyn L. Elder and Bethany Davila[1]*

Spies Like Us: Gamifying the Composition Classroom and
Breaking the Academic Code     187
    *Jessica E. Slentz, Kristin E. Kondrlik, and Michelle Lyons-McFarland*

## Where We Are: Latinx Compositions and Rhetorics     210

In Defense of Latinx     210
    *Christine Garcia*

Chicanx/Latinx Rhetorics as Methodology for Writing Program
Design at HSIs     212
    *Aydé Enríquez-Loya and Kendall Leon*

Crafting a Composition Pedagogy with Latino Students in Mind     216
    *E. Domínguez Barajas*

Latinx and Latin American Community Literacy Practices *en Confianza*     219
    *Steven Alvarez*

Identity, Decolonialism, and Digital Archives     222
    *Cruz Medina*

Decolonial Options and Writing Studies     226
    *Iris Ruiz and Damián Baca*

Problematizing *Mestizaje*     230
    *Eric Rodriguez and Everardo J. Cuevas*

Speaking from and about Brown Bodies: A Personal and Political
Story of Sharing Identities     234
    *Nicole Gonzales Howell*

## Book Reviews     237

*Decolonizing Rhetoric and Composition Studies: New Latinx Keywords
for Theory and Pedagogy,* edited by Iris D. Ruiz and Raúl Sánchez     237
    Reviewed by *J. Paul Padilla*

*Cross-Border Networks in Writing Studies,* by Derek Mueller, Andrea

Williams, Louise Wetherbee Phelps, and Jennifer Clary-Lemon  242
  *Reviewed by Chen Chen*

*The Meaningful Writing Project: Learning, Teaching, and Writing in Higher Education,* by Michele Eodice, Anne Ellen Geller, and Neal Lerner  246
  *Reviewed by Rick Fisher*

*From Boys to Men: Rhetorics of Emergent American Masculinity,* by Leigh Ann Jones  251
  *Reviewed by Timothy Ballingall*

*Ambient Rhetoric: The Attunements of Rhetorical Being,* by Thomas Rickert  256
  *Reviewed by Mark Christopher Lane*

*Reclaiming Accountability: Improving Writing Programs through Accreditation and Large-Scale Assessments,* edited by Wendy Sharer, Tracy Ann Morse, Michelle F. Eble, and William P. Banks  260
  *Reviewed by Maggie Collins*

*Women, Writing, and Prison: Activists, Scholars, and Writers Speak Out,* edited by Tobi Jacobi and Ann Folwell Stanford  264
  *Reviewed by Annie Osburn*

# Contributors  269

# From the Editor

This issue includes a Where We Are section devoted to Latinx Compositions and Rhetorics. The call for submissions sought contributions that would "shed light on and contextualize the work happening by, with, and for Latinx communities within the field of composition studies." We received a tremendous range of submissions, from which we selected the eight essays in this issue that provide a clear indication of the vital, innovative, challenging work happening in Latinx studies. These essays offer definitions of key terms (Garcia; Rodriguez and Cuevas), address writing program design at HSIs (Enríquez-Loya and Leon), describe Latino-centered pedagogies (Domínguez Barajas), detail literacy researcher practices (Alvarez), delve into decolonialism and digital archival work (Medina), advocate for decolonial approaches to writing studies (Ruiz and Baca), and offer storytelling as a mode of identity and political work (Gonzales Howell).

Serendipitously, before conceiving of this Where We Are section, we had already accepted Carol Severino's self-study "'Multilingualizing' Composition," Steven Alvarez's course design for "Taco Literacy," and Cristyn L. Elder and Bethany Davila's course design, "Stretch and Studio Composition Practicum: Creating a Culture of Support and Success for Developing Writers at a Hispanic-Serving Institution." As a result, conversations about language difference, cultural identity, and Latinx rhetorics are not confined to the special section but are threaded throughout this issue, including the book review section, where J. Paul Padilla reviews Iris D. Ruiz and Raúl Sánchez's *Decolonizing Rhetoric and Composition Studies*. My hope is that writing researchers will continue to view *Composition Studies* as a welcoming home for cross-cultural research and pedagogy and for resistant political discourse.

Elsewhere in this issue, authors consider writing objects, writing manuals, writing bodies, slow writing practices, and—zooming out from these sites and practices—writing and rhetoric doctoral curricula and the vanishing presence of linguistic study. Cydney Alexis's material culture analysis of Moleskine notebooks will likely cause you to do an inventory of how your own writing tools (and those of your students) relate to identity formation. In Kristine Johnson's study of the limitations of writing advice manuals, she urges scholars to apply their expertise to advice for scholarly writers. Focusing attention on bodily based pedagogy, Janine Butler draws on Deaf Studies, embodiment theory, and multimodality to illustrate how teachers communicate meaning through bodily performance. Elizabeth Tomlinson and Sara Newman detail their research on how writers with an autism spectrum disorder approach writing tasks, a project that leads them to advocate for pedagogies informed by Universal Design for Learning. Describing what she calls slow writing and reading as a writer,

Michelle Tremmel reveals the advantages of a writing pedagogy that is attentive to pacing and guided by slow instruction. Carrie Byars Kilfoil details the disappearance of linguistics from rhetoric and composition doctoral programs and argues for a return to matters of language and language difference, issues recently animating the field through the lens of translingualism.

This issue is rounded out by a third course design by Jess Slentz, Kristin E. Kondrlik, and Michelle Lyons-McFarland describing a gamified undergraduate writing and research class organized around themes of espionage and government intelligence. The authors illustrate how role-playing and targeted competitions function in the class and in relation to student learning. We close the issue with seven book reviews carefully curated by Kelly Kinney, book review editor extraordinaire, who is now also serving as department head at her institution, the University of Wyoming!

Thank you for reading, subscribing, asking your library to subscribe, visiting us online at our Facebook page, and sharing this issue with colleagues and students. Think of *Composition Studies* for *your* next writing project.

*L.M.*
*Cincinnati, Ohio*
*September 2017*

# Articles

## "Multilingualizing" Composition: A Diary Self-Study of Learning Spanish and Chinese

*Carol Severino*

Using her own experiences of keeping a journal while learning advanced Spanish creative writing and beginning Chinese during the same semester, the author illustrates that composition teachers' second language learning experiences—intimate and challenging encounters with a second language that multilingual composition students experience every day—can develop the cross-language and cross-cultural knowledge as well as the humility and empathy necessary both to "multilingualize" not only one's teaching, but the field of composition as a whole. She shows how teachers' second language learning studies might supplement or replace some of the translingual writing literature that often naively duplicates and redundantly reinvents or rediscovers the longstanding, research-based, sociolinguistic and multilingual perspectives on language from applied linguistics, second language acquisition, and second language writing.

---

## Compositionists as Second Language Learners and Second Language Teachers

In contrast to composition teachers, English as a Second Language (ESL) teachers have long recognized how much their own second-language learning experiences inform and even transform their pedagogy (Bailey, Curtis, and Nunan; Birch; Flowerdew; Lowe; Spencer, "Informing Language Teaching," "The Language Teacher"; Waters et al.). They testify that studying other languages deepens their understanding of language-learning processes and makes their relationships with students more empathetic and peer-like. Teachers' second-language learning experiences—their "apprenticeship of observation," of witnessing and evaluating their teachers in action—can be even more powerful than their teacher preparation, as teachers spend an average of 3,000 days as students, but only 75 in teacher preparation (Lortie 208). Indeed, the special contributions of non-native English-speaking teachers who themselves learned English as a second language are now recognized and researched, thus countering the long-standing privileging of the native speaker (Braine; Ellis, "Teaching from Experience"; Kami-Stein).

However, because composition has been recovering from an unconscious assumption that native-English-speaking writing instructors are teaching classes of native-English-speaking students (Horner; Matsuda, "Myth"; Silva, Leki, and Carson), we have been slower to realize the value of our own second language learning experiences, or even the value of our multilingual students' own languages other than English. Our ignorance of other languages is ironic considering multilingual students are enrolled in most of our classes, and the CCCC's *Guideline on the National Language Policy* advocating universal U.S. multilingualism (revised in 2015) is already 29 years old.

Even more relevant, CCCC's *Statement on Teaching Second Language Writing and Writers*,[1] first published in 2001 (revised in 2009, and reconfirmed in 2014), urges us to "*take responsibility* for the regular presence of second language writers in writing classes, to understand their characteristics, and to develop instructional and administrative practices that are sensitive to their *linguistic* and cultural needs" (italics mine). With its emphasis on *responsibility*, the statement strongly suggests that composition teachers are also second language writing teachers; its emphasis on *linguistic needs* confirms Jessica Williams' view of second language writing teachers as also second language teachers ("Teaching"). It follows then that composition teachers are by necessity also second language teachers although undoubtedly we need more education about addressing language matters (Ferris et al.; Ferris and Hedgcock).

## Composition, Translingualism, and Second Language Writing

Reconceptualizing composition teachers as both second language learners and second language teachers can help heal the longstanding "disciplinary division" between composition and applied linguistics and ESL (Matsuda, "Composition and ESL"; Matsuda, "Wild West"). A focus on language learning and teaching could also clarify the differences between the translingual approach to composition, which stresses readers' accommodations of multilingual writers, and the second language writing approach, which emphasizes writers' second language writing development. According to the open letter to writing studies editors and leaders, translingual writing "stresses the fluidity, malleability and discriminatory potential of languages" but has not fully taken on the *responsibility* to help writers increase their second language proficiency (Atkinson et al. 384, italics mine). Second language writing recognizes multilingual writers' desires to develop their English proficiency in order to reach their academic and professional goals; these goals may or may not involve code-meshing or code-switching between languages in their writing, often claimed as a key feature of translingual writing (Arnold; Guerra; Matsuda, "Lure"). In particular, second language writing argues that the English proficiency goals of resident bilingual students—that is, immigrants or children of immigrants who may be emergent bilinguals not fully literate in their home languages—are especially important to address (Atkinson et al.; "The Future"). Shawna Shapiro et al. confirm that translingual discussions "often overlook…multilingual students' own goal to continue developing as English language users. In other words, a focus on appreciation [of language differences] alone may leave behind classroom practices that are explicitly aimed at promoting English language development" (31-32).

Of course, translingual and second language writing approaches also overlap in significant ways; for example, both value the resources from other languages that second language students employ when writing in English. Perhaps because of this similarity, the two approaches have become conflated and confused both in theory and in practice (e.g., job postings and faculty search and hiring processes), which could result in teachers without second language writing expertise mistakenly tasked with developing multilingual students' potential in English writing (Atkinson et al.). Situated within second language writing in its emphasis on language development, the study I describe here also attempts to distinguish these two approaches from one another by emphasizing learning additional languages.

The CCCC *Statement on Teaching Second Language Writing and Writers* recommends that composition teacher preparation and graduate study require courses in second language writing theory and research as well as second language practicum experiences. A particularly powerful type of second language practicum-like experience, as introduced and enacted in this article, is when composition teachers become second language learners themselves and use diaries to reflect on their experiences and connect them to teaching multilingual writers. Language learning diary studies necessitate a greater focus on continued language learning as an integral part of second language writing (Manchón, *Writing Development* 3) to combat what Trimbur calls the "ritualized forgetting" about languages other than English (qtd. in Horner 5). These studies benefit from integrating concepts from second language writing with concepts from composition to illuminate the challenges facing second language writers. This conceptual integration, Tony Silva, Ilona Leki, and Joan Carson argue, could help composition "address its limitations, develop a more global and inclusive understanding of writing, and thus avoid being a monocultural, monolinguistic, and ethnocentric enterprise" (398).

The idea of composition teachers as second language learners has appeared lately on the scholarly radar; several articles have recommended that teacher-scholars "retool their knowledge of additional languages" (Horner, NeCamp, and Donahue 289), increase foreign language requirements in graduate programs, and "learn more about language—its nature, structure, and function" (Matusda, "The Lure" 483) to "understand firsthand what it is like to live in a multilingual reality" (Matsuda, "Wild West" 136). We need to retool in order to "multilingualize" composition, to counteract its monolingual biases in teaching and scholarship. These recommendations suggest that composition teachers study additional languages, especially two of the most common home languages of the multilingual students we teach: Spanish, spoken by thousands of resident bilinguals, and Mandarin Chinese, spoken by thousands of U.S. international students enrolled in composition classes across the country. These are the languages of focus in this study.

**Second Language Learning as Professional Development**

Compositionists working on redesigning graduate programs to be more multilingual may be interested in how applied linguistics has creatively programmed second language learning experiences into graduate studies, teacher training, and professional development. For example, at Griffith University in Australia, prospective ESL teachers learned Thai as a second language in a Thailand "study abroad" program during the day and then met with their professors in person in the evening to discuss how their language learning could translate to teaching immigrants and international students in Australia (Birch). Other master's programs feature courses in which the first five weeks are dedicated to learning an unfamiliar language and reflecting on that experience, followed by ten weeks reading related theory and research and discussing teaching applications (Waters et al.).

Another language learning model involves "sudden" foreign language lessons to deepen discussions of language teaching controversies. For example, when Kathleen Bailey was teaching Brazilian English-as-a-foreign-language teachers who believed they should never use their students' native Portuguese in class, Bailey surprised them with an immersion lesson in elementary Korean without using English or Portuguese. Then she asked them to reflect: What had they learned? How did they feel? The teachers reported that some of the Korean grammar lessons had mystified, overwhelmed, and disoriented them. After that "shock" experience, they were more open to using Portuguese in the classroom to teach English (Bailey, Curtis, and Nunan).

Teachers can also pursue second language learning experiences on their own, especially writing to learn that language (Manchón, "Writing to Learn") as well as for the narrative, argumentative, and expository purposes already familiar to them. When teachers make their own language course or tutoring arrangements, they have more control over their own learning than when they participate in "programmed" experiences (Lowe). In addition, they can increase the personal significance of these experiences and transfer them to teaching composition by writing reflectively about them.

## Learner Self-Studies

One form of reflective writing as well as teacher-research (Ray) is the language learner self-study traditionally situated in applied linguistics (Casanave; Ogulnick). More literary versions are found in creative nonfiction, for example, the memoirs of Alice Kaplan and Eva Hoffman. There are many models of language learner self-studies, according to Bailey, a pioneer in this area ("Diary"). One model is when learners record their experiences in a diary or journal soon after they occur and then periodically re-read and analyze the entries for recurring patterns and themes. Or before they start their language learning, they have already decided what theme they will explore, as in Andrew Cohen's self-study of how he acquired Japanese pragmatics—what to say and how to say it appropriately in different rhetorical situations ("Developing"). Another model is when a language learner collaborates with a native speaker; Richard Schmidt and Sonia Frota's study of Schmidt's learning Portuguese contributed to the theory of "noticing" that has influenced second language acquisition (SLA) and could also inform composition (Shapiro et al. 33-34). "Noticing" means that the first step toward acquiring a feature is to notice its presence in others' discourse and its absence or misuse in one's own; for example, an English speaker who uses "para" as the default translation of "for" notices when native Spanish speakers use "por" instead (e.g., *gracias por tu ayuda*. Thanks for your help). Thus, language learning studies have not only resulted in more enlightened teaching but in theoretical contributions to SLA. Because of their relevance to the teaching and experiences of multilingual students, such studies can also enrich composition. (See the Diary Studies Bibliography at http://www.tirfonline.org/resources/references/.)

As a native-English-speaking writing center director and a teacher and researcher of first and second language writing, I am also a life-long second language learner—although by no means am I proficient or an expert in any of the languages I have studied. Barely bilingual in English and Spanish, I am no polyglot. But whenever I can, I take classes and arrange tutorials, record my learning experiences in a diary or journal, and then construct narratives or narrative-based self-studies, using detailed data from my journals to examine language and teaching issues: pedagogical conflicts, error feedback, classroom anxiety, genre struggles, and so on (see, for example, Severino, "A Diary"; Severino, "Ice Cream"; and Severino and Thoms). Applied linguist Patsy Duff and colleagues classify such language-learning journal self-studies as examples of narrative inquiry, a genre that generates insights about the complexity and socio-affective dynamics of language learning experiences (142).

Teachers' own second language learning experiences promote language awareness and pedagogical awareness that have intrigued composition teachers. They learn how different languages work to express the same idea; they learn about different languages' phonological (sound), syntactical (sentence structure), lexical (vocabulary), grammatical, pragmatic, and cultural systems. They come to understand the challenges that these English systems present to their students. If they study less commonly taught and indigenous languages, they learn firsthand the power dynamics between languages and cultures. In addition, being on the receiving end of others' teaching strategies promotes a pedagogical awareness that often reveals contradictions in one's own teaching (Spencer, "The Language Teacher"). For example, I might discourage multilingual students from using bilingual dictionaries in class, but then find myself unable to function without one.

Here I present themes from a Spanish and Chinese learning and journaling experience to show the features of thick description (Geertz) and analysis of a diary study. More importantly, I illustrate that second language learning experiences—intimate and challenging encounters with a second language that multilingual composition students experience every day—can develop the cross-language and cross-cultural knowledge as well as the humility and empathy necessary both to "multilingualize" not only one's teaching, but composition as a whole.

## My Diary Self-Study

During a recent research leave, I embarked on a journal self-study of learning two different languages at two different levels at the same time. I continued my study of Spanish by auditing Advanced Spanish Creative Writing in a semester-long, twice-a-week, three-credit course with Hernan (a pseudonym), a Latin American professor and novelist from whom I had taken two such previous courses, and who conducts his classes entirely in Spanish. I also started learning Mandarin Chinese in an eight-week, ninety-minute-a-week, non-credit community Confucius Institute course, and then arranged to do "tandem tutoring" with the same Chinese teacher, Yi (another pseudonym). For the eight weeks that followed the course, Yi helped me individually with Chinese and I helped her with English. Yi conducted both the class and the tutoring in English. The Spanish and the Chinese classes were both small; Spanish had eight students, including three native Spanish speakers, and Chinese had five native English-speakers. I already had a rich background in Spanish, having used it on and off with varying degrees of fluency for decades. But disgracefully, given that I and the tutors I supervise work with hundreds of Chinese students every year, I did not even know how to say "thank you" in Chinese. I would be starting from the very beginning.

My motivation for taking Spanish was to maintain an advanced level of Spanish for professional and family needs. On the other hand, knowing some Chinese, I hoped, would illuminate my research on the English writing of Chinese students and help me as their teacher and tutor as well as an educator of other teachers and tutors. I had observed some Chinese student writers repeatedly confronting the same language problems because of the stark differences between Chinese and English. I wanted to experience those differences in reverse for myself. I wanted to know, from my own attempts to speak, read, write, and hear it, something about how the Chinese language works. It was only fair to try to walk in my students' shoes even though my Chinese would be at the same level their English was when they were in the first grade. My Spanish, however, is at a similar advanced level as their English, especially in writing, so what I would learn about learning Spanish would also carry over to teaching.

For fifteen weeks, after each class session, I wrote at least one paragraph in English about what happened in classroom interactions, what I learned and struggled with, and how I felt about it. The resulting journal was 43 single-spaced pages and 21,600 words long. Spanish class demanded significant reading, plus frequent writing that received feedback from Hernan and my classmates, producing many interactions; thus, I wrote twice as much in my journal about my Spanish classes as about my Chinese classes. My previous self-studies often focused on pedagogical conflicts with my teachers and then drew implications for improved teaching. But with this journal study, I focused on my language learning, in particular the specific and often related cognitive, affective, and social conditions that enabled or hindered it.

Combing through and analyzing my journal for the conditions present when I experienced learning moments and noting recurring patterns, I noted that my learning was facilitated when comprehensible input (Krashen) and pushed written output (Swain and Lapkin, "Problems") consisted of personally significant vocabulary and structures at the point of need (Britton et al; Freire) while I was performing high involvement tasks (Williams, "The Potential Role(s)"). My learning was also facilitated when that input or output was repeated, recycled, and/or used in different contexts and modes. Likewise, the absence of those conditions made learning difficult or impossible for me because they often limited my ability to "notice" when I was flooded with linguistic data. The very acts of writing in my journal and then again in the self-study about learning particular language features worked to reinforce them, making my journal writing an example of both writing to learn language and of consolidating my language learning (Manchón, "Writing to Learn").

The two overlapping and related journal themes—the conditions for learning or not learning—that I will examine via analysis and narrative are (1) point-of-need input and output in high involvement tasks and (2) their repetition and recycling. For each theme, I first relate corresponding themes from composition and then discuss my learning of particular Spanish and then Chinese features, illustrating my observations with examples and excerpts from my journal. Where applicable, I point to what my experiences imply for teaching and tutoring writing, particularly to and with Chinese students, the largest population of international students in the U.S. (Zong and Batalova).

## Learning Condition 1: Point-of-Need Input and Output

*Spanish*

Because in both my teaching and learning I prefer a communicative approach—based on the principle that a writer uses language to say something to someone—the subtitle of the Spanish Creative Writing Class could not have been more suited to me: "The 'I' in Fiction and Non-Fiction." In the first half of the course, we read published Latin American fiction and wrote our own fiction; the second half followed the same pattern, but for nonfiction. We wrote in both genres based on our life experiences using the first person. My fiction was based on the rise and fall of my rock band; my nonfiction was a letter to my then three-year-old granddaughter about her female, bilingual identity, for her to read in ten years. The third and final project, for which we could choose either fiction or nonfiction, was a travel essay about my trip to Cuba. According to the Involvement Load Hypothesis (Hulstijin and Laufer), such "high involvement" tasks—those with "high values of *need* (i.e., the need to know a word), *search*, (an attempt to find the right word with the desired meaning), and *evaluation* (i.e., the comparison of the word with other candidates for appropriateness—are more likely to promote acquisition" (Williams, "The Potential Role(s)" 324; italics in original).

Personally meaningful, needed language input (Krashen) used as soon as possible in what is called pushed output (Swain and Lapkin, "Problems") facilitated my learning. Analogous concepts in composition are teaching and learning generative words from learners' lives (Freire) at the point of need (Britton et al.). When I formulated the first drafts of these stories, I typed quickly, jotting by hand on a notepad the words I needed but did not know or was not sure of, for the example, *female lead singer, crash the cymbals*, and *guitar chords*. I looked them up when I had already produced some text so as not interrupt the flow of thought. I learned, or if I was already somewhat familiar with them, I consolidated my learning of the words that I looked up as I needed them. Likewise, when we did in-class scene and dialogue writing, I asked Hernan for expressions I did not know in Spanish (*to clear one's throat, to be relieved*) to use immediately in my scene. In the writing center, we also have second language writers write parts of their drafts during their tutoring sessions, so we tutors are available to supply language at their point of need.

I knew I was taking risks by translating idiomatic expressions that resonated with me, for example, *time in the sun, attitude of entitlement, bedroom eyes*, and *mid-life crisis*. In fact, the very act of translating a culturally American rock-band experience that happened in English into Spanish was risky, so I wanted to know through trial and error precisely what worked and what did not. Based on transfer and translating from my first language, reported to be a strategy of even the most advanced users of a second language (Jiang; Murphy and Roca de Larios), I was testing language hypotheses for language structures, and if I found out via feedback they had failed, I modified them (Manchón and Roca de Larios). When it was apparent my hypothesis was wrong, especially when language differences implied cultural differences that we openly discussed, I also experienced a learning moment. As I noted in my journal, when Hernan informed us, "In Latin America, we don't use the term 'mid-life crisis,'" I jokingly asked, "Is that because the crises there happen throughout a man's entire life?" Instead, Hernan said, they use *crisis of one's forties* (or *thirties, fifties*). I thus learned the appropriate expression because of this "language-related episode" (Swain and Lapkin, "Interaction") as well as because of personal significance: the frequency of these crises among friends of friends. But I also learned it at the point of need because I needed it to conclude my story: it was the rhythm guitar player's mid-life crisis that was *the final nail in the band's coffin*, an expression I discovered in class actually does work in Spanish. Reflecting on those personally meaningful expressions in English that were risky to translate and their implications for my Chinese students, I now understand their deep-seated feelings that, despite the risk, they need to use "set-phrases"—common Chinese four-part proverbial or metaphorical sayings of cultural and personal import, for example, *round as pearls* to mean skilled singing, and *smooth as jade* to mean good writing. If the expressions translate well enough into English to be understood by non-Chinese-speaking readers, these writers have communicated in a way that expresses their Chinese voices and identities.

*Chinese*

The Confucius Institute Chinese course was organized by thematic units that would serve prospective English-speaking tourists in China: shopping, food/ordering in restaurants, asking for directions, and visiting landmarks. Because I had no immediate plans to visit China, I was interested in some units more than others, mainly those that would help me express my likes and dislikes, the only communicative point of need I was finding. From week to week, little vocabulary was recycled or used communicatively, and I was overwhelmed with new, not-so-personally meaningful language with too many features for me to "notice" much of anything. My journal entry for one class session reads:

> *We probably spent too much time talking about the New Year* [the previous class session had been a celebration of the New Year organized by the Chinese program] *because then she kept us over, teaching us all the numbers from 1-1,000, how to quote prices, all the measure words, and then how to shop for clothes. It was too much to absorb. I didn't even have control over the numbers from 1-10.... A lot of times we were repeating or reading the pinyin* [transcription in Romanized alphabet] *from the power point without knowing what we were saying. For example, she asked us how to say "you" and none of us realized that it's "ni" from "ni hao" (hello). It's worse than Elementary Accelerated Italian because at least we had that class every day. I knew it wasn't a good idea to try to learn Chinese once a week...*

By the sixth week, I was only slightly less overwhelmed:

> *We had a good time wishing the current weather away. But of course Yi will have to send the power point for me to review the vocabulary. Class always goes very quickly, perhaps because of the cognitive overload of so much new information. My mind is always active, although sometimes confused and reeling. There's no time to wonder even what time it is.*

In the tenth week, when during tandem tutoring Yi introduced me to radicals (components of Chinese characters), I was again frustrated with how much there was to know and to memorize in Chinese. By comparison, Spanish seemed like a native language to me. As I noted:

> *Yi taught me 5 radicals—like learning yet another language. Could there be an even harder dimension to Chinese than the ones I am already familiar with—tones, homophones, and monosyllables? Radicals are not easy because they change with position and with the font. She had me look for them in words and sometimes I could do it and sometimes not.*

In terms of personally significant language learned at the point of need, it was not until the food/restaurant unit in the fourth week that I was finally able to learn something I found personally meaningful, and therefore memorable and learnable: *Wo he hongjiu; wo bu he pijiu.* (I drink red wine; I don't drink beer.) I was so proud I could express something about myself that I repeated these sentences to all my friends and family members, thus internalizing them. Because tandem tutoring gave me more control of my learning, I asked Yi for a way to introduce myself besides the *Wo shi Meiguoren* (I am American) we had learned in class, and she taught me, "I teach students English."

A turning point was when, with the help of WordReference.com and Google Translate, I used the same communicative approach that was working for me in Spanish class and wrote stories even though I barely knew 50 Chinese words! I constructed two short narratives in pinyin, one about a family kayak trip and another about our Easter celebration. In other words, I assigned myself high involvement tasks. Like Hernan, Yi corrected my essays; then, processing her feedback, I rewrote them, asked her to read them aloud, and then imitated her pronunciation. Because of these two stories—input for output at the point of need—I learned more words relevant to my life at the point of need: *walk, lake, beach, kayak, family, granddaughter, old dog, chicken, bunny,* and *candy.*

Likewise, when Yi and I switched roles and read in English a speech Michelle Obama gave to students in China, I asked Yi to give me the Chinese equivalents of key words in the speech. Again at the point of need and interest, Yi taught me how to say *university* ("big study") and *study abroad* ("stay study"). I also pushed my output and learned when I explained that I had to apologize to my department chair for a misunderstanding and tell him *duibuqi* (I'm sorry) and that I hoped he would say *meiguanxi* (don't mention it) in return. Analogously, in composition courses, Chinese students need the freedom to choose their own high involvement topics for researching and writing, and not be confined to those the teacher chooses or to specifically U.S.-relevant topics such as American politics.

When I asked Yi how I should indicate that these stories occurred in the past tense or that I was talking about "chickens" in the plural, she told me it was not necessary. I had known in the abstract that unlike English, Chinese does not inflect its verbs for past tense, nor indicate plurals of unspecified quantity, but my own unchanged raw verbs allegedly describing a past experience and my bare singular nouns that really meant plural clarified for me why Chinese students have problems with tenses and plurals in English. Likewise, I wanted to put "and" between the last two items of every series and a "to be" verb wherever it would occur in English. But Yi told me Chinese only uses "and" when the last two items in a series are nouns; she also crossed out many (but not all) of my instances of *shi* (to be)—graphic reminders of why I need to tell Chinese writers of English to add "and" when they are connecting two verbs, adjectives, or sentences, and to insert "to be" verbs to make their sentences complete and comprehensible. My bare Chinese nouns and verbs also convinced me why tense and plurality in English take longer for Chinese students to acquire.

## Language Learning Condition 2: Repetition and Recycling of Input and Output

*Spanish*

Repeated instructional language, as when Hernan frequently announced we would *abordar* (address) a new theme or write in class to *soltar las manos* (untie our hands) was impossible to forget. He facilitated my learning when he recast my primitive communicative attempt—gesturing at the floor and saying in Spanish "lower and lower"—with the word *hundimiento* (sinking), then repeating it throughout the lecture-discussion to describe the descent of a story's character into addiction.

I learned another recycled word via its repetition followed immediately by using it in another form. By the last month of class, Hernan knew well the procrastination habits of the students, especially their tendencies to contribute only a partial draft to workshop, in effect, depriving themselves of everyone's informed comments on a complete plot with developed characters. Sometimes the writers themselves did not even know yet what would happen in the rest of their stories. On brainstorming day for the third and last project, Hernan reminded four students in a row who were undecided about their story topics that they needed to *aterrizar*-to "land on" or get grounded in an idea for their story so that this time they could finish their draft for the workshop. When it was my turn to tell my story idea, V., one of the procrastinators, joked that he knew that I had already finished my entire draft. "Sí, ya aterricé," I joked. (Yes, I already landed.) Up until that point, I had only known about the denotative meaning of *aterrizar*—when a plane lands. Now, with repeated input and then immediate expressive output to conjugate the verb in the "I" form, I learned the connotative metaphorical meaning, which sheds light on the writing process we teach: sooner or later writers and researchers must stop brainstorming and flying around and *land* on a topic. I can now be more confident that I "know" the word *aterrizar* according to I.S.P. Nation's criteria for "knowing" a word—being cognizant of its various forms and contexts for use.

Because of transfer errors that often result when the first language uses one word that the second language breaks down into two, I needed Hernan's feedback to remind me that a similar context for using a certain word had presented itself. That is, a context for using a word was repeated, but I did not "notice" that it was repeated. In previous courses, Hernan had corrected me whenever I wrote "I later learned that…" using the verb "to learn" (*aprender*). The correct way of expressing that meaning is to use the verb for "to find out" (*enterarse*). Yet to me learning what happened seems so much like learning a skill or subject matter, probably *because* English uses "learn" for both. Hence, it is difficult to recognize when in my writing I have come upon a case of "finding out what happened" versus "learning a skill or subject matter," the same reason Chinese students often confuse "examine" and "test," "tell" and "say," or "question" and "problem," expressed as the same words in Chinese.

Likewise, I am often unable to recognize when contexts are repeated for using the preterit versus the imperfect aspect or vice versa; when I need a reflexive versus a nonreflexive form of a verb; or for that matter, even when I should be looking up which to use, as I get confused by the semantics of duration or movement in the verb itself. Yet I can recite the rules for tenses and reflexives. Like me, Chinese students get frustrated with their persistent grammar errors with tense, passive versus active forms, and plurality, yet it may not help when teachers and tutors simply repeat the rules for using one verb tense rather than another when learners are not even aware that they have arrived at a place in their writing where they need to make such a decision. Second language writers need instruction in how to analyze the contexts for their persistent errors, not a recitation of rules they often know as well as or better than their teachers. As Mike Rose explains, it is as if teachers think that grafting a rule to writers' brains will fix the problem (172). I used to grumble when I found myself responding to the same types of errors in Chinese writers' work, but my own errors that persist despite correction have humbled me into accepting them as an inevitable part of language learning.

*Chinese*

Repetition and recycling are even more important in a beginner's level course, but we students perceived we were not getting enough of it. Because we each had to send Yi a recording of ourselves reading a dialogue each week, but had no model with which to practice, I asked her to record the weekly dialogues and send them to us. Then we were able to replay the authentic conversations of Yi and her Chinese neighbor and practice imitating them. Otherwise, we could not possibly remember how to pronounce the words in sequence with their different tones from one week to another.

I was pleased to discover that the number of words such as *he, hu, huo,* and *ma,* whose meanings vary by tone (for example, *ma* can mean "mother," "horse" or "scold" depending on the tone) is partially compensated for by recurring words which can be used for compounding, for example, *guo* (country), such that *Meiguo* is the U.S. and *Zhonguo* is China; and *yu* (language), such that *yingyu* is English and *hanyu* is Chinese. Knowing some radicals also reinforced my learning since I could sometimes recognize in strings of characters the radicals for *water, grass, mouth, female,* and *person,* associating the symbol with the name for it. In other words, the very structure of spoken and written Chinese incorporates repetition and recycling. Copying the radicals myself with a brush that I dipped in water to write on the "magic" paper Yi gave me (the writing disappears so you can reuse it) was a kinetic mode of repetition that helped me remember, as was using flash cards with a Chinese word on the front and the English translation plus a mnemonic device on the back, a strategy I learned from Andrew Cohen's collaborative diary study with Ping Li ("Learning Mandarin").

Much of the repetition and practice in Chinese, however, was left up to us students. Because Confucius Institute courses are non-credit and ungraded and emphasize culture as much as language, teachers do not stress the need to work independently and regularly to learn the language. Because my Chinese was at such a very basic level and the rewards seemed fewer than those from producing finished pieces of creative writing in Spanish that I was proud of, I had problems motivating myself to study Chinese on my own. As I confessed in the journal:

> *The only way this will work is if I vow to practice Chinese every day or most days, but I'm having a hard time with any kind of resolution, e.g., eating, exercise. I don't want to add something else I won't be able to do.*

## Teachers as Language Learners: Benefits for Teachers, Students, and the Profession

Second language learning experiences not only make our teaching and tutoring more responsive to second language writers but also make us more culturally aware. I now know more about the regions, dialects, and landmarks of China and about the practices of Chinese medicine, subjects I can discuss with my Chinese students. I now know how the genre of nonfiction in Latin American Spanish differs from English nonfiction and why; writers in the *testimonio* tradition of reporting political crimes are reticent to take liberties with dialogue and composite scenes like nonfiction writers in English often do because those literary devices could undermine the credibility of their accounts.

One of the most significant benefits of my language learning experiences is that SLA concepts—comprehensible input, pushed output, high involvement tasks, hypothesis testing, first language transfer/translation, noticing, and knowing a word—have come to life for me; in our haste to de-monolingualize composition, we should not ignore decades of applied linguistics, sociolinguistics, and SLA concepts and research. While advocates of translingual writing helpfully remind us of the dangers of using native-speaker norms as measuring sticks for student writing, they seem less concerned with SLA and its effect on writing development, even when writers themselves want to expand their repertoires and develop more control of vocabulary and sentence structures (Atkinson et al.; Gilyard; Matsuda, "The Lure").

A version of translingualism espoused by Bruce Horner and Laura Tetreault states that languages are abstractions and that discussions of what they call "conventionally demarcated languages" stem from the excesses of monolingual ideology (19). They refer to the "dominance of monolingualist definitions of language and language differences (e.g., French vs. Chinese)" (15). And Suresh Canagarajah has observed, "it is difficult to define where one language ends and the other begins" (423). But if more translingualist teachers endeavored to learn new languages, especially those that are noncognate with English, their view that languages are not "demarcated" by the phonological, syntactic, semantic, and discourse differences supposedly only important to monolinguists would be significantly challenged. Learning two different languages the same semester highlighted not only the obvious realities of language differences but also how proficiency can affect perceptions of such differences; in my case, because of my relatively advanced level as well as linguistic similarities, I experienced more commonalities than differences between Spanish and English. But because I was encountering Chinese for the first time, and its morphology and syntax diverge from those of English much more than they do in Spanish, I perceived more differences than similarities. In fact, it could not have been more obvious to me that English and Spanish are inflected languages without tones, and that Chinese is an uninflected tonal language (which, even after the course, was still unintelligible to me). Language demarcations are not figments of a monolingual imagination. As Keith Gilyard testifies, "When I'm around a group of people who speak a language foreign to me, it amounts to nothing to counsel myself that language is really an abstraction and that those speakers don't really have that language that I don't comprehend" (287).

As Gilyard also notes, translingualists have a tendency to flatten language differences, but this "sameness of difference" view (287) ignores the fact that some writers' writing is further from English writing than others because of different degrees of language differences and individual proficiency levels. Proficiency also affected my attitude toward the code-meshing advocated by translingualists; because of my advanced proficiency in Spanish and my personal and professional goals, like some of Juan Guerra's undergraduate and some of Canagarajah's graduate students writing in English, I did not want to either inadvertently or intentionally code-mesh in Spanish; but because of my very low proficiency and modest goals in Chinese, unintentional code-meshing and influence from English was inevitable. Guerra and Gilyard advocate that we consult our students about their views on code-meshing and other features of translingualism. Composition teachers learning other languages would be additional resources to consult.

Empathy is one of the most obvious benefits of teachers' language learning experiences. Following my Chinese learning experience, I have noticed how my relationships with Chinese students have changed. When they complain about the headaches of English, particularly the system of past and perfect tenses, or word choice complications because of "sound-alike's" (content versus context; insist versus persist), I empathize with them, listing my own headaches—producing the four tones and remembering multiple monosyllabic sound-alike words in Chinese. When students express dismay that they cannot write more fluent prose with fewer errors as they imagine native English speakers do, I mention my own persistent errors in Spanish despite decades of studying and using it.

Now I can better point out features of their English writing they are transferring from Chinese. When they present two items without an "and" between them; when they use *even though* in the dependent clause and *but* in the independent clause that follows, I note how with those features, English does not behave like Chinese, an observation they welcome. After a one-semester non-credit course, I know so little Chinese and less about how the language works linguistically, but sadly, it may be more than what most of their other U.S. teachers know.

Some might argue that composition teachers, especially graduate students, have little or no time to learn languages, but many rhetoric and composition graduate programs already have foreign language requirements for reading that could be modified to include writing—the very construct students are studying in their graduate programs. Many universities sponsor language tutoring units that connect prospective language learners to native speaking tutors, especially for less commonly taught languages not usually offered by foreign language departments, for example, Finnish, Quechua, and Tagalog. In addition, public libraries have free online language learning programs such as Mango. Composition teachers with immigrant parents, grandparents, or great-grandparents could pursue their own heritage languages to put themselves in the shoes of their Latino and Asian American composition students also enrolled respectively in Spanish and Chinese. Or they could collaborate with native-speaking Chinese and Spanish foreign language teachers and propose to their department administrators to audit one another's classes, conduct diary studies, and write articles together. After all, almost every college has both a writing program and a foreign language program, and most university administrators profess to value interdisciplinary collaboration. In Victor Villanueva's words, we should act on "the richness of language multiplicity" so "we can have greater community in learning from one another" (qtd. in Horner 10).

Second language learning diary studies are grounded in concrete personal experience, resulting in thick descriptions and linguistic analyses representative of scholarship in second language writing. It would indeed benefit our students, ourselves, and composition as a field to use studies of teachers' language learning to supplement or replace some of the translingualism literature that naively duplicates and redundantly reinvents or rediscovers not only longstanding sociolinguistic and multilingual views of language (Matsuda, "Wild West"; Shapiro et al. 49), but aspects of critical pedagogy (Gilyard 285). These language learning studies would be grounded in the field of second language writing, in turn grounded in applied linguistics and SLA. Translingualism needs to acknowledge and then learn about the hard work and the long, slow process of learning other languages (Jordan; Matsuda, "The Lure") and the fields of applied linguistics, SLA, and second language writing that have rigorously researched that process and ways to advance it. Diary studies could play an essential part in developing composition teachers' language awareness, sensitivity, and empathy, preparing them more effectively to help second language writers with their second language and second language writing development.

**Notes**

1. Many terms exist to describe the writing of bi- and multilinguals in languages other than their primary language for writing if indeed they have one, including writing in English as an additional language. As synonymous with multilingual writers, I prefer to use the terms second language writers in alignment with the CCCC statement and the field of second language writing.

**Works Cited**

Arnold, Lisa R. "'This is a Field that's Open, not Closed': Multilingual and International Writing Faculty Respond to Composition Theory." *Composition Studies* 44.1 (2016): 72-88. Print.

Atkinson, Dwight, et al. "Clarifying the Relationship between L2 Writing and Translingual Writing: An Open Letter to Writing Studies Editors and Organization Leaders." *College English* 77.4 (2015): 383-86. Print.

Bailey, Kathleen M. "Diary Studies of Classroom Language Learning. The Doubting Game and the Believing Game." *Language Acquisition and the Second/Foreign Language Classroom*. Ed. E. Sadtono. Singapore: Regional Language Centre, 1991. 60-102. Print.

Bailey, Kathleen M., Andy Curtis, and David Nunan. *Pursuing Personal Development: The Self-as-Source*. Boston: Heinle, 2001. Print.

Birch, Gary. "Language Learning Case Study Approach to Teacher Education." *Perspectives on Second Language Teacher Education*. Ed. John Flowerdew, Mark Newell Brock, and Sophie Hsia. Hong Kong: City Polytechnic of Hong Kong, 1992. 283-94. Print.

Braine, George. *Nonnative Speaker English Teachers: Research, Pedagogy, and Professional Growth*. New York: Routledge, 2010. Print.

Britton, James, et al. *The Development of Writing Abilities (11-18)*. London: Macmillan, 1975. Print.

Canagarajah, Suresh. "Clarifying the Relationship between Translingual Practice and L2 Writing: Addressing Learner Identities." *Applied Linguistics Review* 6.4 (2015): 415-40. Print.

Casanave, Christine P. "Diary of a Dabbler: Ecological Influences on an EFL Teacher's Efforts to Study Japanese Informally." *TESOL Quarterly* 46.4 (2012): 642-70. Print.

Cohen, Andrew. "Developing Pragmatic Ability: Insights from the Accelerated Study of Japanese." *New Trends and Issues in Teaching Japanese Language and Culture*. Ed. Haruko M. Cook, Kyoko Hijirida, and Mildred M. Tahara. Honolulu: U of Hawaii P, 1997. 133-59. Print.

Cohen, Andrew, and Ping Li. "Learning Mandarin in Later Life. Can Old Dogs Learn New Tricks?" *Contemporary Foreign Language Studies* 396.12 (2013): 5-14. Print.

Conference on College Composition and Communication. *Guideline on the National Language Policy*. CCCC, Mar. 2015. Web. Accessed 7 June 2017. <http://www.ncte.org/cccc/resources/positions/nationallangpolicy>.

Conference on College Composition and Communication. *Statement on Teaching Second Language Writing and Writers*. CCCC, Nov. 2014. Web. Accessed 7 June 2017. <http://www.ncte.org/cccc/resources/positions/secondlangwriting>.

Duff, Patsy, et al. *Learning Chinese: Linguistic, Sociocultural, and Narrative Perspectives*. Boston: de Gruyter, 2013. Print.

Ellis, Elizabeth. "Teaching from Experience: A New Perspective on the Non-Native Teacher in Adult ESL." *Australian Review of Applied Linguistics* 25.1 (2002): 71-102. Print.

Ferris, Dana, et al. "Responding to L2 Students in College Writing Classes: Teacher Perspectives." *TESOL Quarterly* 45.2 (2011): 207-34. Print.

Ferris, Dana, and John Hedgcock. *Teaching L2 Composition: Purpose, Process, and Practice*. 3rd ed. New York: Routledge, 2014. Print.

Flowerdew, John. "Language Learning Experience in L2 Teacher Education." *TESOL Quarterly* 32.3 (1998): 529-36. Print.

Freire, Paulo. *Pedagogy of the Oppressed*. 30th Anniversary Edition. New York: Continuum, 2000. Print.

"The Future of SLW at CCCC: Why CCC and SLW Need Each Other." Symposium on Second Language Writing. Arizona State U, Tempe, AZ. 15 Nov. 2014. Address.

Geertz, Clifford. *The Interpretation of Cultures*. New York: Basic, 1973. Print.

Gilyard, Keith. "The Rhetoric of Translingualism." *College English* 78.3 (2016): 284-89. Print.

Guerra, Juan. "Cultivating a Rhetorical Sensibility in the Translingual Writing Classroom." *College English* 78.3 (2016): 228-33. Print.

Hoffman, Eva. *Lost in Translation: A Life in a New Language*. New York: Penguin, 1989. Print.

Horner, Bruce. "Introduction: From 'English Only' to Cross-Language Relations in Composition." *Cross-Language Relations in Composition*. Ed. Bruce Horner, Min-Zhan Lu, and Paul Matsuda. Carbondale: SIUP, 2010. 1-17. Print.

Horner, Bruce, and Laura Tetreault. "Translation as (Global) Writing." *Composition Studies* 44.1 (2016): 13-30. Print.

Horner, Bruce, Samantha NeCamp, and Christiane Donahue. "Toward a Multilingual Composition Scholarship: From English Only to a Translingual Norm." *CCC* 63.2 (2011): 269-300. Print.

Hulstijn, Jan, and Batia Laufer. "Some Empirical Evidence for the Involvement Load Hypothesis in Vocabulary Acquisition." *Language Learning* 51.3 (2001): 539-58. Print.

Jiang, Nan. "Semantic Transfer and its Implications for Vocabulary Teaching in a Foreign Language." *Modern Language Journal* 88.3 (2004): 416-32. Print.

Jordan, Jay. "Fast Movements, Slow Processes." *Composition Studies* 44.1 (2016): 144-46. Print.

Kami-Stein, Lia D., ed. *Learning and Teaching from Experience: Perspectives on Nonnative English-Speaking Professionals*. Ann Arbor: U of Michigan P, 2004. Print.

Kaplan, Alice. *French Lessons*. Chicago: U of Chicago P, 1993. Print.

Krashen, Stephen D. *Principles and Practices in Second Language Acquisition*. Oxford: Pergamon, 1982. Print.

Lortie, Dan. *Schoolteacher: A Sociological Study*. Chicago: U of Chicago P, 1975. Print.

Lowe, Tim. "An Experiment in Role Reversal. Teachers as Language Learners." *ELT Journal* 41.2 (1987): 89-96. Print.

Manchón, Rosa., ed. *Writing Development: Multiple Perspectives*. Berlin: deGruyter Mouton, 2012. Print.

Manchón, Rosa M., and Julio Roca de Larios. "Writing to Learn in FL Contexts: Exploring Learners' Perceptions of the Learning Potential of L2 Writing." *Learning to Write and Writing to Learn in an Additional Language*. Ed. Rosa Manchón. Amsterdam: John Benjamins, 2011. 61-82. Print.

Matsuda, Paul. "Composition and ESL: A Disciplinary Division of Labor." *CCC* 50.4 (1999): 699-721. Print.

---. "It's the Wild West Out There: A New Linguistic Frontier in U.S. College Composition." *Literacy as Translingual Practice: Between Communities and Classrooms*. Ed. A. Suresh Canagarajah. New York: Routledge, 2013. 128-38. Print.

---. "The Lure of Translingual Writing." *PMLA* 129.3 (2014): 478-83. Print.

---. "The Myth of Linguistic Homogeneity in U.S. College Composition." *College English* 68.6 (2006): 637-51. Print.

Murphy, Liz, and Julio Roca de Larios. "Searching for Words: One Strategic Use of the Mother Tongue by Advanced Spanish EFL Writers." *Journal of Second Language Writing* 19.2 (2010): 61-81. Print.

Nation, I.S.P. *Learning Vocabulary in Another Language*. 2nd ed. Cambridge: Cambridge UP, 2013. Print.

Ogulnick, Karen. *Onna Rashiku (Like a Woman): The Diary of a Language Learner in Japan*. Albany: SUNY, 1998. Print.

Ray, Ruth. *The Practice of Theory: Teacher-Research in Composition.* Urbana: NCTE, 1993. Print.

Rose, Mike. *Lives on the Boundary.* New York: Penguin, 1989. Print.

Schmidt, Richard W., and Sylvia Frota. "Developing Basic Conversational Ability in a Second Language: A Case Study of an Adult Learner of Portuguese." *Talking to Learn: Conversation in Second Language Acquisition.* Ed. Richard Day. Rowley: Newbury, 1986. 237-326. Print.

Severino, Carol. "A Diary Self-Study of an Adult Italian Learner's Course Experience." *Entre Lenguas* 8 (2002-3): 5-17. Print.

---. "'Ice Cream in the Cold Wind': Struggles with a Second Genre in a Second Language." *Writing on the Edge* 24.1 (2013): 41-48. Print.

Severino, Carol, and Joshua Thoms. "Journal-Based Self-Studies of L1 English/L2 Spanish Speakers Learning L3 Kichwa in Ecuador and L3 Guaraní in Paraguay." *Entre Lenguas* 13 (2007): 61-75. Print.

Shapiro, Shawna, et al. "Teaching for Agency: From Appreciating Linguistic Diversity to Empowering Student Writers." *Composition Studies* 44.1 (2016): 31-32. Print.

Silva, Tony, Ilona Leki, and Joan Carson. "Broadening the Perspective of Mainstream Composition Studies: Some Thoughts from the Disciplinary Margins." *Written Communication* 14.3 (1997): 398-428. Print.

Spencer, Shelley A. "Informing Language Teaching through Language Learning." *Profile* 6 (2006): 187-97. Print.

Spencer, Shelley A. "The Language Teacher as Language Learner." *Reflective Writing: A Way to Lifelong Teacher Learning.* Ed. Jill Burton, Phil Quirke, Carla Reichmann and Joy .Kreeft Peyton. TESL-EJ, 2009. 31-48. Web. Accessed 18 Mar. 2014. < http://tesl-ej.org/books/reflective_writing.pdf >.

Swain, Merrill, and Sharon Lapkin. "Interaction and Second Language Learning: Two Adolescent French Immersion Learners Working Together." *The Modern Language Journal* 82.3 (1998): 320-37. Print.

---. "Problems in Output and the Cognitive Processes They Generate: A Step Towards Second Languge Learning." *Applied Linguistics* 16.3 (1995): 371-91. Print.

The International Research Foundation for English Language Education (2014). "Diary Studies on Language Learning and Teaching." Accessed 7 June 2017. http://www.tirfonline.org/resources/references/

Waters, Alan, et al. "Getting the Best Out of 'the Language Learning Experience.'" *ELT Journal* 44.4 (1990): 305-15. Print.

Williams, Jessica. *Teaching Writing in Second and Foreign Language Classrooms.* Boston: McGraw Hill, 2005. Print.

---. "The Potential Role(s) of Writing in Second Language Development." *Journal of Second Language Writing* 21.4 (2012): 321-31. Print.

Zong, Jie, and Jeanne Batilova. "International Students in the United States." *Migration Information Source.* Migration Policy Inst., 12 May 2016. Web. Accessed 7 June 2017. <http://www.migrationpolicy.org/article/international-students-united-states>.

# The Symbolic Life of the Moleskine Notebook: Material Goods as a Tableau for Writing Identity Performance

*Cydney Alexis*

Writing is considered a sacred act and the writer a sacred cultural figure. People use objects when trying to access this desired identity. How a person approaches and uses an object is intimately connected to family, sense of self, writing history, relation to peers, media connections, social awareness, and life story. Hence, turning to objects is one way of uncovering the very complicated identities that perform the practice of writing and for understanding the writing process itself. In this essay, I turn to the Moleskine notebook, a popular writing object, to show how three writers develop, navigate, and maintain their writerly identities and writing practices through this seemingly simple object.

---

We may impose our identities on possessions and possessions may impose their identities on us.

—Russell W. Belk (1988)

During an interview, a writer tells me about a duffle bag the older kids carried around his high school campus. For him, this bag marked entry into a new stage of schooling; it helped him to imagine a future as a high school student. This is just one object of many that surfaced during my three-dozen "life story" (Atkinson) interviews[1] with people about the materiality of their writing environments, or "habitats," as I have described them elsewhere (Alexis, "The Writing Habitat"). Other participants mentioned the Trapper Keeper, a highly desired object that parents often would not purchase due to its cost and perceived superfluousness. The Trapper Keeper carries middle-class identity associations, and many students I spoke to could remember whether they did or did not have one and could cite the reason why.

Memories such as these, which tie objects together with identity and schooling, resonate with the way objects hang out in writing studies research, a field whose interest in material objects has been steadily mounting for the last decade. Objects are rarely the central focus of study in writing studies research, save some notable exceptions (Baron; Boyle and Barnett; Haas; Wyche; Wyche-Smith). Social scientists Mihalyi Czikszentmihalyi and Eugene Rochberg-Halton note that researchers in their fields of psychology and sociology, respectively, "tend to look for the understanding of human life in the internal psychic processes of the individual or in the patterns of relationship between people; rarely do they consider the role of material objects" (1). I find that this holds, as well, for writing studies. In writing studies, we see objects accompanying writers or writers using them as sets or props for desired purposes (Emig; Prior and Shipka), providing space or a stable frame or stage for literate activities (Brandt and Clinton; Gere; Heath), and greasing the wheels towards or hampering access to literacy (Bartlett; Brandt). Objects, in fact, are referenced all over the place in writing research. Yet it's safe to say that we do not know what objects are *doing* in writing studies. This is because writing studies scholars have not yet fully engaged with rich work by scholars of material culture studies and consumer culture research (referenced herein as consumer research, for brevity) who, for decades, have been theorizing and researching the relationship between humans and material goods and proving that even the smallest, seemingly insignificant object has a story to tell about the humans who use it (Arnould and Thompson; Belk; Czikszentmihalyi and Rochberg-Halton; Deetz; Epp and Price; Miller; Prown, "Mind" and "Style"; Schlereth).

We know from the possessions literature that rather than one single object, a "constellation" of relevant objects is necessary when an individual performs a particular *identity*[2] or practice (such as that of "athlete," for example) (Kleine III, Kleine, and Kernan; Reed II; Reed II et al.; Solomon). Individuals attach to particular possessions in intense ways, weaving them into self-concept as reflecting "me" (Belk; Czikszentmihalyi and Rochberg-Halton; Kleine, Kleine, and Allen). In other words, people use possessions to perform "purposive identity work" (Epp and Price) as well as to express a particular "social identity" (Reed II; Kleine III, Kleine, and Kernan).

Humans express their selves through possessions; they also rely on possessions to memorialize past events and identities (Belk; Czikszentmihalyi and Rochberg-Halton; Kleine III, Kleine, and Kernan) and attach intensively to possessions that reflect an identity that they have achieved (Kleine III, Kleine, and Kernan) or that they wish to embody (Reed II et al.; Solomon). Individuals who have the ability to imagine "possible selves," or future selves performing a particular task, identity, or trade, are more likely to complete tasks successfully themselves (Markus and Nurius; Oyserman et al., "Possible" and "Socially"). Considering the demonstrated power of objects in the process of becoming possible selves, and people's reliance on object constellations to perform identities and trades, we should be asking deeper questions about how objects assist, even shape, writers in learning, negotiating, and maintaining their writing practices and writing identities.

Elsewhere, I have remarked on the importance of material culture and possessions research to our field and explored how material writing environments impact writing practice (Alexis, "The Writing Habitat"). In this article, my goal is to take a deeper look at a particular object, the Moleskine notebook, which came up unprompted in one of my interviews and—it was impossible to miss—was exploding in popularity around me. Because of this, I solicited two more life story interviews with users of Moleskines to better understand this notebook phenomenon. I argue here that the Moleskine notebook, a seemingly simple object, is a "facilitating artifact" for the performance of the identity of 'writer'(Kleine III, Kleine, and Kernan 229). Specifically, artifacts such as the Moleskine "stimulate reflexive self-evaluations leading to self-definitions" (Laverie et al.) The Moleskine also plays complex roles in the lives of those who incorporate it into their writing practice. Moleskine users often internalize the Moleskine parent company's branding of the object as a literati and artist notebook, which I demonstrate in the pages that follow. In order to do this, I present a brief history of the Moleskine notebook and its emergence in popular culture. The Moleskine is a tableau onto which people project their hopes and fears about writing. In other words, it is interwoven with ideas about what it means to be a writer as well as people's lived experience of being writers. Not all writers attach to the objects they work with or incorporate objects into their self-concept. Those who do, do so to varying degrees. Here, I present the stories of three of the writers I interviewed whose narratives about writing with Moleskines reflect three different integrations of this object into their writing lives, writing identities, and writing practices. "Biographies" of objects, Kopytoff asserts, are useful because they reveal what might otherwise resist analysis; they can also help researchers to catalogue how objects are plucked out of the commodity realm to be used in novel ways by consumers (66-68). And yet these objects, as you will see, also shape the way writers approach their craft.

**Becoming a Writer, With Possessions**

Fiona, a graduate student in English, remembers the time when she began to journal. She was in grade school, and she was causing trouble as a result of not being scholastically challenged. At nine years of age, a teacher recommended journaling. Around this time and through this practice, her writing identity emerged:

> At the time I started journaling, I would have been sharing a room with my younger sister, who wasn't engaged with reading or writing . . . It was all a part of a process of claiming identities that were different from each other, and so by being the child who wrote, and by being the child with books and notebooks, I had an identity that was

separate from the children on either side of me that hadn't identified with those things.

David, a writing program administrator, narrates a similar story. He was a freshman in college when he came across the Moleskine notebook (see fig. 1).

Figure 1. The Classic Moleskine, by Jochen Handschuh.³

At this time, he was trying to become a writer. He began reading writers' notebooks and writing in his own, and he began to attach to and fetishize this particular material object: "Fetishize is not too heavy a word . . . I became so fixated on them . . . At that time I was getting into writing. I was an English major. I was reading a lot. I was sort of discovering reading, really, for the first time. I was fantasizing about being a writer . . . I started reading writer's notebooks . . . I started reading the notebooks of Albert Camus."

I present these two stories in support of the idea that objects help writers to do the following:

- Imagine what it means to be a writer ("I was fantasizing about being a writer")
- Carve out identities for themselves ("By being the child who wrote," "I was getting into writing," "I was . . . discovering reading"), often in relation to important others ("It was all a part of a process of claiming identities that were different from each other," "I had an identity that was separate from the children on either side of me," "I was reading the notebooks of Albert Camus")
- Compel the desire to write by imitating the object use or practices of published writers ("I started reading writers' notebooks")
- Maintain writing identities over time

In consumer research terms, individuals have a self-identity (or identities) that is both personal and social. They draw from the social world cues that help them imagine and perform that self-identity. Goods, and the media surrounding them, trigger certain identity performances and also help individuals to maintain and perform identity (Kleine III, Kleine, and Kernan; Reed II; Reed II et al.). One who writes, then, will receive cues from the material world regarding an identity and the materials that might be used to perform it. David's narrative, for example, demonstrates how people utilize objects to imagine how to "think, feel, and be like" writers (Reed II et al. 315).

Fiona and David have personal identities as writers that developed around goods. They share something else in common: They both have had intense relationships with one particular notebook, the Moleskine, which, in Dorothy Holland and Jean Lave's terms, is a cultural symbol that helps them to understand and perform the work of a writer. And they are not alone.

**The Moleskine Phenomenon**

By now, you are likely familiar with the classic Moleskine pictured in figure 1. But unless you are a dedicated Moleskine user, and even if you are one, you may not be familiar with the expansiveness of the Moleskine phenomenon, which has progressed far beyond offering the one iconic type pictured above. It is not an exaggeration to say that users constitute a sort of cult. A simple search in newspaper archives yields hundreds of articles about the Moleskine. A Google search for "Moleskine" reveals hundreds of thousands of user photographs and blog entries and detailed images and accounts of writers' and artists' (often obsessive) uses of this object. A Moleskine user created a fan blog (*Moleskinerie.com*) that achieved such popularity that the company eventually assumed control and now runs the blog. On Flickr, users upload hundreds of thousands of images, such as the one pictured in figure 2.

The Moleskine company manages a Flickr group called "Moleskinerie" with more than 22,000 members and 116,000 uploaded photos. In 2014, Moleskine Spa reported 98.7 million euros in sales; Moleskine anticipates its market growing to 300 million people by 2020 ("Q4" 2014). More impressive than the numbers, however, is the company's awareness of its branding and its unmitigated success in marketing this object as an artist and literati companion. Each of the classic Moleskines are bound, covered in faux leather, held together symbolically and literally by a plastic band, and contain a pocket attached to the back cover into which is inserted a "history" of the notebook: "Moleskine is the legendary notebook, used by European artists and thinkers for the past two centuries, from Van Gogh to Picasso, from Ernest Hemingway to Bruce Chatwin." This "history" inscribes a promise to users: that they can tap into an exoticized literary and artistic heritage created by legendary writers and artists. The original Moleskine parent company Modo & Modo branded not only its creative past, but also its aesthetic present:

A simple black rectangle with rounded corners, an elastic page-holder, and an internal expandable pocket: a nameless object with a spare perfection all its own, produced for over a century by a small French bookbinder that supplied the stationery shops of Paris, where the artistic and literary avant-gardes of the world browsed and bought them. A trusted and handy travel companion, the notebook held invaluable sketches, notes, stories, and ideas that would one day become famous paintings or the pages of beloved books. ("Moleskine World")

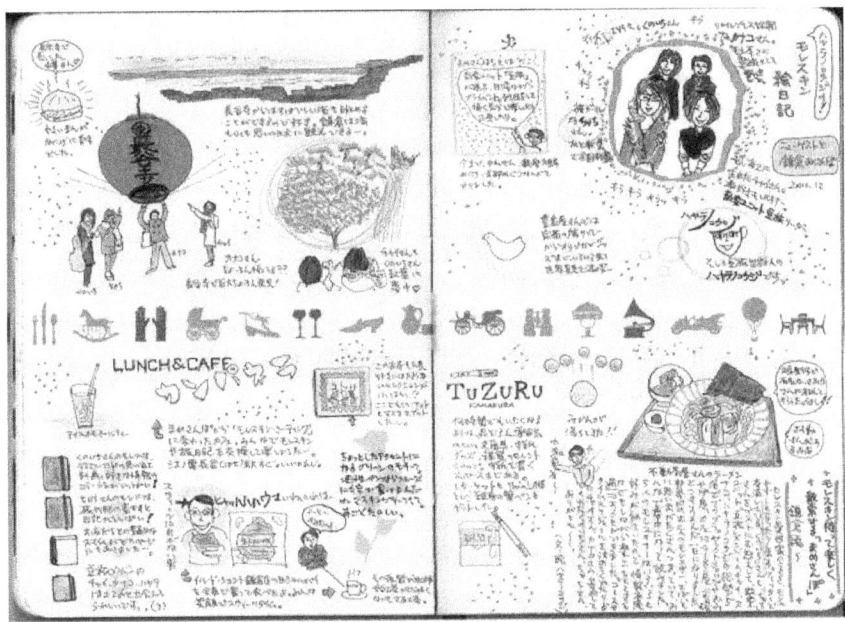

Figure 2. Kouji Hayateno's Moleskine.

The words "simple," "nameless," "spare," and "small" are purposefully used to convey a classic aesthetic, one that foregoes the contemporary clutter of logos, overdesign, and corporate identity so that the brand might locate itself in the cultural longing for a perceived simpler, analog time. Moleskine personifies the notebook as a "companion" and suggests that by using it to write, one might someday become a Hemingway. Despite the company's expansiveness, it builds goodwill by conveying an image of a local artisan product.

Within this context, it is not difficult to understand why David, mentioned earlier, found the Moleskine compelling as an object that would help him to tap into the mindset and culture of being a writer. Moleskine now sees itself this way as well. In 2014, the company asserted that it is the "only brand that has successfully established itself as an identity marker starting from a notebook," although it did not describe itself in these terms when I first started researching the company in 2009 ("Q4"). Moleskine's identity-based branding is not unusual in today's market, as companies often "create or (re)position products and brands to embody a particular social identity oriented lifestyle" (Reed II 286). The company has been able to market not just a product, or a constellation of products, but also a community. The company now asserts, indeed, that it "sells much more than a notebook."[4]

What Moleskine is selling has been communicated well by journalists and bloggers who have prolifically published their thoughts on this object:

> In this digital age where everything is electronic and online . . . there is an unsurprising movement towards the simple pleasures of paper notebooks . . . the tactile nature of good-quality paper and the scratch of a pen as you write on it seems to enhance, even *sanctify*, the act of writing. (Shapshak 4, emphasis added)
>
> Writing in a Moleskine is different from writing on an ordinary piece of paper. There's a certain respect and reverence for your thoughts and ideas. It's not as transient as a scrap of paper, and there is nothing as disposable as a Word document . . . . It doesn't make what you're writing special, it makes that you're writing special. (Roderick, qtd. in Shapshak 4)

Moleskine has successfully connected its product with a simpler time, and the act of writing with an analog lifestyle. You can hear this in a bookstore manager's statement that "It's also nostalgic, to put your pen to paper . . . It creates that sense of literature" (qtd. in Shapshak 4). This is ironic since the company markets digital products, such as a journal application available for both Mac and Windows platforms, and since its popularization has largely happened via the web.

Another irony casts a shadow over this whole business: The company's marketing narrative is largely spurious. "It's not even clear that Hemingway used a Moleskine at all," Joe Lavin writes. "He merely mentioned that in Paris he wrote part of a novel in a notebook that fit in his pocket." Indeed, small, anonymous, unnamed notebooks were produced by Parisian bookbinders until the 1980s. As the story goes, author Bruce Chatwin named this anonymous book the "Moleskine" upon discovering that the last family-run, artisanal bookbinder in Tours had gone out of business when its factory burned down ("Le Moleskine n'existe plus," Chatwin exclaimed in his novel *Songlines* [*Moleskinerie*]). Before this, Moleskine was a "Franglais generic term for stout waxed canvas: a waterproof cover that protected the contents of your protected notebook from rain, spilt milk and bodily fluids" (Bywater 7). In 1997, a Milanese Italian design company, Modo & Modo, began producing the notebook we now know as the Moleskine, patented the name, and "began one of the most audacious branding exercises of recent decades" (Bywater 7).

Despite Moleskine's fabricated branding, this object has entered actual writers' lives, as David conveyed to me. After interviewing David, I conducted targeted interviews with other self-professed Moleskine users, two of whose stories I present here alongside his in order to understand how the branding played out in the lives of people who had integrated this notebook into their practices.

**Objects as Expressions of Self**

Fiona discovered the Moleskine notebook once her journaling practice had developed and now, as an adult, she attaches quite strongly to this notebook for aesthetic and practical purposes. As a vast body of work has demonstrated, individuals cultivate, define, negotiate, and maintain their identities through attachment to goods (Belk; Csikzentmihalyi and Rochberg-Halton; Epp and Price; Kleine, Kleine, and Allen; Schultz et al.; Wallendorf and Arnould). Individuals generally attach to possessions over which they have a strong degree of control (Belk), that relate to parts of their selves that they value or that they admire in their social worlds (Kleine, Kleine, and Allen; Schultz et al.), towards which they hold a strong emotional charge or "cathexis" (Kleine, Kleine, and Allen 327), and that represent past associations or current ties (Czikszentmihalyi and Rochberg-Halton), as well as well-established parts of one's individual personality (Kleine, Kleine, and Allen) or family identity (Epp and Price). Attachments can tell a person's life story.

I learned a lot about Fiona's story—and personal relationships with writing objects—through her attachment to the Moleskine. Since grade school, when her teacher recommended she start journaling, she has used notebooks for uninhibited personal writing, for recording thoughts and feelings. Later, the Moleskine became so incorporated into her journaling practice that she stopped using other kinds of notebooks. She calls herself a "compulsive" writer in these notebooks. Their dominant use is not for writing projects, academic writing, or even lists; she uses them to record her thoughts in stream-of-consciousness format. She cites the Moleskine as a site of "unclogging" and contrasts the writing she does there with academic writing, which causes anxiety and blockage. In class, she sits with two notebooks. She takes academic notes in a generic notebook while she simultaneously uses the Moleskine to record her thoughts and emotions. The Moleskine, then, is a record of her mental life, thoughts, and emotions—aspects of her being.

Fiona always carries a Moleskine notebook fairly close to her body. She does not carry just any type; she prefers the small navy-blue version pictured in Figure 3, the inside of which is comprised of graph paper.

Figure 3. Fiona's Moleskines.

She's been using this type of Moleskine for years; what you see pictured is only a fraction of the total collection. She buys purses that have Moleskine-sized pockets, so that she can keep one near, if her clothing does not accommodate the notebook. Others have recognized her use of this object, frequently giving her Moleskine gifts. She told me this makes her feel badly because she will not use any type except the blue graph paper style, so she ends up giving away the gifted Moleskines.

Fiona's investment in this artifact, which is attached to her person at most times, is an example of what Belk calls "self-extension" (139). Possessions come to be revered as part of the self and in some cases literally extend the self, as is the case with some prosthetic devices. But a large component of this phenomenon is metaphoric. Belk argues that "a key to understanding what possessions mean is recognizing that, knowingly or unknowingly, intentionally or unintentionally, we regard our possessions as parts of ourselves" (139). Indeed, after the brain and face, humans will rate possessions as much, and sometimes more of, a part of their self-concept than body parts. In short, "the feeling of identity invested in material objects can be extraordinarily high" (144). It is this investment that leads Fiona to characterize her relationship to the Moleskines as "stewardship"; she feels responsible not necessarily for the writing contained in them but for the value they have as objects.

Fiona has associated objects with identity work since she was young. She cultivated the identity of writer to distinguish herself from her four siblings. In my interview with her, she quickly expressed the idea that because her family was large, "self-definition was related to having and owning things . . . it was really just a way of saying, 'I am an individual person.'" She described back-to-school shopping trips as "chaotic," her family as "territorial," and the home governed by an "economy of theft and exchange." If something was left in a common area, it disappeared. At holidays, gifts of different colors were given to each child. This is an example of objects being pulled out of the commodity realm and "singularized" as they are used in the expression and maintenance of identity (Epp and Price 821).

"Singularization" is an individuated experience of making meaning from a thing and decommodifying it by integrating it into one's life (Epp and Price 821). For Fiona, this takes the form of selecting particular Moleskines that reflect her identity and purpose. For other Moleskine users, singularization takes on even more dramatic forms. Figure 4, for example, shows a trend called a "hack": user-designed customizations of objects.

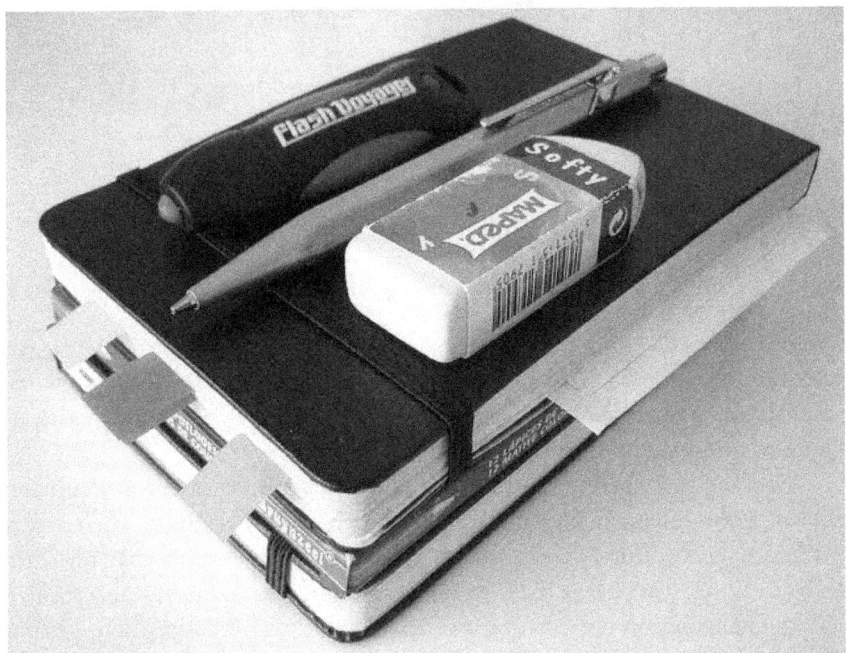

Figure 4. Moleskine Travel Kit, by Dimitri Popov.

All one has to do is type "Moleskine hack" into Google to access a vast resource for individuating one's Moleskine (a more recent example of this phenomenon can be observed by searching with the hashtag #bulletjournal on Instagram). Figure 5 depicts a user's hand-cut tabbed and labeled Moleskine.

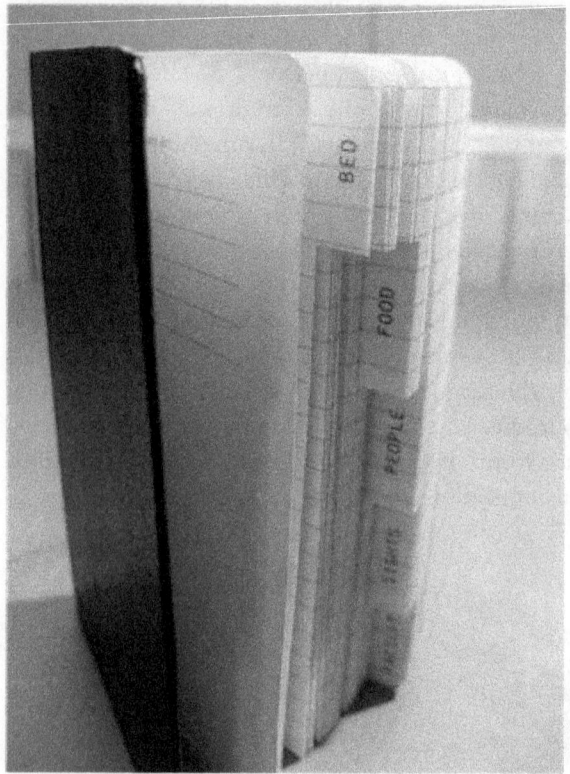

Figure 5. The Hacked Moleskine, courtesy of gtdfreak.

The elaborate tabbing and hacking systems discussed above can help a writer to transform and ritualize what might otherwise be seen as mundane work (such as keeping a calendar) or to organize what is perceived as already singular and as a representation of selfhood: one's writing.

Hacking and cutting up Moleskines appears to contradict a dominant thread in the discourse around this object, which is that due to their cost,[5] aesthetics, and cultural resonance, they have a "sacred" status that prevents them, at times, from being used. As Belk et al. note, "in an increasingly secular world, consumption has become a sacred act; through consumption, people "sacralize experience" and objects are treated as "set apart, extraordinary, or sacred" (1, 2, 9-12). "I have tons of Moleskine," one person writes, "All empty . . . It's terrifying to aim anything that resembles a writing implement at it. I've gone back to those sordid, crass pedestrian notebooks" (Dalisay). However, it is also possible that hacking the notebooks makes them more sacred, not less.

## Objects and Affiliation

Fiona's story represents the ways that objects are used as self-expression in service of building an identity around writing. Her use of the Moleskine is also fairly uncomplicated. She performs only one type of writing in her Moleskines and avoids using them for more stressful genres. She does not appear to use her notebooks for many of the oft-cited reasons in popular discourse: to counter the digital, to achieve writerly status, or to bring gravitas to her ideas. Rather, her story exemplifies how the "strongest attachments form with things that mark a realized identity development path," in this case, as a person who journals (Kleine, Kleine, and Allen 341).

David's story raises other points: First, what happens when our narrative around an object consumes our ability to use it; second, how objects reflect our affiliations with important others, such as peers, family, and friends; and, third, how our identities (around writing) intersect with and get bound to objects in ways that make their study an important component of understanding writing practice.

Throughout my interview with David, he narrated relationships with material goods that had a sacred tone. He told me a story about a poem ("Ezekiel's Wheel," by Geoffrey Hill) that he carried around in his wallet; he did not understand the poem and this lack, for him, represented an identity conflict. In his words, "it was an object that I was carrying around as a kind of way of dealing with a larger problem, which was that I was not a poet." He folded the poem up with the desire to continue carrying it around until he could understand it. The folded-up poem became even more weighted when one day he was working at a potter's wheel in a ceramic studio and the man who normally occupied that wheel entered the shop; the man's name, he realized, was Ezekiel. And he was sitting at Ezekiel's wheel. He shared this story as a means of explaining the series of coincidences and religious intersections that occurred during this time period, as he was trying to understand and forge his identity as both a person and writer. That day, he was uncomfortable because he was a novice ceramicist sitting at an expert potter's wheel. The folded-up poem was one object onto which he had projected ideas about himself.

This tension of wanting to become something that he is not, yet witnessing it in others and trying to access it, is observable in his childhood and in what I read as the emergence of his identity as a writer, which developed with and against his siblings and peers. David grew up in a family of three and shared a room with his brother, against whom he defined his identity. His brother was a musician whose part of the room was occupied by musical equipment. David asked his parents to buy him a desk at a young age. He was trying to claim space in a room he shared with his brother, demarcate territory, and signal his developing writerly persona (Alexis, "The Writing Habitat" 86). This resonates with Fiona's use of private, material space to claim an identity tied to writing. Possessions were not only tied to self-definition, but Fiona also successfully argued for her own room because she needed space and time to write, and she was the only child of five siblings who won this private space (86). In both cases, the material (object or space) is used for self-definition, for oneself internally and against others.

David grew up close to two male friends with and against whom he defined his identity. Speaking about who influenced his writing most, he says:

> The people I think of as influential were the people I was competing with more than anything. I remember two friends . . . every year or every semester there would be an award for language arts, an award for social studies, a little medal, in grade school. And the three of us always won it . . . . But it was somewhat uncomfortable because one of them was a real reader, a pathological reader and he was extremely imaginative and my mother sometimes used him as a—to try and get me to read. She'd say, "Nate reads all the time." And I'd say, "I don't want to do that." You know, it would really bug me . . .

What struck me throughout David's interview is his perception of himself in relation to others who are practicing similar activities or, put another way, the deep influence that close others have on our developing literate identities and sense of self when young. This tension between self and others ricochets throughout my interview with him, as he describes his developing persona as one who writes. His awareness of others continues in college, where David meets the woman who would later become his wife. He describes trying to doodle in his notebooks to make them interesting to her. He says, "I would spend hours a day just writing in these notebooks. I'm not an artist at all, so I was fiddling around with visual design stuff, but not effectively." Yet as he describes his fascination with his wife's artistry, he also narrates a tension with how he perceives his own use of Moleskines. Whereas he felt that his notebooks were not to be "sullied with class notes," her notebooks reflected another orientation: "That's something that kind of both upset me and fascinated me about her notebooks when I first started flipping through them. She would just write on anything and everything. She'll be writing, you know, a poem or a story and there'll be some information about a doctor's appointment and then class notes from a history class."

David's interview displays the degree to which he is conscious of how identities and orientations manifest in material goods. He narrates a story about giving a Moleskine to a cousin who was embarking on a long vacation:

Since that time he's become this compulsive journaler in these notebooks. Recently he picked up one of mine and flipped through it and said, "This is just a list. It's lists of stuff to do, like to-do lists, and mine's a story." And I said, "Yes. I don't have time to do that." I felt kind of sad to hear that. And he was just observing something, saying, "We do this really differently." So yes, I still use these notebooks. I have tons of them, but they're more of just information than anything else.

David feels angst that he is not a "real" writer, by which he means a writer of fiction and poetry; he sees himself as just writing down plain "information." He worries that he is profaning the sacred space of the Moleskine. Part of the Moleskine's sacrosanct quality for David is its design. As he says,

I have a sentimental attachment to [the Moleskine]. I like the way it looks. But I don't know the first thing about design. I wish I could look at a building or a painting and discern the language of design . . . And I envy people who can do that. And I feel that rather than being literate in that way, I'm pretty much at the mercy of that kind of visual rhetoric or design rhetoric.

The awe he feels for the Moleskine, then, is bound up with conflict over his own identity as a writer and his relation to others who write. Although he earned high honors in his discipline and is a successful writer and administrator, he laments, "I wish I were a better writer than I am. I wish I were a scholar, but I am not. I am a writing teacher." The Moleskine seems to lodge, or at least help us to unravel, anxieties about what it means to be a creative and productive writer. There is some "identity conflict" (Reed et al. 311) between his desire to be a writer and what he "principally understands himself to be" (Schatzki 54).

The Moleskine is an object that is bound to and reveals identity negotiation. In a sense, David uses this object to understand who he is. His relationship with the Moleskine demonstrates how the triad of self, other, and possessions intertwine with identity work. It supports Kleine, Kleine, and Allen's conclusion that identity research focused only on "the self as me," and not the self in "relations with others," is incomplete (341). As they write, "Self-identifying possessions reflect who I am as a unique individual, and/or who I am as I am connected to others" (341).

At a critical moment in his development as a writer, David, like Fiona, found the Moleskine and identified in it something valuable to his self-narrative. Through this object, he tries to understand and define his writing identity and his relation to others. At the same time, it is undeniable that the Moleskine also reveals more troubled feelings David holds about writing and his relationship to others who write. It is possible that David's sacred connection with the Moleskine has affected his ability to use the object freely. Housed in it is a tension between the writer he imagined, continues to imagine, and perceives himself to be.

**Integrated Object Use**

If Fiona's story communicates the idea of objects reflecting "who I am as a unique individual" and David's "who I am as I am connected to others," Lily, also a graduate student at the time of our interview, provides another perspective. Like Fiona and David, she could narrate the history of the Moleskine notebook, though initially she did not know or remember that the narrative is inserted in the back of the book. Unlike Fiona and David, however, Lily resists the Moleskine's narrative and is even a bit hostile to the company's association of writing with masculinity, through its references to the classic male literary canon via mentions of Picasso and Hemingway and through its use of stark black leather design motifs. She bought her first oversized bound Moleskine because she could not find another that she liked better and that had large enough pages to house her work.

What fascinated me about Lily's use of the Moleskine was, on the one hand, her lack of attachment to the object, and on the other, that her use of it was the most integrated and broad of those whom I interviewed. As you can see in Figures 6 and 7, Lily uses the Moleskine for all types of writing: taking class notes, mapping paper ideas, and sketching PowerPoint presentations.

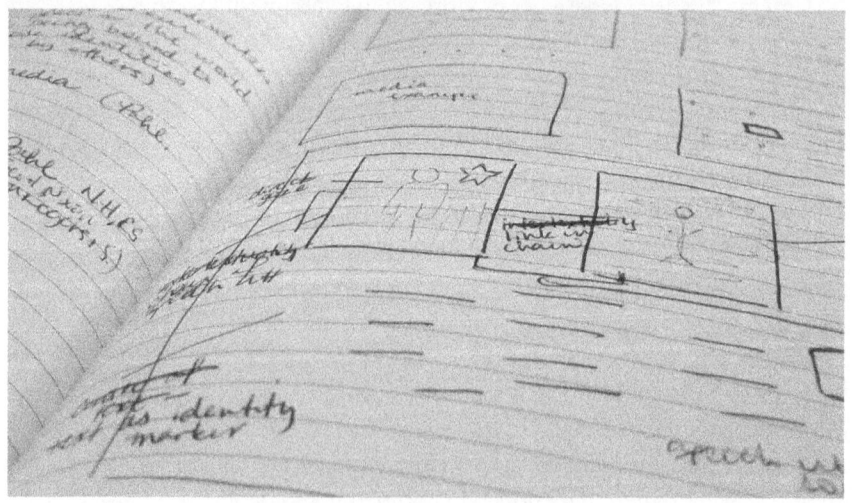

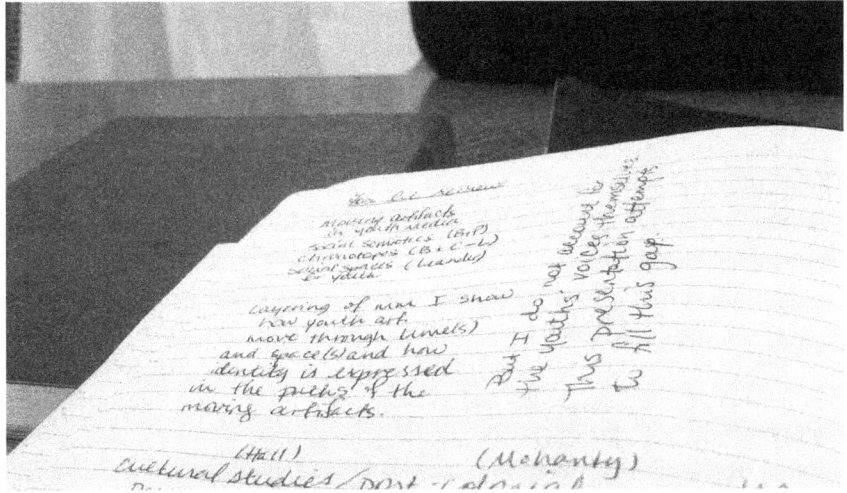

Figures 6 and 7. Lily's Moleskines.

Lily is fond of drawing in Moleskines, as opposed to drawing on loose paper, because this keeps her drawings "contained." For her, invention, space, and the Moleskine are linked; of the Moleskine's large dimensions, she said, "I like the ideas to come out; I like that space." This example illustrates how, in purchasing products, writers link aesthetic concerns to utilitarian or process-related ones. Lily chose this design because it was big enough that her hand could rest on the page while she writes, because of its narrow rule ("wide rule is a waste of space"), its binding ("the ring on spiral-bound notebooks always gets caught on my backpack") and its black cover, though she also dislikes that the cover is "boring" and "gendered masculine." Lily switched to the Moleskine in graduate school. Because they are bound, she states, they "have a kind of permanence that other notebooks don't." She feels her writing is being "preserved." Although she seems fairly unattached to the Moleskine, she did speak about writing in strong positive tones: "I have an emotional attachment to the act of writing and keeping my life ordered or keeping the ideas going or the creativity that can be engendered through the act of writing in this book . . . I am emotionally attached to thinking through ideas in this way." Her reference to "attachment" highlights how one can be invested not in an object, but in the practice that accompanies it. Understanding how and why writers rely on objects, even if, as in David's case, they might have a negative impact on practice, is important for our field.

Surprisingly, Lily told me that she hates writing, but likes every stage of the process where she is the primary audience. When I asked her if the Moleskine helps her manage her displeasure with writing, she answered, "Yes, absolutely . . . I enjoy writing in the Moleskine . . . because there's no risk to it . . . this stage is what gets me out of writer's block . . . in fact, I sometimes will just take this to the coffee shop and not my computer . . . because it will help me to get over just the fear of having to actually do the writing of it." This accords with Fiona's view of the Moleskine as a site of "unclogging." Lily often keeps the Moleskine side-by-side with her computer, and she goes back and forth between taking notes and working at the computer, in the same way that Fiona utilizes two Moleskines side by side, with one reserved for stream of consciousness writing.

For Lily, then, the Moleskine is a tool and a space that helps her to produce writing, to begin the creative part of the practice of writing that she loves. It is a stress reliever when she is working on less pleasurable tasks like the academic writing that is so central to her career. But it is not an object of obsession, affection, or attachment. In fact, Lily noted that if and when she finds another notebook that offers what the Moleskine does, she will switch. The Moleskine has not been integrated into her self-concept. This could possibly be because, unlike David and Fiona, Lily found the Moleskine at a much older age, once her identity as a writer and understanding of her writing practice needs were already cemented. In addition, the notebook's branding conflicts strongly with her sense of self, as it is connected to the male canon through the Hemingway myth.

Of the writers with whom I spoke, Lily has the most untroubled history with and most integrated use of the Moleskine. Whereas Fiona has attached the Moleskine to a segmented part of her writing practice, Lily's lack of attachment allows her to use it in complex, integrated ways. Her use of the Moleskine asks us to consider whether it might be the case that writers use objects in the least segmented or restrictive ways, and for the most broad purposes, when intense and positive attachments are not present.

## Conclusion

In this essay, I have attempted to understand the significance of one material object in writers' lives as a means of portraying the complexity of the relationship between writers, writing goods, and the practices and rituals that support literate performance. Rather than suggesting that all writers who use this object use it in the same way, I hope instead to point to similar types of work performed by material objects as writers attach to them for a variety of reasons.

Fiona, David, and Lily have different relationships to the Moleskine. Fiona has found a consistent use of this notebook; as a result, her practice is compelled, not thwarted, by this object. In contrast, the Moleskine appears to be a vexed object for David, one that initially signaled possibility and now reflects his feeling that he has not embodied the identity he wished to achieve.

I am careful to say "his feeling" because experience suggests that many who write on a daily basis for their work (and I'd include many academics in this category, including the majority of those whom I interviewed) do not see themselves as *writers* per se. David's internal sense of what *writing* means is a problem for writing studies, as only certain types of writing are marked off as "creative" and hence valuable, which I believe has led to the devaluing of the majority of writing performed by those who do it for their profession (for more information, see Alexis, "Stop Using"). Through the Moleskine, David will likely continue to work through his anxieties regarding his writing identity, anxieties that manifested during our various discussions of what this tiny object means in his and his family members' writing lives. David retains this object in his writing life because it was instrumental in helping him to envision a possible self as a writer, an identity that he still attempts to embody. At the same time, his competing and more easily inhabitable identity as an administrator troubles his relationship with the Moleskine since he does not see administrative writing as appropriate for this particular symbolic material possession. David's identities are in tension and motion, a liminal state that the Moleskine reveals. Yet a commonality binds David's and Fiona's narratives: The Moleskine is performing identity work, inviting an attachment, providing an entry into a desired identity or practice, and spurring internal reflection. In this way, the material object presses its own identity on writers, dictating certain types of disciplinary performance. Lily actively resists the identity components of the notebook; they do not reflect her "me." Her case compels consideration of whether attachment increases or hinders complex, broad, untroubled use of a possession.

The Moleskine notebook is just one facilitating artifact through which writers perform critical identity work that is an instrumental component in the development of a writing practice. Becoming a writer is composed of many instances in which one both imagines what writers do and performs similar acts. A chief way that this imagining occurs at a young age is through goods. Writers lean on chosen objects such as desks, pens, knick-knacks, and notebooks to begin to occupy a desired self and to practice it alone and, perhaps more importantly, for and with others. A practice of writing, then, cannot be understood without considering the various tools and settings with and within the habitats in which writers work—beginning with the kitchen in childhood, the bedroom in adolescence, and numerous other sites, both public and private, as adults. Writers practice their craft with a strong awareness of their relation to those around them, whether it is the identities of siblings and peers or of authors in a literary canon.

Siblings, peers, family members, and others who surround us as we are developing and articulating a writing self play important roles. Hence, rather than study writers in isolation (Emig; Flower and Hayes; Prior and Shipka), we need to study them in relation to the others they write with, against, and around. Besides the institutional and structural "sponsors" who support writing work is the vast network of what one of my students termed lowercase "s" sponsors who enable and disable our access to literate resources (Brandt).[6] These sponsors are at the very least a tableau against which we project desired selves. Writing is considered a sacred act and the writer a sacred cultural figure. People trying to access this desired identity use objects. How a person approaches and uses an object is intimately connected to that person's family, sense of self, writing history, relation to peers, media connections, social awareness, and life story. Turning to objects, and to facilitating artifacts, is one way of uncovering the very complicated identities that perform the practice we call "writing."

## Notes

1. For this project, I conducted 28 interviews with people who currently or formerly wrote regularly for school or work. The majority of my participants, at the time, were undergraduate and graduate students. However, a little over a third were not. Schoolteachers comprised nearly 20% of my study participants. I am interested in this population because teachers not only use objects in their own practices but also design writing environments for students. I also interviewed three generations of one family (two of these individuals were retired), and four individuals who identify as fiction and poetry writers or writers who work in business and administration.

2. A brief sketch of what I mean by *identity* is useful here, since writing studies has yet to treat in depth the subject of *writing identity* as a distinct type of identity with associated practices and object constellations. Cross-disciplinary research on identity has established that there is indeed a self that has some degree of control over one's own actions (Erikson; James; Sartre) that develops in stages and emerges from some form of group belonging (Erikson), and that gets shaped over time, both due to personal interests and associations and historical and social forces that impact the individual (Holland and Lave; Holland et al.). I find compelling Holland et al.'s articulation of identity as "a central means by which selves, and the sets of actions they organize, form and re-form over personal lifetimes and in the histories of social collectivities" (270). Holland and Lave refer to these as "personal identities" and note that they can be evoked "via cultural symbols" that help one to learn expectations for behavior in a particular realm. Additionally, Reissman notes that when constructing identities, individuals often perform identity to a desired end, often "involv[ing] their audience in 'doing' their identities" (5). A succinct definition of identity has been forwarded by consumer researchers Reed II et al. as "any category label to which a consumer self-associates either by choice or endowment" (312). Building on the above, I define identity as any category label or positionality to which a person self-associates either by choice or by endowment, due to identification with that label or because the performance of it will lead to some desired end. Identity is not a stable category and is not singular; hence, individuals may self-associate with more than one identity category and these identifications may shift over time.

3. This image is protected under a Creative Commons license: https://creativecommons.org/licenses/by-nc/2.0/legalcode.

4. Moleskine's commentary on its own success is fascinating. About its customer base, Moleskine writes, "They are global, they share a number of basic cultural elements, they want tools to help them bridge analog and digital, they are relatively less price sensitive. And, most importantly, they live on the move, and need brands that can help them convey their identity" ("Q4"). Moleskine explains its appeal as providing "distinctive aspirational values, supported by a strong reason to believe, a unique cultural heritage, which we maintain relevance [sic] by constantly engaging with expressions of contemporary culture."

5. Moleskine's Wikipedia page indicates that there is some fan controversy over the Moleskine's high cost in light of its production in China, a notoriously cheap labor market.

6. I am indebted to Rowan University graduate Lauren Buck for this point, which she raised in my fall 2014 section of Evaluating Writing.

## Works Cited

Alexis, Cydney. "Stop Using the Phrase *Creative Writing*." *Slate* 6 Jan. 2017. Web. 4 Apr. 2017. <http://www.slate.com/articles/life/inside_higher_ed/2017/01/let_s_banish_the_phrase_creative_writing.html>. Rpt. in *Bad Ideas About Writing*. "Creative Writing Is Unique Category." Edited by Drew Loewe and Cheryl Ball. Morgantown: Digital Publishing Institute, 2017. Print.

---. "The Writing Habitat: Objects, Environment, Practice." *Rhetoric, through Everyday Things*. Ed. Scot Barnett and Casey Boyle. Tuscaloosa: U of Alabama P, 2016. 83-95. Print.

Arnould, Eric J., and Craig J. Thompson. "Consumer Culture Theory (CCT): Twenty Years of Research." *Journal of Consumer Research* 31.4 (2005): 868-82. Web. 1 Apr. 2017. <http://www.jstor.org/stable/10.1086/426626>.

Atkinson, Robert. *The Life Story Interview*. Thousand Oaks: Sage Publications, 1998. Print.

Barnett, Scot, and Casey Boyle, eds. *Rhetoric, through Everyday Things*. Tuscaloosa: U of Alabama P, 2016. Print.

Baron, Dennis. "From Pencils to Pixels: The Stages of Literacy Technology." *Passions, Pedagogies, and 21st Century Technologies*. Ed. Gail E. Hawisher and Cynthia L. Selfe. Logan: Utah State UP, 1999. 15-33. Print.

Bartlett, Lesley. "To Seem and to Feel: Situated Identities and Literacy Practices." *The Teachers College Record* 109.1 (2007): 51-69. Print.

Belk, Russell W. "Possessions and the Extended Self." *Journal of Consumer Research* 15.2 (1988): 139-68. Web. 1 Apr. 2017. <http://www.jstor.org/stable/2489522>.

Belk, Russell W., Melanie Wallendorf, and John F. Sherry, Jr. "The Sacred and the Profane in Consumer Behavior: Theodicy on the Odyssey." *Journal of Consumer Research* 16.1 (1989): 1-38. Web. 1 Apr. 2017. <http://www.jstor.org/stable/2489299>.

Brandt, Deborah. *Literacy in American Lives*. New York: Cambridge UP, 2001. Print.

Brandt, Deborah, and Katie Clinton. "Limits of the Local: Expanding Perspectives on Literacy as a Social Practice." *Journal of Literacy Research* 34.3 (2002): 337-56. Print.

Bywater, Michael. "The Touch of Genius; This Notebook Will Help You Paint Like Van Gogh, Sketch Like Picasso and Write Like Hemingway—or at Least That's What Its Makers Would Have You Believe." Michael Bywater Finds Out Why Everyone's Buying It." *Independent* 3 Aug. 2003, Sun.: Features 7. Web. 26 Aug. 2016.

Czikszentmihalyi, Mihaly, and Eugene Rochberg-Halton. *The Meaning of Things: Domestic Symbols and the Self.* Cambridge: Cambridge UP, 1981. Print.

Dalisay, Jose. "In Praise of Moleskine." Comment by Raymond Arzadon on Jose Dalisay's blog entry. Web. 23 Oct. 2011. <http://homepage.mac.com/jdalisay/blog/PenmanSept07.html>.

Deetz, James. *In Small Things Forgotten: The Archaeology of Early American Life*. New York: Anchor-Doubleday, 1977. Print.

Emig, Janet A. *The Composing Processes of Twelfth Graders*. Urbana: NCTE, 1971. Print.

Epp, Amber, and Linda Price. "The Storied Life of Singularized Objects: Forces of Agency and Network Transformation." *Journal of Consumer Research* 36.5 (2010): 820-38. Web. 1 Apr. 2017. < http://www.jstor.org/stable/10.1086/603547>.

Erikson, Erik H. *Identity and the Life Cycle*. New York: Norton, 1980. Print.

Farry, Oliver. "G2 Etcetera: Why I Love Moleskines." *Guardian* [Manchester] 20 April 2004, final ed.: 23. Web. 18 Aug. 2016. <http://go.galegroup.com/ps/i.do?id=GALE%7CA115558205&v=2.1&u=ksu&it=r&p=ITBC&sw=w&asid=05a7569ccfa03ddc0e79254713e3965d>.

Gere, Ann Ruggles. "Kitchen Tables and Rented Rooms: The Extracurriculum of Composition." *CCC* 45.1 (1994): 75–92. Print.

gtdfreak. "infobook-after-50." 6 Jan. 2007. Online Image. Flickr. 28 April 2017. <https://www.flickr.com/photos/gtdfrk/347593171/in/pool-51462541@N00>.

Haas, Christina. *Writing Technology: Studies on the Materiality of Literacy*. Mahwah: Lawrence Erlbaum Associates, 1996. Print.

Handschuh, Jochen. "Moleskine." 31 July 2006. Online Image. Flickr. 28 April 2017. <https://goo.gl/kZZ19h>.

Hayateno, Kouji. Untitled Photograph. Permission to use granted via email 14 Feb. 2013. Facebook message.

Heath, Shirley Brice. *Ways with Words: Language, Life, and Work in Communities and Classrooms*. New York: Cambridge UP, 1983. Print.

Hill, Geoffrey. *Canaan*. New York: Penguin, 1996. Print.

Holland, Dorothy, et al. *Identity and Agency in Cultural Worlds*. Cambridge: Harvard UP, 1998. Print.

Holland, Dorothy, and Jean Lave. "Social Practice Theory and the Historical Production of Persons." *Actio: An International Journal of Human Activity Theory* 2 (2009): 1-15. Web. 18 Aug. 2016. <http://www.chat.kansai-u.ac.jp/publications/actio/pdf/no2-1.pdf>.

James, William. *The Principles of Psychology, Volume 1*. New York: Henry Holt, 1890. Print.

Kleine III, Robert E., Susan Schultz Kleine, and Jerome B. Kernan. "Mundane Consumption and the Self: A Social-Identity Perspective." *Journal of Consumer Psychol-*

*ogy* 2.3 (1993): 209-35. Web. 1 Apr. 2017. <http://search.ebscohost.com/login.aspx?direct=true&db=aph&AN=4815974&site=ehost-live>.

Kleine, Susan Shultz, Robert E. Kleine III, and Chris T. Allen. "How is a Possession 'Me' or 'Not Me'? Characterizing Types and an Antecedent of Material Possession Attachment." *Journal of Consumer Research* 22.3 (1995): 327-43. Web. 1 Apr. 2017. <http://www.jstor.org/stable/2489618>.

Kopytoff, Igor. "The Cultural Biography of Things: Commoditization as Process." *The Social Life of Things: Commodities in Cultural Perspective*. Ed. Arjun Appadurai. Cambridge: Cambridge UP, 1986. 64-94. Print.

Latour, Bruno. "On Interobjectivity." *Mind, Culture, and Activity* 3.4 (1996): 228-45. Web. 18 Aug. 2016. DOI: 10.1207/s15327884mca0304_2.

Laverie, Debra A., Robert E. Kleine III, and Susan Schultz Kleine. "Reexamination and Extension of Kleine III, Kleine, and Kernan's Social Identity Model of Mundane Consumption: The Mediating Role of the Appraisal Process." *Journal of Consumer Research* 28.4 (2002): 659-69. Web. 1 Apr. 2017. <http://www.jstor.org/stable/10.1086/338208>.

Lavin, Joe. "Novel Going Nowhere? Must Be Your Notebook: Pricey, Leather-Bound Moleskine Journals Have 'Wannabe Writer' Written All Over Them." *Gazette* [Montreal] 26 Sept. 2005, final ed.: D4. Web. 26 Aug. 2016.

Markus, Hazel, and Paula Nurius. "Possible Selves." *American Psychologist* 41.9 (1986): 954-69. Print.

Miller, Daniel. "Why Some Things Matter." *Material Cultures: Why Some Things Matter*. Ed. Daniel Miller. London: University College London P, 1998. 3-24. Print.

"Moleskine Store." *The Official Moleskine Website*. Moleskine SpA, 14 Nov. 2010. Web. 18 Aug. 2016. < http://www.moleskine.com/us/>.

"Moleskine World." *MOLESKINE*, 7 Apr. 2017. <http://www.moleskine.com/us/moleskine- world>.

"Moleskinerie: Legends and Stories." *Moleskine*. Moleskine SpA, 14 Nov. 2010. Web. 18 Aug. 2016. <http://www.moleskinerie.com>.

Oyserman, Daphna, Deborah Bybee, and Kathy Terry. "Possible Selves and Academic Outcomes: How and When Possible Selves Impel Action." *Journal of Personality and Social Psychology* 91.1 (2006): 188-204. Web. 18 Aug. 2016. <https://goo.gl/4g8ib1>.

Oyserman, Daphna, Larry Gant, and Joel Ager. "A Socially Contextualized Model of African American Identity: Possible Selves and School Persistence." *Journal of Personality and Social Psychology* 69.6 (1995): 1216-32. Web. 18 Aug. 2016. <http://dx.doi.org/10.1037/0022-3514.69.6.1216>.

Popov, Dimitri. Moleskine Travel Kit. 1 Sept. 2006. Online Image. Flickr. 28 April 2017.

Prior, Paul, and Jody Shipka. "Chronotopic Lamination: Tracing the Contours of Literate Activity." *Writing Selves, Writing Societies: Research from Activity Perspectives*. Ed. Charles Bazerman and David R. Russell. Fort Collins, CO: The WAC Clearinghouse, 2003. n. pag. Web. 18 Aug. 2016. <http://wac.colostate.edu/books/selves_societies/prior/>.

Prown, Jules David. "Mind in Matter: An Introduction to Material Culture Theory and Method." *Winterthur Portfolio* 17.1 (1982): 1-19. Web. 28 Apr. 2017. <http://www.jstor.org/stable/1180761>.

---. "Style as Evidence." *Winterthur Portfolio* 15.3 (1980): 197-210. Web. 26 Aug. 2016. <http://www.jstor.org/stable/1180742>.

"Q4 2014 Moleskine SpA Earnings Call-Final." *Fair Disclosure Wire*, 11 Mar. 2015. Web. 18 Aug. 2016.

Reed II, Americus. "Activating the Self-Importance of Consumer Selves: Exploring Identity Salience Effects on Judgments." *Journal of Consumer Research* 31.2 (2004): 286-95. Web. 26 Aug. 2016. <http://www.jstor.org/stable/10.1086/422108>.

Reed II, Americus, Mark R. Forehand, Stefano Puntoni, and Luk Warlop, "Identity-Based Consumer Behavior." *International Journal of Research in Marketing* 29.4 (2012): 310-21. Web. 26 Aug. 2016. <https://lirias.kuleuven.be/handle/123456789/373484?>.

Reissman, Catherine Kohler. "Narrative Analysis." *Narrative, Memory, and Everyday Life*. Huddersfield: U of Huddersfield, 2005. Web. 17 May 2017. <http://eprints.hud.ac.uk/4920/>.

Rodriguez, Juan. "Following the Paper Trail; In a City with No Shortage of Writers, Both Legendary and Aspiring, the Right Canvas Can Make All-Okay, Some-of the Difference." *Gazette* (Montreal) 16 Aug. 2007, final ed.: D8. Print.

Sartre, Jean-Paul. *Being and Nothingness: A Phenomenological Essay on Ontology*. New York: Philosophical Library, 1943. Print.

Schatzki, Theodore R. *The Site of the Social: A Philosophical Account of the Constitution of Social Life and Change*. University Park: Pennsylvania State UP, 2002. Print.

Schlereth, Thomas J. *Material Culture Studies in America*. Nashville: American Association for State and Local History, 1982. Print.

Schultz, Susan E., Robert E. Kleine III, and Jerome B. Kernan. "'These Are a Few of My Favorite Things': Toward an Explication of Attachment as a Human Behavior Construct." *Advances in Consumer Research* 16.1 (1989): 359-66. Web. 1 Apr. 2017. <http://search.ebscohost.com/login.aspx?direct=true&db=buh&AN=6487731&site=ehost-live>.

Shapshak, Toby. "A Moleskine Love Affair." *Business Day* [South Africa] 28 April 2007, weekend rev. ed.: 4. Print.

Solomon, Michael R. "The Role of Products as Social Stimuli: A Symbolic Interactionism Perspective." *Journal of Consumer Research* 10.3 (1983): 319-29. Web. 26 Aug. 2016. < http://www.jstor.org/stable/2488804 >.

Wallendorf, Melanie, and Eric J. Arnould. "'My Favorite Things': A Cross-Cultural Inquiry into Object Attachment, Possessiveness, and Social Linkage." *Journal of Consumer Research* 14.4 (1988): 31-47. Web. 1 Apr. 2017. <http://www.jstor.org/stable/2489159>.

Wyche, Susan. "Time, Tools, and Talismans." *The Subject is Writing: Essays by Teachers and Students*. Ed. Wendy Bishop. 1st ed. Portsmouth: Boynton/Cook, 1993. 111-23. Print.

Wyche-Smith, Susan Lee. "The Magic Circle: Writers and Ritual." Diss. University of Washington, 1988. Print.

# Writing by the Book, Writing Beyond the Book

*Kristine Johnson*

> Writing has become more visible in academia through writing advice manuals and the faculty development activities they inspire. In this article, I examine writing advice manuals and argue they are epistemologically current-traditional, which limits how well and how far they can support scholarly writers. Writing advice manuals and composition scholarship offer conflicting visions of scholarly writing knowledge about writing, particularly with respect to the writing process and the place of rhetorical invention. I finally call on scholars in composition studies to attend to invention in scholarly writing through reflection, research, and teaching.

---

Joining a faculty writing group sounded suspiciously like joining a self-help group: there was a book to buy, so-called simple steps to follow, weekly meetings to attend, and enthusiastic testimonials from members of the group. As a composition scholar and writing teacher, I was reluctant to believe that any writing group, particularly one focused on behavior and accountability, would offer me a wholly new approach to scholarly writing. But it was ultimately this testimonial from my well-published friend that persuaded me to join: "Writing group changed not only my scholarly productivity but also my life!" After my first year on the tenure track, I associated scholarly writing with stress and fear. Finding time for research among my teaching and administrative duties had been difficult, and I struggled to define my scholarly agenda beyond graduate school and the dissertation. I eventually bought the book, *How to Write a Lot: A Practical Guide to Productive Academic Writing*, committed to its methods, and began attending weekly meetings.

I had always been conscientious about writing regularly (if not always productively) and setting realistic goals, but writing group aimed to turn these good intentions into unbending habits. My group followed the method Paul J. Silvia outlines in *How to Write a Lot*: each writer keeps a daily log of words written, time spent writing, and notes about each writing session; formulates small, concrete goals for each writing session; and attends a weekly group meeting to report on successes and failures and announce goals for the upcoming week. Because of writing group, I can report that I completed the first full draft of this essay in sixty-nine writing sessions, each of which lasted an average of two hours; I can also report that I achieved my daily word goal 83% of the time (somewhat below the 97% Silvia achieved in the year before publishing *How to*

*Write a Lot*). Because of writing group, I have a one thousand-line spreadsheet that provides detailed evidence of my writing process across nearly four years.

Through writing group I encountered an active, popular moment that encourages faculty and graduate students to write more productively and publish more successfully. During the last two decades, a number of writing advice manuals—a genre I define later in the essay—have been published to support scholarly writers: *Writing Your Dissertation in Fifteen Minutes a Day*; *Writing Your Journal Article in Twelve Weeks*; *Professors as Writers: A Self-Help Guide to Productive Writing*; *The Clockwork Muse: A Practical Guide to Writing Theses, Dissertations, and Books*; and *How to Write a Lot: A Practical Guide for Productive Academic Writing*. While some manuals focus on only dissertations and others address multiple scholarly genres, they share a central assumption: scholarly writers inherently possess valuable, publishable ideas and requisite writing skills; to be successful, they need only to foster better writing behaviors.[1] This assumption exists in writing across the curriculum and faculty development scholarship that promotes accountability-focused writing groups, writing retreats, and writing bootcamps (Baldi, Sorcinelli, and Yun; Elbow and Sorcinelli; Fajt, et al.; Gray, Birch, and Madson; Salem and Follett; Schick et al.). And as scholarly writers come together through social media, the assumption has been popularized in events such as Academic Writing Month (AcWriMo). Writers join AcWriMo each November through Facebook and Twitter, and they commit to a process outlined in many writing advice manuals: "Set yourself some crazy goals; Publicly declare your participation and goals; Draft a strategy; Discuss what you're doing; Don't slack off; Publicly declare your results" (Williams). AcWriMo is highly publicized in the *Chronicle of Higher Education*, on academic blogs, and across social media; in November 2014, #AcWriMo generated over two thousand tweets from faculty and graduate students across the disciplines.

Writing group indeed produced quantitative changes in my scholarly writing. I generated more words and wrote for more hours than I had previously, which helped me feel I was leading a more productive, balanced life. In the competitive, high-stakes environment of scholarly publication, focusing on quantity was both comforting and mathematically logical: writing more words should result in more publications. Yet writing group did not produce qualitative changes in my writing, and it often drove me away from the hard, sometimes meandering work of deep intellectual engagement. It did not make me more confident about the value of my ideas or give me new things to say. Further, immersing myself in this scholarly writing movement prompted questions about my identity as a writing teacher. In the composition classroom, I taught students that finding interesting ideas requires intellectual work and that the writing process is recursive and sometimes surprising—commonplaces rehearsed in most undergraduate composition textbooks. In my own writing life, I convinced myself that my ideas were worth pursuing and plodded through my essay outlines at three hundred words per day. The beliefs about writing that I shared with students and that I adopted in my own practice were fundamentally conflicting, and I wondered to whom I was being disingenuous.

My argument in this essay is that current, popular perspectives on scholarly writing—most clearly manifested in writing advice manuals—are epistemologically current-traditional, which limits how well and how far they can support scholarly writers. Both in their own writing practices and in their work with other writers, composition scholars should not accept these perspectives uncritically. I begin by analyzing several writing advice manuals, and my analysis is framed by two questions: How do writing advice manuals understand writing and the writing process? And how do they understand rhetorical invention? My analysis reveals that writing advice manuals and composition scholars offer contradictory answers to these questions. I then outline how writing advice manuals focus on behavior rather than process and place invention outside the province of writing. Finally, I call on composition scholars to do the research and teaching that allows us to be present and persuasive in current conversations about scholarly writing. Writing is an increasingly visible part of academia and faculty development, and when we work with other faculty and graduate students, we must promote our own disciplinary values.

**Writing By the Book**

Writing advice manuals are one part of a constellation of current, popular texts and activities that support scholarly writers, but my focus here is writing advice manuals because they generally predate faculty development scholarship on writing, are promoted in events such as AcWriMo, and offer sustained discussions of scholarly writing. Writing advice manuals differ according to focus and audience, and simply analyzing bestsellers is challenging because writing manuals are categorized in unpredictable ways (some as medical reference books and others as grammar guides). In this essay, two principles guided my choice of manuals to analyze. First, I defined *writing advice manual* according to the genre conventions Barbara Kamler and Pat Thomson outline in their research on dissertation advice books: "(a) An expert–novice relationship is produced and reproduced, (b) the process of writing a dissertation is simplified to a series of linear steps, (c) writing advice is packaged as a set of overgeneralized rules, and (d) the texts are emphatic and offer a paradox of reassurance and fear" (509). Although Kamler and Thomson examine only books for dissertation writers, my analysis also includes books for faculty and graduate students. With the exception of manuals with *dissertation* in the title, writing advice manuals consistently group all post-undergraduate scholarly writers together—a move that overlooks particular challenges in graduate student or faculty writing. Second, I analyzed manuals that are regularly endorsed in AcWriMo tweets, online articles offering scholarly writing advice, and the Writing Program Administration listserv. Nearly all of the manuals I analyzed were recommended in a recent WPA-L discussion about faculty writing workshops, which suggests a need for compositionists to subject writing advice manuals to closer examination.[2]

**Writing and the Writing Process**

I began my analysis of writing advice manuals by posing this question: how do these texts understand writing and the writing process? Although most writing advice manuals do not employ the same vocabulary found in composition textbooks, they do offer a clear vision of writing and the writing process. The manuals consistently define writing as a physical behavior, and as such, they focus on behaviors and habits that support or inhibit generating text easily and productively. Scholars struggle to balance teaching, service, administration, and personal lives with the demands of research and publication, and writing advice manuals promise strategies for increased productivity and publishing success. Beyond defining writing as a physical behavior, the manuals also address affective elements of writing such as anxiety, identity, and isolation. They address emotion within a behavioral frame, however, arguing that writing should be an emotionally detached activity and that behavior is ultimately the solution to all affective concerns.

The idea that writing is simply a physical behavior originates in research from Robert Boice, a psychologist interested in writing blocks and fluency in writing. In *Professors as Writers: A Self-Help Guide to Productive Writing*, an early book in the writing advice manual genre, he argues that successful scholarly writing is a simple matter of contingency management: "Make writing a daily activity, regardless of mood, regardless of readiness to write. Make a more regular, recurrent activity contingent on writing for a minimum period of time first" (79). He encourages scholarly writers to establish a set of "stimulus control procedures" such as writing in a regular space, writing for between thirty minutes and two hours each day, setting goals and sub-goals for each writing session, and keeping charts of time spent writing and pages generated (78–80). Boice is particularly influential in conversations about scholarly writing because he makes a claim in *Professors as Writers* that many writing advice manuals repeat: the physical behavior of writing generates more creative thoughts.[3] For Boice, ideas do not initiate discourse, and the scholarly writing process moves in one direction; generating text may prompt ideas and creativity, but ideas do not prompt writing.

Writing advice manuals explicitly or implicitly reinforce the idea that behavior—not inquiry, dissonance, or other rhetorical exigencies—initiates writing. In *How to Write a Lot*, Silvia defines writing as behavior and takes great care not to frame it as a creative process: "Writing productively is about actions that you aren't doing but could easily do: making a schedule, setting clear goals, keeping track of your work, rewarding yourself, and building good habits" (3–4). Writing is strictly a set of "concrete behaviors, such as (a) sitting on a chair, bench, stool, ottoman, toilet, or patch of grass and (b) slapping your fingers against the keyboard to generate paragraphs. . . . Let everyone else procrastinate, daydream, and complain—spend your time sitting down and moving your mittens" (Silvia 7–8). He finally defines writing in such strongly behaviorist terms that he invalidates the possibility of blocking: "Writer's block is nothing more than the behavior of not writing. Saying you can't write because of writer's block is merely saying that you can't write because you aren't writing. It's trivial. The cure for writer's block—if you can cure a specious affliction—is writing" (45–46). By framing writing as a behavior to be controlled and monitored, Silvia offers readers reassurance and seemingly clear answers: writing problems are resolved through the physical act of writing.

Beyond classifying writing as a behavior, writing advice manuals also define scholarly writing as a series of physical, sequential behaviors. Sonja Foss and William Waters, in *Dissertation Destination: A Traveler's Guide to a Done Dissertation*, outline twenty-nine steps (which can be completed in just over one thousand hours) for researching and writing a dissertation. They reassure readers that completing each step in order prevents writing blocks. For example, if the writer follows these steps, "the literature review almost writes itself. . . . You are literally writing your way through the pile [of notes and citations] as you type the second excerpt, the third excerpt. . . . You have to add introductions, overviews, your argument about the excerpts, and transitions between the excerpts, but those are easy now because you see your argument" (94). In *Writing Your Journal Article in Twelve Weeks: A Guide to Academic Publishing Success*, Wendy Belcher guides writers through sixty steps (five tasks per week for twelve weeks) for revising a paper for publication. And in *The Clockwork Muse*, Eviatar Zerubavel describes scholarly writing as "a mountain with stairs," promising that climbing each "mental stair" listed in the book is "relatively simple, instead of a single seemingly unaccomplishable task you will actually be dealing with a series of relatively unproblematic mini-tasks that you clearly *can* manage" (39). These manuals identify the primary challenge of scholarly writing as behavioral rather than intellectual, and they promote simplicity over complexity.

Writing advice manuals are primarily interested in changing behavior, but they also emphasize the connection between writing and emotion—particularly negative emotions such as anxiety and fear. Silvia and Belcher each acknowledge writing anxiety as a barrier to productivity, but they believe emotional problems have behavioral causes and therefore behavioral solutions. Silvia recognizes the "insecurities, feelings of avoidance and defensiveness, or inner mental blocks that hold people back" (3), but he contends that blocking and fear are resolved by physically writing. Belcher addresses the issue of not being emotionally ready to write by arguing that emotion follows action (she agrees with Silvia that simply writing will produce positive feelings about writing). She also encourages scholarly writers to learn techniques for "thinking positively about your life and work" and integrating positive behaviors—such as lighting candles, playing songs, or doing stretches—with each scheduled writing session (32). Neither Belcher nor Silvia claim that scholars will overcome negative emotions by developing new writing skills or strengthening their ideas; both argue that better behaviors allow scholarly writers to manage and overcome negative emotions.

Boice is highly attentive to the effect of writing anxiety and negative emotions on scholars' ability to write. He discusses a range of emotional issues that include disliking writing, lacking confidence, writing anxiety as measured by the Daly–Miller Writing Apprehension Test, depression, phobias, and writing cramps (24–28). After arguing that these affective issues are fundamentally behavioral, he forwards one specific behavior: automatic writing. According to Boice, automatic writing "releases your inner writer . . . establishes momentum, bypasses internal censors, generates rhythm and voice, and builds confidence in abilities to be spontaneous, playful, and creative" (96). Scholarly writing suppresses the spontaneous mind, and practicing automatic writing—writing such as copying from sources and taking notes on sources—will resolve blocks and negative emotions. Boice argues that practicing automatic writing each day will "build progressively more length and substance" (58) into a scholarly writing project and will eventually produce a full draft. Although automatic writing may seem to align with expressive theories of composition that promote freewriting and unhindered expression, Boice is more interested in behavior than in self expression.[4] The purpose of generating text is to generate text, not to resolve intellectual questions or develop a personal voice.

Ultimately the themes of behavior and affect converge when the writing advice manuals argue that behavior is the best solution to affective issues. They characterize behavior, affect, and writing success as virtues acquired through practice: by practicing the behavior of writing, professors and graduate students become writers. Writers develop positive associations with writing by writing. Writers write. Although each manual offers a unique perspective, their authors share foundational assumptions, which are appealing for their clarity. If complex intellectual and emotional challenges can be addressed through spontaneous writing, twenty-nine steps, a spreadsheet, or a weekly writing group meeting, then many scholarly writers surely may want to avoid deliberately difficult writing with indeterminate steps and changeable goals.

## Rhetorical Invention

Writing advice manuals define writing as a physical behavior, which downplays the role of ideas and thinking in writing. Yet the purpose of scholarly writing is not only to produce knowledge but also to produce *new* knowledge, so I continued my analysis by asking this question: How do these texts understand rhetorical invention? Before I examine invention in writing advice manuals, I must note one caveat: some authors, including Boice and Silvia, work in the social sciences, where particular kinds of knowledge are discovered through the scientific method rather than the writing process. One reason for scholarly writing in the social and natural sciences is to "write up" data gathered through experimental or other empirical methods. However, these writing advice manuals do not consider the possibility that writing itself may help scholars support or elaborate their conclusions or even generate new interpretations of their data—inventive work that happens even when writers are working from empirical data.

Writing advice manuals first make a clear, Ramist separation between writing and thinking. Silvia believes invention is not part of the writing process because scholarly writing does not solve problems or produce insight: "You're not crafting a deep narrative or composing metaphors that expose mysteries of the human heart. . . . Novelists and poets are the landscape artists and portrait painters; academic writers are the people with big paint sprayers who repaint your basement" (45). The work of scholarly writing is to commit knowledge to written form in the most stark, utilitarian manner possible. Silvia does claim that planning is an integral part of writing and that "people who write a lot also plan a lot" (30), but he does not view planning in the way we understand it in composition studies. In their study of cognitive processes, for example, Linda Flower and John Hayes define planning and goal setting as inventional activities; successful writers are effective planners because they are able to define and manage global and local goals simultaneously (371–75). Silvia reduces planning to time management and assigning oneself appropriate daily writing tasks.

After separating writing and thinking, the writing advice manuals claim that writing-to-discover interferes with the more important work of writing-to-produce. They operate under the behaviorist assumption that errors—writing in circles or composing a dead-end draft—should be avoided, while composition scholars would claim that missteps can be generative. In *Destination Dissertation*, Foss and Waters encourage readers not to begin writing until they have completed significant inventive work such as identifying the research question, selecting the data and methodology, and outlining literature review areas. They claim that exploratory writing interferes with text production: "Beginning to write now will significantly delay the completion of your dissertation because you will be delaying its real start. When you begin writing before you've made the key decisions about your dissertation . . . you usually get stuck fairly quickly" (35). Foss and Waters acknowledge that dissertation writers must find an idea (something for which they do not offer much guidance), but they dissuade students from writing to learn, from finding "a vague idea of a topic . . . and writ[ing] on your proposal, hoping to figure out what you want to research" (26). In *The Clockwork Muse*, Zerubavel admonishes writers to make their "writing [process] more 'linear' . . . to make sure that your writing moves in a linear fashion rather than 'in circles,' so that you indeed end up with a fully completed thesis, dissertation, or book" (83). Both manuals lead writers away from complexity, suggesting that writing should simply transfer stable ideas to written form.

Separating writing and thinking finally precludes the possibility for drafting and revision to be sites of invention. Belcher places invention, as planning and as inquiry, outside the scope of her work, explaining that researching and writing a scholarly article in only twelve weeks is unrealistic. But she also discounts invention as part of scholarly writing: "Most books on academic writing assume that the most difficult part of writing is arriving at good ideas. This may be difficult for undergraduates, but it is not for graduate students or junior faculty. In my writing workshops, good ideas abound. The real problem is how many good ideas languish in unfinished, unpublished articles" (xii). Although invention may certainly take place while completing the sixty steps, Belcher does not address why and how discourse is initiated, and her sequential approach does not allow the writing process to be recursive. She instead claims that "revision is the heart of good writing and that many scholars are unpublished not because they have bad ideas, but because they have never learned how to improve their drafts" (xiii). For Belcher and other advice manual authors, ideas exist in stable form apart from writing, and consequently, revision has the capacity to improve words rather than ideas.

**Writing Beyond the Book**

Composition scholars should be critical of writing advice manuals because they are epistemologically current-traditional, focusing on behavior over process and rejecting rhetorical invention. While it is not my intention simply to criticize writing advice manual authors (two of whom are behavioral psychologists) for their philosophical allegiances, it is my aim to expose the limits of behaviorism for supporting scholarly writers and fostering rhetorical invention—limits that composition studies recognized decades ago in its turn toward process pedagogy and disciplinarity. The disciplinary work of composition studies has been to establish a body of declarative and procedural knowledge about writing. According to Elizabeth Wardle and Doug Downs, procedural writing choices originate in declarative knowledge about writing: "How one plays the game depends on what game one thinks one is playing . . . it is clear that the story we tell ourselves about the nature of writing—our conceptions of what writing is and how it ought to work—will powerfully shape how we go about doing it" (279). Writing advice manuals offer a temptingly clear vision of the scholarly writing game, a vision that cannot be reconciled with declarative knowledge produced in composition studies. Although focusing on behavior may seem to address problems of competition and scarcity in scholarly publishing, it creates new issues by directing writers away from the discovery, questioning, and intellectual engagement that make writing and ideas matter.

Behaviorism is interested in external behavior rather than internal processes, and research in behavioral psychology attempts to explain internal events in behavioral terms.[5] In her work on teaching grammar, Constance Weaver explains that traditional (decontextualized, drill-based) grammar instruction stems from behaviorism, which defines learning as habit formation and encourages students to avoid mistakes that would prevent them from forming good habits (18). She argues that traditional grammar instruction is ineffective precisely because of these behaviorist assumptions. Composition pedagogy, however, stems from constructivism and cognitive psychology, which instead defines learning as hypothesis formation and encourages errors that ultimately produce more sophisticated hypotheses (18). Early in its existence, composition studies shifted the focus of writing instruction from behavior and written products to cognition and writing processes. Rhetorical invention figured prominently in this shift because, as Janice Lauer notes, invention "is the only one [canon of rhetoric] that directly addresses the content of communication as well as the process of creation, thus dealing with one of the most visible parts of published rhetorical performance, the content, and one of the most often invisible—the process by which a writer produced that content" (*Invention* 1–2). Early composition research on cognition and heuristics further illustrates how invention extended the province of writing beyond the behavioral to the intellectual: invention addresses the ideas a writer conveys and the process that commits ideas to a product.

Writing advice manuals reject or ignore rhetorical invention as it was theorized in early composition scholarship, where the writer is the primary site and agent of invention. In cognitive studies of writing, the writing process was characterized as a process of discovery. Flower and Hayes claim that "goal directed thinking is intimately connected with discovery" (378) and identify tagmemics and the classical topics as discovery procedures (382). Invention was characterized as a way of solving rhetorical problems, and scholars claimed that it can and should be taught as a techne. Richard Young, for example, is careful to define writing as a techne rather than a knack because he believes that elements of the discovery process are subject to conscious, teachable actions (344-45). These perspectives on writing and invention had clear pedagogical implications; scholars claimed that teaching invention—especially with heuristics—would yield better writing than simply relying on chance or habit. Lauer argues that transcendent, flexible, generative heuristics increase "the chances of discovering insight" and help writers "retrieve past meanings and to symbolize new associations" ("Toward a Metatheory" 268). Writing advice manuals stand in clear contrast to these neoclassical positions on writing and invention, defining scholarly writing and insight as a knack rather than a teachable art. They position discovery outside the province of writing and consign it to either the scientific method or the realm of skills that scholarly writers should already possess. And because they understand the writing as a set of linear behaviors rather than a recursive process, they do not provide writers with multiple directions and probable judgments.

Compositionists may be hesitant to endorse neoclassical, agent-centered claims about invention (and therefore may be hesitant to critique writing advice manuals on those grounds), but writing advice manuals also reject or ignore postmodern understandings of invention.[6] Postmodern theorists, concerned that early perspectives on invention perpetuate the subject/object split of technological thinking, characterize invention instead as an experience of questioning and destabilizing. The task of writing, Lynn Worsham argues, is not to synthesize new associations but "to defamiliarize and denaturalize. Its task is to make strange and uncanny what is familiar and comfortable" ("The Question" 233). If writing should destabilize, then invention should not be deliberately controlled with heuristics. Victor Vitanza instead calls for aleatory procedures that embrace chance, the excluded middle, and the "monsters of thought" (186). Postmodern scholarship ultimately questions the assumption that writers are the primary agents of invention, whether invention is a hermeneutic or productive activity. In his work on genre and invention, Anis Bawarshi shifts the focus from how writers articulate desire to how they *acquire* desire (2); he emphasizes that writers "both invent and are invented by the genres that they write" (12). Writing advice manuals clearly promote writing as a stabilizing activity, and they assign writers agency to control genres, transfer knowledge to written form without interference, and overcome the "monsters of thought" that may inhibit productivity.

By placing invention—in its neoclassical or postmodern sense—outside the province of writing, writing advice manuals reduce scholarly writing to scribing. Michel Carter differentiates writing and scribing, arguing that the two are not points on a continuum but wholly different acts: "*Scribing* is... the kind of literate composition that is characterized not by beginnings but by *the* beginning, a way of knowing and being in the world marked by continuity, equilibrium, orientation to that which comes before" (115). Because scribing does not recognize uncertainty and the instability of knowledge, it is epistemologically current-traditional; indeed it is "a sort of copying because, like 'utterance,' it is the generation of text without questioning, challenging, without upsetting, without interpretation, at best only ornamenting what is already there" (Carter 115). But *writing* and rhetorical invention embrace the unknown because writing always takes place "on the threshold between order and disorder, the known and unknown, being and becoming, location and dislocation" (116). Writing advice manuals encourage generating text—scribing—above other aims because they assume writing neither discovers nor creates knowledge and that knowledge is stable. However, if the primary aim of scholarly writing is to extend beyond the known, then writing advice manuals cannot fully support scholarly writers as they aim to make contributions to a discipline.

Discerning the role of invention in scholarly writing specifically is difficult because composition studies has focused little attention on the writing practices of (and writing pedagogy for) graduate student writers and paid virtually no attention to faculty writers. Compositionists who address scholarly writing, however, affirm invention as a value. Laura Micciche describes a graduate course in critical writing and calls for composition studies to conceptualize writing instruction as a vertical endeavor through graduate school because "critical writing is not a mere extension of undergraduate writing practices and is not best learned by tacit immersion" (497). Her critical writing course teaches rhetorical theory, genre theory, and rhetorical grammar, and it includes feedback at all phases of writing (486–93). And most significantly, the course addresses invention through a "pedagogy of wonder" (480). Learning how to wonder fosters inquiry, which Micciche defines as the "process of asking questions for which one does not have answers—a hermeneutical endeavor that requires considerable practice as writer and attentiveness as reader" (480). By positioning writing on the threshold of the unknown, Micciche brings invention into the province of what scholarly writers can learn and be taught, assigning writing the power to generate knowledge and solve problems.

Invention leads writers toward complexity and dissonance, and some composition scholars define difficulty as both a disciplinary value and a characteristic of scholarly writing. E. Shelley Reid argues that teaching assistant preparation courses should include "difficult" writing assignments that require exploration and inquiry—that is, assignments with inventive challenges. Reid notes that students often arrive at graduate school with little experience struggling as writers, and she fears that "people who do not believe that premise [that writing well is difficult] themselves only go through the motions as writing teachers" (W202). By engaging writing teachers in difficult writing, "we help them discover for themselves what the discipline of writing education really involves" (W217). Reid hopes teachers will empathize with students as a result of their struggle, and her larger hope speaks to the value of invention because it is through invention that writers encounter the discipline. In an article in the *Chronicle of Higher Education*, Lynn Worsham addresses intellectual difficulty in her lament over "fast food scholarship." She argues that "too many academics—veterans and neophytes alike—are producing scholarship that appears to have traded careful, methodical, fully developed intellectual work for quick and dirty publication" ("Fast-Food"). Worried that a publish-or-perish mentality has overshadowed the goal of intellectual mastery, she contends that true intellectual work "requires deep dedication and a willingness to labor long after the amateur would have quit." Certainly some scholarly projects are simply more difficult or time-consuming than others, and it is questionable if scholarly projects accrue value with time. Like Micciche and Reid, Worsham links scholarly writing with intellectual engagement. Because ideas matter in scholarly writing, invention must also matter.

**Professors as Writers, Writers as Professors**

Writing advice manuals and the activities they inspire have made writing more visible in academia, encouraging scholars to see themselves as writers. Although Silvia encourages scholarly writers to adopt serviceable, mechanistic writerly identities (evidenced in his basement painting analogy), he nonetheless forwards writing as a distinctive part of professional identity. Composition studies should welcome this attention to writers and writing, yet as writing teachers and scholars, writing program administrators, and writing center directors, we should not so easily accept these perspectives on scholarly writing. Increased attention to scholarly writing offers composition studies an opportunity to develop knowledge with value both within and beyond our discipline; it further challenges us to promote faculty and graduate student development programs that foster invention and engage ideas, supporting writers beyond advice manuals, bootcamps, and AcWriMo schedules.

Empirical studies of student writers and professional and technical writers are well established in composition studies, yet studies of faculty and graduate student writers—specifically in composition studies—are rare. Current attention to scholarly writing and writerly identity suggests that this kind of research is timely, and one of my aims in this essay has been to reveal a gap in current thinking about scholarly writing. Studies of faculty and graduate writers may provide counter narratives to the pervasive behaviorist narrative, and they may help us better communicate how rhetorical invention actually functions in scholarly writing. When attending to invention in scholarly writing, we might address these questions: What is the nature of daily writing practices and habits? What kinds of questions do writers ask to invent new ideas? How did published authors invent subject matter for particular books or articles? How do writers know when to give up on an idea? How does the peer review process influence invention and revision? What are the behavioral, emotional, and intellectual challenges in scholarly writing? While I would not argue that results from these studies should simply be codified and taught, I believe they may provide valuable frameworks for faculty and graduate student development programs; they may provide knowledge that supports the likely significant number of scholarly writers whose primary concerns are not behavioral. Uncovering actual writing practices may reveal difficulty, complexity, and dissonance, and it may describe how physical writing behaviors and rhetorical invention interact.

Beyond pursuing this research agenda, teachers and scholars in composition studies should promote faculty and graduate student development programs that encompass invention, engage ideas, and push writers toward complexity—programs that encourage writers in ways that are consistent with our disciplinary values. Promoting these development programs does not mean wholly rejecting writing advice manuals and the activities they inspire, but it does mean recognizing their limitations. The texts compositionists recommend and the programs we create must recognize writing as an inventive act that positions writers on the threshold of the known and unknown, an act of discovery and questioning. For example, a text by a compositionist and writing center director, Irene Clark, *Writing the Successful Thesis and Dissertation: Entering the Conversation*, includes a chapter, "So What? Discovering Possibilities," with invention activities that help any scholarly writer "'listen' to conversations of published colleagues—that is, read deeply in relevant texts—in order to have something that members of the community will regard as 'worth considering'" (7). Clark explicitly aligns herself with a process approach to composition, and her work does not strongly exhibit any of the four genre conventions that Kamler and Thomson outline, particularly the packaged set of overgeneralized writing rules. Beyond evaluating materials based on genre markers, those who lead faculty and graduate student development programs may ask these questions when selecting materials: Does the text or program address elements of writing beyond drafting behavior? Does it represent writing as a recursive process? Does it define ideas as changeable?

Effective writing programs may combine behavioral goals with a focus on inquiry and intellectual complexity. Angela Clark-Oates and Lisa Cahill argue that writing centers are uniquely equipped to support faculty writers because they are physically and philosophically designed to foster literacy events—critical, interpretive conversations between readers and writers (111–13). When writing centers house faculty writing groups, they "provide faculty writers the opportunity to dialogue with interested and invested readers, provide access to individuals who can serve as an approximation of an audience and as a testing ground for the development and organization of ideas" (124). Writing centers may position scholarly writing as a social act and offer space for scholars "to experiment with and discuss their writing" (124). At Elon University, Peter Felten, Jessie Moore, and Michael Strickland combined a retreat structure (focused writing time with no distractions) with a focus on publishing teaching and learning scholarship: discussion of genre challenges, feedback at multiple phases of the writing process, and faculty facilitators who kept "feedback focused on content and organization as opposed to editing and stylistic suggestions that might not be relevant until after the writers revised" (50). Compositionists like those at Elon are equipped to offer expertise that moves faculty and graduate student development programs beyond physical writing habits to rhetorical habits of mind, beyond timely completion to wonder, beyond behavioral accountability to intellectual engagement. Writing behaviors, time to degree, and accountability are not unimportant, but they do not encompass what it is to be engaged in an activity that bridges order and disorder, the known and unknown.

Current, popular perspectives on scholarly writing highlight the reality that faculty and graduate students are writers. Composition studies should confront and embrace this reality through empirical research and strong faculty and graduate student development programs, but it is also my hope that this attention to scholarly writing will prompt all compositionists to reflect on their writing practices and processes. Assumptions about scholarly writing may powerfully influence our interactions with other writers, including undergraduate writers. Felten, Moore, and Strickland hoped their program would change the culture of undergraduate writing on campus because the faculty had to "trade places with their students, working with peer editors and regular deadlines, which encourages them to see student writers in a different light" (47). Although results from the program are anecdotal and "assessing the impact of such residencies on WAC pedagogy is slippery at best," the Elon leaders report that the "goal of raising faculty awareness of writing process complexity has been achieved and will have some impact on pedagogy across the curriculum . . . through working intensively on their own writing processes, [participants] have been moved to a clearer understanding of what their students encounter in course-based writing" (46). Faculty writing experiences influence student experiences, and all benefit when teachers recognize that undergraduate and scholarly writing share foundational elements. Making categorical distinctions frames either scholarly writing or undergraduate writing as artificial: faculty writers may narrow their own writing to scribing yet ask their students to practice invention, or they may copy from sources during automatic writing yet tell their students to generate insight.

Joining a writing group and keeping a daily writing log changed my scholarly writing and made *writer* a more central part of my identity, yet the value of writing group for me was the questions it raised: When is simply generating text not enough? When is a writing problem actually an invention problem? Which writing difficulties are productive, and which are indicative of an ill-formed rhetorical problem? When should I use writing to open up new ideas, and when should I use it to close them down? As Reid describes, engaging in difficult writing and reflecting on my writing practices helped me identify with students and other faculty writers, and it led me to important questions about the nature of writing itself. In an academic culture increasingly attentive to writing, composition studies can ask and even answer these questions, and our work can support scholarly writers across the disciplines.

## Notes

1. While the writing advice manuals I analyze indeed state explicitly that graduate students and faculty possess the ideas and skills for success, some compositionists have named this assumption as harmful (Clark; Micciche; Sullivan).

2. On October 29, 2014, recommendations were solicited on WPA–L for a book to give faculty and graduate student participants in a scholarly writing workshop. The following texts were recommended: *Professors as Writers* by Robert Boice (recommended five times); *How to Write a Lot* by Paul Silvia (two times); *Writing Your Journal Article in Twelve Weeks* by Wendy Belcher; *The Clockwork Muse* by Eviatar Zerubavel; *Becoming an Academic Writer* by Patricia Goodson (the recommender noted this text is derivative of Boice's); *Habits of Highly Productive Writers* by Helen Sword; and *Revising Prose* by Richard Lanham. I neither asked for these recommendations nor offered suggestions.

3. The claim is based on his 1985 study in *College Composition and Communication*, where he found that external contingencies such as a daily writing schedule "facilitate…the appearance of creative ideas for writing" (477).

4. In his work on faculty writing development with Mary Deane Sorcinelli, Peter Elbow notes that he does not ask scholarly writers to freewrite at writing retreats because freewriting is a private exercise, "not a way to produce a public finished product" (21). He is nonetheless interested in the "freewriting muscle" and the ability "to utter words and thoughts about the topic at hand entirely without mentally rehearsing them beforehand" (21).

5. David Wallace analyzes four behaviorist discussions of composition pedagogy, which were published in the 1960s and 1970s. He defends these approaches first by noting that they played "an important role in the transition from product to process

pedagogies" (103), and second, by explaining that they are empirical rather than positivist. Wallace addresses pedagogical practices that include a "series of stimuli provided by instructors or peers, responses by students, and feedback from instructors or peers" (104). While he examines behaviorism as it emerged in early process pedagogy (pedagogy that included peer feedback and student reflection), I am concerned with behaviorism as it existed before process pedagogy and as it exists in current perspectives on scholarly writing.

6. Another area of postmodern invention scholarship addresses digital and multimodal writing. Because scholarly writing manuals and the activities they inspire almost exclusively address traditional, text-based scholarly production—a move that certainly reflects a limited vision of scholarly writing—I do not extend my discussion of invention here to multimodal composition. Instead, I have made an argument about the ways that writing advice manuals limit and reject rhetorical invention, and their focus on text-based genres is further limiting.

## Works Cited

Baldi, Brian, Mary Deane Sorcinelli, and Jung H. Yun. "The Scholarly Writing Continuum." *Working with Faculty Writers*. Ed. Anne Ellen Geller and Michele Eodice. Logan: Utah State UP, 2013. 38-49. Print.

Bawarshi, Anis. *Genre and the Invention of the Writer: Reconsidering the Place of Invention in Composition*. Logan: Utah State UP, 2003. Print.

Belcher, Wendy Laura. *Writing Your Journal Article in 12 Weeks: A Guide to Academic Publishing Success*. Los Angeles: Sage, 2009. Print.

Boice, Robert. "The Neglected Third Factor in Writing: Productivity." *CCC* 36.4 (1985): 472–80. Print.

---. *Professors as Writers: A Self-Help Guide to Productive Writing*. Stillwater: New Forums, 1990. Print.

Bolker, Joan. *Writing Your Dissertation in Fifteen Minutes a Day: A Guide to Starting, Revising, and Finishing Your Doctoral Thesis*. New York: Owl Books, 1998. Print.

Carter, Michael. *Where Writing Begins: A Postmodern Reconstruction*. Carbondale: SIUP, 2003. Print.

Clark, Irene. *Writing the Successful Thesis and Dissertation: Entering the Conversation*. Upper Saddle River: Prentice Hall, 2007. Print.

Clark-Oates, Angela, and Lisa Cahill. "Faculty Writing Groups: Writing Centers and Third Space Collaborations." Geller and Eodice 111–26. Print.

Elbow, Peter, and Mary Deane Sorcinelli. "A Faculty Writing Space: A Room Of Our Own." *Change* 38.6 (2006): 17–22. Print.

Fajt, Virginia, et al. "Feedback and Fellowship: Stories from a Successful Writing Group." Geller and Eodice 163–74. Print.

Felten, Peter, Jessie L. Moore, and Michael Strickland. "Faculty Writing Residencies: Supporting Scholarly Writing and Teaching." *Journal on Centers for Teaching and Learning* 1 (2009): 39–55. Print.

Flower, Linda, and John R. Hayes. "Cognitive Process Theory Of Writing." *CCC* 32 (1981): 365–87. Print.

Foss, Sonja, and William Waters. *Destination Dissertation: A Traveler's Guide to a Done Dissertation*. Lanham: Rowman & Littlefield, 2007. Print.

Geller, Anne Ellen, and Michele Eodice, eds. *Working with Faculty Writers*. Logan: Utah State UP, 2013. Print.

Goodson, Patricia. *Becoming an Academic Writer: 50 Exercises for Paced, Productive, and Powerful Writing*. Los Angeles: Sage, 2012. Print.

Gray, Tara, A. Jane Birch, and Laura Madson. "How Teaching Centers Can Support Faculty as Writers." Geller and Eodice 95–110. Print.

Kamler, Barbara, and Pat Thomson. "The Failure of Dissertation Advice Books: Toward Alternative Pedagogies for Doctoral Writing." *Educational Researcher* 37.8 (2008): 507–14. Print.

Lanham, Richard. *Revising Prose*. 5th ed. New York: Longman, 2006. Print.

Lauer, Janice M. *Invention in Rhetoric and Composition*. West Lafayette: Parlor Press, 2004. Print.

---. "Toward a Metatheory of Heuristic Procedures." *CCC* 30.3 (1979): 268–69. Print.

Micciche, Laura R. with Allison D. Carr. "Toward Graduate-Level Writing Instruction." *CCC* 62.3 (2011): 477–501. Print.

Reid, E. Shelley. "Teaching Writing Teachers Writing: Difficulty, Exploration, and Critical Reflection." *CCC* 61.2 (2009): W197–W221. Print.

Salem, Lori, and Jennifer Follett. "The Idea of a Faculty Writing Center: Moving from Troubling Deficiencies to Collaborative Engagement." Geller and Eodice 50–72. Print.

Schick, Kurt, et al. "Writing in Action: Scholarly Writing Groups as Faculty Development." *Journal on Centers for Teaching and Learning* 3 (2011): 43–63. Print.

Silvia, Paul J. *How to Write a Lot: A Practical Guide to Productive Academic Writing*. Washington: American Psychological Association, 2007. Print.

Sullivan, Patricia A. "Writing in the Graduate Curriculum: Literary Criticism as Composition." *JAC* 11.2 (1991): 283–99. Print.

Sword, Helen. *Stylish Academic Writing*. Cambridge: Harvard UP, 2012. Print.

Vitanza, Victor J. "From Heuristic to Aleatory Procedures; or, Towards 'Writing the Accident'." *Inventing a Discipline: Rhetoric Scholarship in Honor of Richard E. Young*. Ed. Maureen Daly Goggin, Urbana: NCTE, 2000. 185-206. Print.

Wallace, David. "Reconsidering Behaviorist Composition Pedagogies: Positivism, Empiricism, and the Paradox of Postmodernism." *JAC* 16.1 (1996): 103–17. Print.

Wardle, Elizabeth, and Doug Downs. "Looking into Writing-about-Writing Classrooms." *First-Year Composition: From Theory to Practice*. Ed. Deborah Coxwell-Teague and Ronald F. Lunsford. Anderson: Parlor Press, 2014. 276–319. Print.

Weaver, Constance. "Teaching Grammar in the Context of Writing." *English Journal* 85.7 (1996): 15–24. Print.

Williams, George. "November is Academic Writing Month." ProfHacker. *The Chronicle of Higher Education*. 24 Oct. 2012. Web. 15 Oct. 2014. <http://chronicle.com/blogs/profhacker/november-is-academic-writing-month/43608>.

Worsham, Lynn. "Fast-Food Scholarship." *Chronicle of Higher Education*. 12 Dec. 2011. Web. 15 Oct. 2014. <http://chronicle.com/article/Fast-Food-Scholarship/130049/>.

---. "The Question Concerning Invention: Hermeneutics and the Genesis of Writing." *PRE/TEXT* 8.3-4 (1987): 197–244. Print.

Young, Richard. "Arts, Crafts, Gifts, and Knacks: Some Disharmonies in the New Rhetoric." *Visible Language* 14.4 (1980): 341–50. Print.

Zerubavel, Eviatar. *The Clockwork Muse: A Practical Guide to Writing Theses, Dissertations, and Books*. Cambridge: Harvard UP, 1999. Print.

# Bodies in Composition: Teaching Writing through Kinesthetic Performance

*Janine Butler*

This article calls on composition instructors to reflect consciously on how we can use our bodies kinesthetically to perform multimodal writing processes through gestural, visual, and spatial modes. Teaching writing through kinesthetic performance can show students that our bodies are being constructed via interaction with audiences, akin to the way our compositions are always co-constructed by readers. Gestures that embody multimodal composition can create an inclusive pedagogical space in which instructors and students interact with differences through various modes of communication. More specifically, I draw on scholarship on Deaf studies, embodiment, and multimodality to show that performance and composition represent embodied experiences in which we rhetorically negotiate multiple meanings and interpretations with our audiences. Textual vignettes throughout the article describe how I perform in the classroom to show students different elements of a nonlinear, multimodal writing process. I share five pedagogical gestures that illustrate kinesthetic strategies for guiding students through new rhetorical situations, genres, and media. I encourage instructors to continually adapt the pedagogical gestures presented here in interaction with students' embodied differences.

---

I know that embodiment necessitates an action. It requires movement. It's not the body's relationship to the mind that marks something as embodied, but the body's relationship to space, time, and other bodies or objects. . . . [B]odies are always in relation to the world around them, to the other bodies, and that, truly, there is no good or bad body.

—Daisy Levy (in Powell et al., 2014)

## Kinesthetic Bodies in Composition

*Hello, I'm Ms. Butler and I'm your instructor for this course. I'm Deaf and communicate through American Sign Language (ASL).[1] The interpreters for this class will be interpreting ASL into English and English into ASL. We'll be expressing ourselves to each other in different ways through the compositions we create here.*

I begin this article the same way I begin the first day of class each semester—by articulating my embodiment as a Deaf composition scholar who communicates through visual, spatial, and gestural modes to welcome different ways to compose meaning. Students in my classes generally do not know ASL and are not processing the signed grammar and syntax, so to make the writing process manifest, I emphasize gestures and body language when performing writing concepts through multimodal strategies, including three-dimensional movements. My kinesthetic performance through visual, spatial, and gestural modes is a call to composition students and instructors to use our bodies to interact with other bodies and the compositions we create to express ourselves.

Harnessing the potential of teaching writing through kinesthetic performance can contribute to pedagogies that aim to create space for student performance of differences in the classroom. Our bodies are multimodal and our compositions are multimodal: We juxtapose, arrange, or disarrange modes to compose meaning. We might zoom into images in audio-visual presentations to accentuate meaning just as we might stand up taller or lean forward to draw attention to our presence as composition teachers working with students. Instructors can use their bodies to physically recreate—or embody—the process of combining multiple modes to create meaning. Through my embodied pedagogy, I bring together visual, spatial, and gestural modes into a *kinesthetic* rhetoric that encapsulates how we articulate ourselves through the movement of our bodies.

Composition instructors can physically interact with abstract ideas to make them tangible to students. To perform the concept of rhetorical situation in class, for example, I turn my body to one side to personify the writer, then to another side to personify the audience, and turn my entire body into the text that connects the two as I move from one side to the other. The context becomes the movement of my hands and arms in a circle around the space of the rhetorical situation. Abstract information becomes concrete through different modes that can dramatize visual-spatial connections. Such kinesthetic re-creations of the writing process demonstrate that we interact materially with composition through multiple modes. Instead of equating "multimodal" and "composition" with "digitized, screen-mediated texts" in ways that could limit "the kinds of texts students produce for our courses" (Shipka W348), we can perform the multimodal nature of communication in and through the body.

Teacher-scholars are designing effective learning opportunities for students to experience writing as a physical and embodied process (e.g., Dolmage; Dunn; Fleckenstein; Palmeri) and to perform in the classroom (e.g., Fishman, Lunsford, McGregor, and Otuteye; Jones; Love). Patricia A. Dunn is prominent among those who incorporate physical activities and performances to support students' "aural, visual, kinesthetic, and spatial" ways of knowing and expressing meaning (11). To create an inclusive space for students to perform their writing processes, I build on Dunn's efforts and call for composition instructors to perform embodied differences. Teaching writing through kinesthetic performance shows that meaning is not stable, linear, or monomodal, and that we instructors welcome multiple communication styles. We produce gestures that will be interpreted variously by others just as students compose with multiple modes to construct meaning for audiences.

Kinesthetic movement involves an awareness of both our bodies and our interactions with other bodies and media—including texts, the technologies we use, and the writing process. The kinesthetic nature of composing becomes apparent when I discuss visual design and arguments with students. I move my hands and arms to embody the malleability of visual-spatial arrangement. *How do the elements of the image work with or against each other to create the visual argument? If each element is strategically placed, what is the effect of their arrangement? Look at the diagonal angle in the upper left corner. I'm mirroring the diagonal with my right arm raised up. My left hand becomes the gaze of the woman in the left margin of the image. She's staring towards the diagonal. And there's empty space inbetween that I'm recreating by moving my right hand in an oval shape. Now, let's frame the image and push it back as if we're interpreting it. What is the combined effect of the elements and their spatial arrangement?* In class-wide discussions, I use my performances to guide and respond to students' comments. In individual conversations, I ask students to keep the visualization in mind as they continue analyzing or designing their own visuals.

The value of embodied performance has been studied by others, notably Leeann Hunter, whose experiences as a child of Deaf adults led her to develop a student-centered composition pedagogy informed by Deaf culture. Hunter has asked her students to perform through gestures in nonverbal skits, and these performances encourage students to reflect "on the visual and spatial affordances of expressing concepts with our bodies." Her pedagogical examples "illustrate how the hearing classroom could benefit from practices that engage in embodied discourses and visual-spatial metaphors." Just as Hunter suggests that non-deaf students benefit from communicating through their bodies, so I insist that we instructors could perform kinesthetic composition as a continual practice throughout the semester to model the embodied process of composing ourselves with students.

Throughout this article, I keep the spotlight on instructors' bodies to encourage conscious reflection of how we present ourselves kinesthetically in the classroom. I want us to remember, however, that these embodied performances involve interactions with students; they are designed to help students become more comfortable with composing in different modes, and are developed in response to students' own responses to instructors. As Levy indicates in the epigraph to this article, embodiment requires "an action . . . [and] movement. It's not the body's relationship to the mind that marks something as embodied, but the body's relationship to space, time, and other bodies or objects" (Powell et al.). We perform our embodiments via interactions with other bodies in the spaces we share. Without our students, our gestures would have no purpose because kinesthetic composition is the embodied and active movement of meaning through interactions with other bodies, modes, and media in the classroom.

In this article, scholarship on Deaf studies, embodiment, and multimodality intersect to show that both performance and composition are physical processes of expressing our differences through the juxtaposition of multiple modes. Throughout this article, I create *textual vignettes* that describe how I embody different elements of the nonlinear writing process with students. These vignettes demonstrate a variety of approaches for physically recreating the kinesthetic nature of multimodal composition through everyday interactions with students. I conclude the article with five pedagogical gestures that illustrate kinesthetic strategies that composition instructors can adapt for different learning spaces.

In order to support students' multiple learning styles and physical engagements with writing, instructors should first perform different ways to interact with other bodies, modes, and media in the composition process. This article replicates this interactive performance by discussing the embodied performance of composition instructors in dialogue with different pedagogical approaches. Recognizing that composition is always already kinesthetic allows us to experience writing as embodied meaning.

## Kinesthetically Performing Multimodal Composition

Kinesthetic composition makes manifest that embodied differences influence how we engage in the world and the choices we make in expressing ourselves through different modes. I use ASL, facial expression, gesture, and posture to show students that communication is not primarily any one mode in isolation and that we do not have to "speak" flawless academic English to connect with our audiences. Instructors and students can likewise connect through various embodied and technological modes; for instance, gestures can perform copy-and-paste functions to show that revision is tangible, not abstract.

When composition instructors communicate through different modes, we make manifest that embodiment "is about understanding what difference one's body makes to the experience of being in the world" (Mitchell 16). Our bodies—and the differences between our bodies—shape how we interact with other modes and bodies in the spaces we share. To quote Maureen Johnson, Daisy Levy, Katie Manthey, and Maria Novotny's key concept statement on embodiment, "all bodies do rhetoric through texture, shape, color, consistency, movement, and function" (39). Our bodies compose through gestural, visual, spatial, and other modes of expression.

Here is an example of how we could make the multimodal composing process tangible. During a workshop session in my class, a female student explained that she was unsure how to write a seven-page rhetorical analysis of a video, so we watched a segment together to assess our reactions. While the video played, I interacted with the screen and with her: *Pause at this moment. Observe the amount of action occurring on screen in this five-second clip alone. You could write an entire page on these five seconds alone. Think about how you could do that. Watch: My hands are framing the video. My left hand opens up as it becomes the words fading out near the lower right corner; my right hand is the swoosh of these lines; then the fading in on the left, the sudden drop on the right. How are they all working together in these five seconds?*

During the rest of the class session, this student developed a visual outline of what she saw. Upon noticing her closely observing the video and sketching notes, I decided to continue my kinesthetic approach with other students. At the end of the project, several students remarked that this strategy helped them. My hands recreated the temporal and spatial sequencing of the video in tangible form and articulated the nonlinear process of composing.

I use the term *articulated,* instead of voiced, to emphasize that spoken language is not the exclusive mode of communication and that gesture is a meaningful component of communication. Sherman Wilcox defines gestures as coordinated actions and patterns of movement—including facial expressions, body language, and posture—that *articulate* meaning (44). David F. Armstrong, William C. Stokoe, and Wilcox frame "both spoken and signed languages as systems of gestures" (5) that "overcome[s] such arbitrary distinctions" between what we consider to be linguistic and what we consider to be nonlinguistic (8). We perform through the language of gestures with our audiences. As Kristin L. Arola, Jennifer Sheppard, and Cheryl E. Ball's *Writer/Designer* explains when defining the five modes of multimodal communication to students, the gestural mode "provides an important way of connecting . . . to other people" (13). Gestures materialize the connections we make with each other and with our compositions, such as when we smile and place our hands over our heart to wordlessly show others that we have been moved by their poignant essays.

Kinesthetic performance and gesture show that we share meaning through connecting bodies and modes. Leland McCleary reminds us "of the essentially embodied nature of the interaction through which we construct our worlds [because] both oral and gestural modalities of language are mediated through the body" (112). Kinesthetic performance also shows that, as Rebecca Sanchez argues, separating texts from bodies is an act of "disassociat[ing] language from human corporeality" and from the external world (25). Making meaning through physical movement transforms abstract ideas into concrete and tangible experiences.

Gesture and body language can articulate abstract ideas that may not be stated as easily through linear or verbal forms. While gestures cannot replicate the syntax and grammatical structure of ASL, gestures can express complex meaning in nonlinear form. Consider the similarities between multimodal composition and sign language in Margalit Fox's description of sign language as that which

> assembles its words in another mode, where the possibilities for structure go far beyond straight lines. . . . A language in the visual mode can . . . encode its signals simultaneously. . . . Whereas words are linear strings, signs are compact bundles of data, in which multiple units of code—handshape, location and movement—are conveyed in virtually the same movement. (101)

Fox's description of the affordances of sign language is remarkably similar to how we describe the affordances of multimodal compositions: we can express complex, nonlinear meaning through kinesthetic movements in three-dimensional space. While gestures are not the same as ASL, gestures can embody the juxtaposition of multiple modes. We can use our bodies kinesthetically to reorient our ideas and reconstruct our compositions. I cup my hands side-by-side to visualize paragraphs and I move my cupped hands to recreate the movement of paragraphs, sentences, and thoughts. I encourage students: *Don't force yourself to write the very first sentence of the introduction, then the introduction, then the first body paragraph. That linear approach may not work for you. Start writing wherever your thoughts begin or where your thoughts are flowing at the moment.* My arms and hands cascade vertically and horizontally to replicate the flows of a stream.

I remember a particular student who embraced my kinesthetic suggestions to let his thoughts flow in predrafting sessions. He struggled to write down ideas for his first project, so I suggested that he open up his mind and let the words flow without worrying about organization during the predrafting stage. He came back in the next session and used physical gestures to describe how he had written down everything that came to mind. Throughout the semester he used gestures to show me how he repeated this kinesthetic strategy with each project to help him get his thoughts down on paper. His experience suggests that we can reconceptualize writing as a physical performance and find the connections between our ideas and writings.

The benefits of interactive communication become salient through scholarship on the embodied nature of ASL literature, most prominently H-Dirksen L. Bauman, Heidi M. Rose, and Jennifer L. Nelson's *Signing the Body Poetic*, an edited collection on signed poetry, stories, and performances that brings together English essays and ASL performances on DVD. In a separate piece, Bauman examines the inherent cinematic nature of ASL poetry that "weds vision with movement" through the "simultaneous foregrounding of the visual-spatial-kinetic dimensions of experience" (35). He emphasizes the viewer's role in co-creating the communicative experience: "the ASL text is always a human body, projecting its own visual-spatial-kinetic experience, awakening similar lived experiences in the minds and bodies of the viewers" (44). We can identify two implications of embodied performance and composition: audiences are active participants in interpreting kinesthetic performances, and performers intentionally interact with audiences to co-construct a shared experience. Similarly, in *Deaf Subjects*, Brenda Jo Brueggemann observes that writing and sign language are both rhetorical performances in interaction with an audience and asks if perhaps the two are more connected than we have realized. I reply with a resounding, "*yes!*" and add that without knowing ASL, teachers can still use gesture to co-construct meaning with audiences and students. For instance, facial expressions can perform changes in tone and inflection in both alphabetic and aural-visual compositions—and we can ask audiences how they might be interpreting these changes in tone and inflection in order to better understand how we express ourselves.

Kinesthetic performance reflects Gunther R. Kress and Theo van Leeuwen's theory of multimodal communication in which our bodies and voices are materials that we can physically articulate to express meaning. The kinesthetic approach extends the New London Group's statement that, "in a profound sense, all meaning-making is multimodal" (81). For instance, I perform brainstorming as a recursive and physical movement of ideas. I raise a hand to my head and rotate my hand in the process of thinking through ideas, then move both hands to one side to brush aside an idea. We can encourage students to recreate this recursive process as they develop and articulate ideas for projects.

Such kinesthetic performances show that writing is an embodied act in which we interact through multiple modes. Performing in the classroom supports Kristie Fleckenstein's "literacy of bodysigns, a literacy in which we are neither writers nor bodies, but writing bodies" and in which meaning relies "on our physical participation in the world" (46). While Fleckenstein describes physical activities that support composition students' embodied literacies—or shared ways of knowing and making meaning within the world—I remind instructors that, in addition to integrating embodied activities in our classrooms, we can actively engage with students through our pedagogical performances.

Kinesthetic performances consciously oppose "the dominant discourse surrounding the teaching of writing [that] focuses on texts and thoughts, words and ideas, as though these entities existed apart from the bodies of teachers, writers, audiences, communities" (Dolmage 110). We construct meaning through interactions with other bodies, technologies, and modes. Our pedagogies should therefore embody the rhetorical nature of communicating to audiences who actively interpret our differences.

**Pedagogical Gestures that Embody Multimodal Composition**

Given the interconnections among body, movement, spatiality, and language, I propose five pedagogical gestures for kinesthetically engaging with the physical and nonlinear processes of composition. As there is no single approach for implementing these gestures, I suggest that composition instructors adapt them to complement students' various learning and communication practices. Instead of condensing your gestures into a one-day activity or asking students to observe your performance as part of a single assignment, consider attending to your body as a source of meaning-making throughout the course.

*Gesture #1: We appreciate that various bodies perform kinesthetic composition.*

Teacher-scholars have demonstrated the value of performance in composition pedagogies. Jenn Fishman, Andrea Lunsford, Beth McGregor, and Mark Otuteye request that we "expand our curricula and our pedagogies to make room for [student] performance in the writing classroom" (226). Meredith Love shows that performance studies can enhance writing pedagogy by opening "the definition of 'composing'" to more possibilities for student expression (14). Leigh A. Jones asks her students to explore the authority available to them as they perform different roles through podcasting and other writing assignments (82). These instructors' experiences suggest that students can explore meanings and experiment with technologies, take on new tasks and create various media, and develop a stronger understanding of the compositional choices they make. However, if instructors want to support students' diverse pathways to knowledge—as Dunn and Jason Palmeri insist we should—then we should also perform such multimodal writing processes as part of our instruction.

Composition teachers can engage in kinesthetic composition to draw attention to the different ways in which teachers engage with students. In a notable instance of attending to teachers' bodies in interaction with students, Mary Dixon and Kim Senior's study of photographs of teachers and students marks the fluid relationships, contours, and connections across bodies and presences in the classroom. Just as importantly, Laura R. Micciche, Hannah J. Rule, and Liv Stratman's audio and video recordings of their teaching and interacting with students provide multimodal documentation of how they use their bodies and voices to perform their identities as teachers. We can all consciously enhance our gestural performances—with and without technology—to interact meaningfully with students.

Kinesthetic composition does not require us to use our hands or bodies in the same way—instead, our bodies differently articulate our own movements and meanings. The gestural suggestions in this article do not include photographs or videos because I do not make assumptions about the physical capabilities of instructors or students. I do not recommend that every instructor enact the same exact gestures, especially if anyone feels uncomfortable performing or interpreting body language. I do, however, want to promote greater awareness of how we embody meaning when teaching writing.

Each one of us articulates meaning through different bodily qualities. While I might choose to explain disciplinary conventions for different genres by rearranging headings and paragraphs with both of my hands, another instructor might use one arm to do so, and yet another instructor might use her legs to move around the room. Using different movements reinforces that writing is a physical act rooted in our embodiments regardless of capabilities, and this variety reflects how we all compose through different modes to express ourselves. For instance, one learner might feel inclined to integrate visual design elements into her alphabetic essay while another learner might implement more systematic elements. Different learning styles do not make one composition better than another, just as different embodiments do not make one performance more meaningful than another. At the same time, differences in identities will affect how students and instructors (mis)interpret each other's gestural and written compositions.

*Gesture #2: We show that bodies can be (mis)read and (mis)interpreted.*

Each time we produce and interpret a text or body, we mediate (i.e., construct and transform) the meaning of both. When introducing the concept of textual analysis, I have shown students that a text is anything that can be read or interpreted. *My body is a text that you can analyze. Right now you can read my body to sense my emotions and interpret what I'm expressing. If I'm optimistic or happy you can read the meaning based on my bodily comportment.* I have observed students suddenly observing my bodily gestures when I make these statements—which leads me to agree with Melanie Yergeau, who states, "I think that *text* properly refers to living, breathing bodies. . . . My body is text personified." Our gestural compositions—the gestures that we use to make meaning—are read and interpreted by others.

If we are texts personified, then when we compose *and* when we perform, we enact embodied rhetorics, or what A. Abby Knoblauch defines as "the purposeful effort by an author to represent aspects of embodiment within the text he or she is shaping" (58). We can represent our bodily differences through changes in posture to explain ethos (credibility) and stance (attitude towards a topic). *Look at me: I am standing tall and firm while moving my hand down to resemble a politician at a podium. I am projecting my argument and stance to the audience, I am working to demonstrate my credibility, and I am using my body and words to convince you to agree with me. In contrast, when I step over to the side and slouch, I do not demonstrate a clear idea of what I am trying to state and I cannot project my credibility to the audience.* The visual change in posture seems to make the concepts tangible to students and reinforces how we interpret each other's gestural and written compositions.

Performing kinesthetic movements shows that our bodies—and our compositions—are collaborative creations of our own and of others' interpretations of us. In her discussion of embodiment, Anne Frances Wysocki reminds us that internal experiences within our bodies are always in tension with our awareness of our bodies as being perceived and "objectified through others' mediations of us" (16). To borrow Yergeau's phrase, "every person is jointly authored and constructed." A student might misunderstand my neutral facial expression as disappointment while another may not be sure how to react to the movement of my body across the room. These same students might feel tension when writing because they are aware that an audience will read their work and may misinterpret their intentions. The similarities between performing and composing are apparent: Our written and gestural compositions are jointly constructed and mediated by multiple bodies and modes.

Now, we might ask ourselves: If compositions are co-constructed and transformed by different bodies, how might students interpret our gestures in different ways? You might perform a single movement or gesture and ask students to share their interpretations of the single performance—then ask students to consider how they interpret written work. How do different gestures or performances change the construction of identity? When reading compositions, how do different modes or arrangements change the interpretation of a writer's text? These discussions should develop recognition that others are interpreting us when we communicate—just as others will interpret our compositions and engage in "particular readings of our identities" that we cannot always anticipate (Williams 8). This collaborative process demonstrates to students that instructors are always performing roles as teachers in the classroom *and* that we are asking students to perform their identities through composition.

If we discuss with students how they interpret identities based on performances, then teachers and students might be better equipped to consider rhetorical agency as—to borrow from Stephanie L. Kerschbaum—a "rhetorical negotiation between speakers and audiences, a negotiation in which individuals do not have full control over their own identity" ("On Rhetorical Agency" 60). We continually negotiate meaning through social and written interactions with each other's differences. Rhetorical negotiation is not sequential but is recursive as we read each other's stances, performances, and gestures and respond to others' readings of us.

*Gesture #3: We connect through underprivileged modes and technologies.*

Our kinesthetic performances will be interpreted in various ways by students through rhetorical negotiation just as their compositions may be inscribed with different meanings by others. Our intended meanings shift when mediated through bodies, texts, and spaces. No single performance or composition will have a fixed meaning; rather, kinesthetic composition recognizes, in the spirit of cultural rhetorics, the "rhetorical power in building relationships between multiple traditions, multiple histories, multiple practices" (Powell et al.). By making meaning through relations of embodied differences, kinesthetic composition creates a space for multiple meanings. No single mode or body is necessarily empowered or privileged to the exclusion of other modes or bodies.

What meanings can we discover when we communicate through underprivileged modes? Kinesthetic composition is at its heart multimodal and embodied; we arrange and combine modes as one way of making meaning. This does not exclude those who may not see our bodies or compositions on the screen. Here is what we might do: Describe verbally, or compose through alphabetic text, how our body replicates—or becomes—the composition of an interactive presentation, a graphic novel, a blog post with links and images. Describe the spatial arrangement and sensation of movement as we navigate through a series of slides or hyperlinks. Accentuate different modes of communication that do not privilege the aural or the visual mode in isolation.

Even when we do not privilege a single mode, we will still have to negotiate rhetorically the multiple and unstable meanings that we create through our interactions with others. There are those who do not benefit from physical communication or those with body language and behavior that may not reflect our own behavior—just as our behavior might not reflect theirs. Instead of identifying any particular condition here, I want to instead focus on how we can circulate meanings without disempowering certain bodies.

How can we, for example, negotiate rhetorical meaning with students who are resistant to our gestures? I am reminded of a dedicated female student who clearly attended to my body language but seemed to struggle to maintain eye contact with me during our conversations. In our one-on-one discussions during class, I would direct our attention to her screen or paper so that we could interact through media. Offsetting immediate contact allowed us to connect through technology and helped her compose through media. By gesturing with my hands to her laptop screen or printouts, we could kinesthetically rearrange and reimagine her compositions without keeping the focus on the face or eyes. In this way, the body was an extension into the composition. Throughout the semester, she seemed quite comfortable continuing to work with me, asking me for help, and coming to me with any questions.

We can interact with bodily and written texts through multiple modes. For instance, I try to project information on screen as often as possible to reinforce what is being discussed in class and I use my body to interact with what is on screen if possible. If there is a list of bullet points on screen and I discuss two of the points, I run my hand across both points, circle them, or put a hand under certain words. Granted, bodily interaction with the screen is not always possible, since in some classrooms the screen is located above our heads. In that case, we can use the mouse as a technological extension of the body. This allows us to connect kinesthetically through digital modes.

I have not taught a blind student or a student who could not see my performances, but I like to imagine a descriptive audio service that would thoroughly describe how I use my body and facial expressions to emphasize and show meaning. If possible, I would also request a copy of the descriptive audio transcript to be able to assess and improve the expression and interpretation of my gestures. The goal would be to include all student bodies in the multimodal space.

*Gesture #4: We create an inclusive space that combines bodies, modes, and media.*

Performing different movements and gestures demonstrates the value of different embodiments in multimodal composition. James C. Wilson and Cynthia Lewiecki-Wilson argue that transforming how bodies are perceived will "require an understanding of embodiment as difference" instead of "'difference' as defect and deficit" (18). In the same spirit, Kerschbaum treats difference "as rhetorical performance" that is "dynamic, relational, and emergent" ("On Rhetorical Agency" 57); in other words, we rhetorically negotiate our constructions of difference through interactions with each other. Instead of trying to stabilize or erase difference, these scholars ask us to create a space for all bodies to perform our differences in negotiation with each other.

My use of sign language reveals my relational difference in classrooms with hearing students, where I also use the gestural, visual, spatial, and kinesthetic modes to embody multimodal communication. As Kerschbaum writes, "deafness, like any other identity category, is to be understood both through the contexts in which we communicate and act *and* by our embodiments of it" ("Avoiding" 617, emphasis in original). My kinesthetic performances embody my deafness and the value of communicating through different modes. My difference is rhetorically negotiated during every interaction with students. Since this meaning-making tension reflects the tension of writing to an audience, instructors should continue to negotiate differences rhetorically with students through performance and composition.

Bringing kinesthetic composition to the classroom supports Margaret Price's request that we design inclusive kairotic spaces, or "areas of academe where knowledge is produced and power is exchanged" (Yergeau et al.). In classrooms where knowledge is predominantly produced through one mode (such as the verbal/aural mode), certain students will be marked as absent due to their inability to fully participate. For instance, I once taught a hard-of-hearing female student with whom I could communicate through sign language. There were times when I could have signed with her to the exclusion of other students, but I never did so. In Price's words, we would have been marking the other student bodies as absent because they could not participate in the signed exchange (Yergeau et al.).

Signing, and excluding non-signing bodies in the process, would empower a single student and prevent others from accessing the learning space. In contrast, performing composition through multiple modes does not privilege sound (or ASL) over other modes, artificially separate bodies from the act of writing, or impose a linear process of writing. When we perform multimodal composition, we rhetorically negotiate how we interpret each other's embodiments and compositions. We work through social and written tension by combining and rearranging different gestures, voices, and technologies. This tension and negotiation will never disappear, but when we do not privilege or empower a single mode of communication or learning style, we will have created a space in which we value interacting with differences.

*Gesture #5: We interact with new and unfamiliar modes and genres.*

Of course, physical performance may not be a natural expression for some bodies, but composing also may not come naturally to many writers. Students will find challenges when working with new assignments, genres, and media—and we can use the challenging moments in our performances to show that writing is a process of finding ways to express ourselves.

We can use movements and gestures to articulate sensations when struggling to describe ideas. Once, two students in my class were analyzing a movie trailer and described the music to me as "dramatic music." I asked them, *What does dramatic music mean? Tell me what you hear. Describe it to me. Okay, let's watch how the interpreter is physically representing the oscillations of the background music by transforming her hand into a wave. As the music reaches its crescendo—and as the action on screen reaches its explosive moment—her hand quickly vibrates along the top of the wave. This vibration extends through her arms down to her body.* The two students' faces showed fascination as they observed the interpreter; they then replayed the movie trailer and moved their bodies along with the music as they imagined descriptions for dramatic music.

Kinesthetic performance of sound reinforces Steph Ceraso's multimodal listening pedagogy, which recognizes that we sense sound not only through the ear, but through vibrations in the body and multiple senses. I have found that when my hands become the intonations of speech and pulses of a beat, students' faces light up in appreciation of a renewed approach to sound. *Sense the vibrations in the air, feel the beat reverberating through your body. How does the fast rhythm affect the movement of your body or what you are envisioning? How does the sound layer with the visuals on screen the way that I lay my hands on top of one another?* Since students have responded positively to musical performances, I would recommend that anyone hesitant to performing composition begin by using gestures to follow the changes in tone and pitch for songs and other aural-based compositions such as speeches in which speakers' inflection, emphasis, and tone changes.

Performing kinesthetic composition seems especially applicable when we are asking students to write in genres that they may find uncomfortable or unfamiliar. Let's close this performance with some gestures that support the interaction of new modes, media, and bodies.

Are students designing comic books or graphic novels? If so, teachers can reinforce a hybrid genre's juxtaposition of images and alphabetic text by speaking and using cupped hands to indicate possible locations for the speech bubble. Place your cupped hands at different locations around your body to show that meaning might be interpreted in different ways depending on the placement of text. Bring your hands closer to your face and ask students if the proximity of the speech bubble to your face shapes how they respond to you. Ask them to consider how they could strategically place text in different locations to construct readers' responses to their graphic novels. This kinesthetic discussion could help guide them through different spatial arrangements for composing in hybrid genres.

Are students creating videos? Teachers can guide them through visualizing the composition without sketching pictures or by finding other ways to draft videos. In discussions with a student on how he could make a video of his presentation accessible, I used my body to show how he could arrange the various visual elements of his recorded presentation, including his body, the slides, and the captions. He carefully watched me and developed a video presentation that was laid out spatially just as we had constructed it with our bodies during the drafting stage. We had co-developed a visual-spatial storyboard that allowed him to successfully execute his vision.

Are students creating interactive presentations? Show students the affordances of a new genre by becoming the paths and frames of the interactive presentation. For instance, when a student wanted to create a business presentation through Prezi, I used my body to advise him about the impracticalities of using animated transitions in a professional context. My hands framed my face and then moved in and out and flipped upside down to recreate the tight rotations and extreme zooms of a presentation that overuses these features. He responded with an appreciative nodding of his head and said he would be conscious to avoid those features in a professional presentation. In this way we can kinesthetically become the content of any new genre, from the pages of a website to the sections of an alphabetic document, to support students composing in new communicative contexts.

Are students struggling with integrating sources in their papers? Integrating quotes in papers is a physical act of combining multiple perspectives in one compositional space. So, performing the act of integrating sources could supplement verbal explanations of how to introduce, cite, and explain quotes. Use your posture or hands to embody the student's perspective. Perform the act of welcoming someone with your hands to symbolize introductory phrases. Change your posture or hands to transition to the quoted material—and even use the gesture for quotation marks. Move to the other side of the quote to sandwich it with the explanation. Show that the quote should be surrounded by the student's perspective. Use this strategy at different points during the writing process to help writers sense the effect of their words on the page.

Are you asking students to rhetorically analyze a text? A student of mine struggled to start writing a rhetorical analysis of two articles. As we discussed how she could go through the articles to find points of analysis, she used the phrase, "pulling information out." I eagerly encouraged that strategy by kinesthetically showing her how she could pull, or draw, information out of each page of her article. She immediately returned to her article and began developing a visual outline of what she pulled out of the article. This was a productive process in which the visceral term we used, *pull*, encapsulated the connection between the text and the reader.

In any of these or other teaching situations, the goal is for students to transfer the performance of the kinesthetic arrangement to their compositions. Whether subconsciously or consciously, they ideally develop a multisensory understanding of how they make meaning through their compositions.

**A Movement through Kinesthetic Composition**

Writing through any modality is an embodied experience that can bring to students' attention their internal experiences and preferences, particularly when they sense the importance of their audiences and content. How might we guide them through new and various rhetorical situations? We can start by interacting through multiple modes of expression, including physical and verbal languages, to capture the tangible qualities of articulating ourselves. This dynamic interaction opens up a space for students *and* instructors to learn through multiple perspectives. Let us begin:

> *In every rhetorical situation—from your academic compositions to your professional performances—you and your audience are co-constructing collaborative or contradictory meanings. Our bodies and our texts are engaged in a continual process of negotiation as we read each other's gestures and inscribe meaning onto other bodies and texts. Recognizing the interactive interpretation of meaning empowers us to articulate our embodied differences in a movement through kinesthetic composition.*

## Acknowledgments

Endless thanks to Erin Frost, the anonymous reviewers at *Composition Studies*, and Laura Micciche for insightful feedback and support.

## Notes

1. The capital *Deaf* is used by members who identify with Deaf culture, a linguistic minority that values face-to-face communication. The lowercase *deaf* describes the physical state of being deaf. I use the capital Deaf when referring to my Deaf cultural identity in this paper and the lowercase deaf when referring to the physical state.

## Works Cited

Armstrong, David F., William C. Stokoe, and Sherman E. Wilcox. *Gesture and the Nature of Language*. Cambridge: Cambridge UP, 1995. Print.

Arola, Kristin L., Jennifer Sheppard, and Cheryl E. Ball. *Writer/Designer: A Guide to Making Multimodal Projects*. Boston: Bedford/St. Martin's, 2014. Print.

Bauman, H-Dirksen L. "Rede*signing* Literature: The Cinematic Poetics of American Sign Language Poetry." *Sign Language Studies* 4.1 (2003): 34-47. Print.

Bauman, H-Dirksen L., Heidi M. Rose, and Jennifer L. Nelson, eds. *Signing the Body Poetic: Essays on American Sign Language Literature*. Berkeley: U of California P, 2006. Print.

Brueggemann, Brenda Jo. *Deaf Subjects: Between Identities and Places*. New York: New York UP, 2009. Print.

Ceraso, Steph. "(Re)educating the Senses: Multimodal Listening, Bodily Learning, and the Composition of Sonic Experiences." *College English* 77.2 (2014): 102-23. Print.

Dixon, Mary, and Kim Senior. "Appearing Pedagogy: From Embodied Learning and Teaching to Embodied Pedagogy." *Pedagogy, Culture, and Society* 19.3 (2011): 473-84. Print.

Dolmage, Jay. "Writing Against Normal." *Composing (Media) = Composing (Embodiment): Bodies, Technologies, Writing, the Teaching of Writing*. Eds. Kristin L. Arola and Anne Frances Wysocki. Boulder: Utah State UP, 2012. 110-26.

Dunn, Patricia A. *Talking, Sketching, Moving: Multiple Literacies in the Teaching of Writing*. Portsmouth: Boynton/Cook, 2001. Print.

Fishman, Jenn, Andrea Lunsford, Beth McGregor, and Mark Otuteye. "Performing Writing, Performing Literacy." *CCC* 57.2 (2005): 224-52. Print.

Fleckenstein, Kristie. *Embodied Literacies: Imageword and a Poetics of Teaching*. Carbondale: SIUP, 2003. Print.

Fox, Margalit. *Talking Hands: What Sign Language Reveals about the Mind*. New York: Simon and Schuster, 2008. Print.

Hunter, Leeann. "The Embodied Classroom: Deaf Gain in Multimodal Composition and Digital Studies." *The Journal of Interactive Technology and Pedagogy* 8 (2015). Web. 17 Dec. 2015. <https://jitp.commons.gc.cuny.edu/the-embodied-classroom-deaf-gain-in-multimodal-composition-and-digital-studies/>.

Johnson, Maureen, Daisy Levy, Katie Manthey, and Maria Novotny. "Embodiment: Embodying Feminist Rhetorics." *Peitho Journal* 18.1 (2015): 39-44. Web. 11 Nov. 2015. <http://peitho.cwshrc.org/embodiment-embodying-feminist-rhetorics/>.

Jones, Leigh A. "Podcasting and Performativity: Multimodal Invention in an Advanced Writing Class." *Composition Studies* 38.2 (2010): 75-91. Print.

Kerschbaum, Stephanie L. "Avoiding the Difference Fixation: Identity Categories, Markers of Difference, and the Teaching of Writing." *CCC* 63.4 (2012): 616-44. Print.

---. "On Rhetorical Agency and Disclosing Disability in Academic Writing." *Rhetoric Review* 33.1 (2014): 55-71. Print.

Knoblauch, A. Abby. "Bodies of Knowledge: Definitions, Delineations, and Implications of Embodied Writing in the Academy." *Composition Studies* 40.2 (2012): 50-65. Print.

Kress, Gunther R., and Theo van Leeuwen. *Multimodal Discourse: The Modes and Media of Contemporary Communication*. New York: Oxford UP, 2001. Print.

Love, Meredith. "Composing Through the Performative Screen: Translating Performance Studies into Writing Pedagogy." *Composition Studies* 35.2 (2007): 11-30. Print.

McCleary, Leland. "Technologies of Language and the Embodied History of the Deaf." *Sign Language Studies* 3.2 (2003): 104-24. Print.

Micciche, Laura R., Hannah J. Rule, and Liv Stratman. "Multimodality, Performance, and Teacher-Training." *Computers and Composition Online* (2012): n. pag. Web. 22 Nov. 2015. <http://www2.bgsu.edu/departments/english/cconline/cconline_Sp_2012/Multimodality_Rev-2011-12/tdm.html>.

Mitchell, Lisa M. *Baby's First Picture: Ultrasound and the Politics of Fetal Subjects*. Toronto: U of Toronto P, 2001. Print.

New London Group. "A Pedagogy of Multiliteracies: Designing Social Futures." *Harvard Education Review* 66.1 (1996): 60-92. Print.

Palmeri, Jason. *Remixing Composition: A History of Multimodal Writing Pedagogy*. Carbondale: SIUP, 2012. Print.

Powell, Malea, et al. "Our Story Begins Here: Constellating Cultural Rhetorics." *Enculturation* (2014): n. pag. Web. 18 Nov. 2014. <http://enculturation.net/our-story-begins-here>.

Sanchez, Rebecca. *Deafening Modernism: Embodied Language and Visual Poetics in American Literature*. New York: New York UP, 2015. Print.

Shipka, Jody. "Negotiating Rhetorical, Material, Methodological, and Technological Difference: Evaluating Multimodal Designs." *CCC* 61.1 (2009): W343-66. Print.

Wilcox, Sherman. "Gesture and Language." *Gesture* 4.1 (2004): 43-73. Print.

Williams, Bronwyn. *Identity Papers: Literacy and Power in Higher Education*. Logan: Utah State UP, 2006.

Wilson, James C., and Cynthia Lewiecki-Wilson. "Disability, Rhetoric, and the Body." *Embodied Rhetorics: Disability in Language and Culture*. Ed. James C. Wilson and Cynthia Lewiecki-Wilson. Carbondale: SIUP, 2001. 1-25. Print.

Wysocki, Anne Frances. "Introduction: Into Between—On Composition in Mediation." *Composing (Media) = Composing (Embodiment): Bodies, Technologies, Writing, the Teaching of Writing*. Ed. Kristin L. Arola and Anne Frances Wysocki. Boulder: Utah State UP, 2012. 1-22. Print.

Yergeau, Melanie. "aut(hored)ism." *Computers and Composition Online* (2009): n. pag. Web. 12 Oct. 2015. <http://www2.bgsu.edu/departments/english/cconline/dmac/html/meta/ 007.html>.

Yergeau, Melanie, et al. "Multimodality in Motion: Disability and Kairotic Spaces." *Kairos* 18.1 (2013): n. pag. Web. 12 Oct. 2013. <http://kairos.technorhetoric.net/18.1/coverweb/yergeau-et-al/pages/space/index.html>.

# Valuing Writers from a Neurodiversity Perspective: Integrating New Research on Autism Spectrum Disorder into Composition Pedagogy

*Elizabeth Tomlinson and Sara Newman*

> This study investigates how individuals with an autism spectrum disorder (ASD) approach writing tasks. We draw from the largest sample of autistic individuals to date in our field to argue for the value of understanding ASD writers through the lens of neurodiversity. The neurodiversity approach focuses on autism as a part of human experience and values adaptive techniques, as opposed to dwelling on a cure for ASD. Our research expands and supports neurodiversity theory through the participants' descriptions of their approaches to writing and the techniques they use to communicate successfully with audiences across areas of their lives—in classrooms, workplaces, and their own personal writings. To better address the needs of all students, on the basis of this research, we advocate for an approach to composition pedagogy that incorporates Universal Design for Learning (UDL) and the classical notion of *mētis*.

---

According to the Centers for Disease Control (CDC), approximately 1 in 68 children in the U.S. have an Autism Spectrum Disorder (ASD) (Baio). Because postsecondary students are not mandated to disclose diagnoses, it is likely that more autistic individuals enter college than records indicate (Jurecic 422; Walsh 7). As the diagnosis is associated with communication skills, ASD is a topic significant to writing studies scholars and instructors. Yet minimal research considers ASD in college and professional writing pedagogy and practice and, when it does so, often focuses on individuals (e.g., Jurecic; Worsham and Olson) or online platforms (Wyatt). Typically, too, these studies do not consider those individuals' own thoughts about ASD and writing. Scholarship from our field provides an important starting place for studying this significant topic, though writing studies has yet to fully incorporate autism research into theory and practice. For example, no work has addressed ASD and writing in light of the new criteria in the *Diagnostic and Statistical Manual of Mental Disorders 5* (*DSM*) nor has writing scholarship fully reckoned with Theory of Mind (TOM), a cognitive studies perspective which claims that autistic individuals are not aware that other people have states of mind (Baron-Cohen, *Mindblindness*).

With these issues in mind, we surveyed 29 autistic individuals, asked them to discuss their own life writing (Couser; Newman), and analyzed the data from a neurodiversity perspective. This social approach to disability views autism as a naturally occurring human variation representing difference, not necessarily a deficit. We discovered these individuals advocate "embracing difference" instead of equating difference with deficit; they are also quite aware of the composing process and their own approaches to it, different audiences, and tasks. These firsthand accounts complement recent research, demonstrating that autistic individuals do indeed have a sense of themselves and their communication skills (Baines; Hacking) as well as an understanding of audience. By asking for the participants' thoughts about writing, we acquired several excellent teaching strategies as well as insights into integrating these strategies into the classroom; we frame these strategies here within the neurodiversity compatible framework of Universal Design for Learning (UDL) and the classical notion of *mētis*. These strategies are consistent with the findings from our data and allow us to interrogate and complicate the assumptions embedded within the new *DSM-5* criteria. Although our neurodiversity perspective is at odds with the *DSM*'s diagnostic stance, we believe we must acknowledge and confront that stance both to lessen the *DSM*'s influence over medical, educational, and social values and to facilitate transitions in these realms to values based on Disability Studies (DS) thinking. This DS approach indicates that instructors must teach from the students' personal identities outward, rather than from labels inward, an approach that requires listening to the students' voices.

## Disability and ASD: From the Medical Model to a Neurodiversity Perspective

Until recently, most writing scholarship approached disability by characterizing affected students in terms of the medical model. According to this model, which grounds the *DSM* and special education theory and practice, disabilities are individual problems to be cured (Lewiecki-Wilson; Linton). DS scholars have called attention to the essentializing inherent in the medical model. They point out its dependence on an artificial binary between deficit and cure and have offered alternatives that characterize bodies in terms of societal norms rather than normality and abnormality (Davis; Linton). These social perspectives on the body are compatible with writing studies, a field that often characterizes communication in terms of the body; in the past, these characterizations tended toward a medical approach but the scholarship is now adopting a social stance (Brueggemann, et al. 371).[1]

Among social DS perspectives, the recent neurodiversity model acknowledges the great variety of human physical manifestations—some rare, some common, and each with its own set of advantages and problems—by considering all human bodies on a physical/mental spectra. "There is no normal style of human brain or human mind, any more than there is one normal race, ethnicity, gender, or culture" (J. Walker 156); instead these characteristics represent diverse rather than deficient aspects of the human condition. Accordingly, the neurodiversity perspective focuses on overall quality of life, recognizes the positive aspects of autism, acknowledges autism as a human experience, and "promote[s] subjective well-being and adaptive rather than typical functioning" (Kapp, et al. 60, 67). The neurodiversity perspective acknowledges what the disabled individual thinks and how s/he identifies (Brueggemann et al.; Linton 12). Temple Grandin notes that neurodiversity takes attention away from current preoccupations with "autism as diagnostic category that produces a sense of identity" (4). This perspective is not only consistent with how many autistic individuals characterize themselves (Monje; Walters; Worsham and Olson) but also shifts cultural conceptions from the medical model to a neurodiversity framework.

At present, the medical model influences scholarly as well as public perspectives on ASD in large part because of Simon Baron-Cohen's widely accepted theories about TOM in regard to autism. For those who theorize autism as a failure of TOM, ASD is both a biological and cognitive defect that manifests in social, communication, and imagination problems (Baron-Cohen, "Autism" 81; Happé, "An Advanced" 130). Autistic individuals may face challenges when planning and executing daily tasks—schoolwork, for instance—and may encounter difficulties seeing the part for the whole. In writing classes, these matters are evident when students have difficulties creating academic essays and writing for an audience. As a result of such common pedagogical practices, autism appears to manifest as communication deficits.

In *Mindblindness,* Baron-Cohen locates autistic "abnormalities" (81) in the following assumption: autistic individuals cannot recognize that other people have minds and intentions, or mental states, other than their own (55). As Baron-Cohen puts it, autistic individuals are "mindblind," by which he means that they cannot understand or communicate with others. As he states, "The gulf between mindreaders and the mindblind must be vast . . . Tragically, mindblindness is not idle thought experiment or a piece of science fiction. For some people, it is very real" (*Mindblindness* 4-5). Despite Baron-Cohen's efforts to understand and help individuals affected by autism, the medical force of his terminology is clear: the autistic individual's experience is a tragic, abnormal reality and requires treatment, if not cure. Such experiences, Baron-Cohen contends, are as yet mysterious to the normal individual, whose experience is knowable. Because the "impaired" "mindblind" individual contrasts with the "normal" "mindreader," or non-autistic person, the concept of "mindblindness" relies on the medical model of disability (Baron-Cohen, *Mindblindness* 4).

In fact, research by Uta Frith and Francesca G.E. Happé, as they respectively acknowledge, demonstrates that the lines between the "autistic" and "non-autistic" are not so clear; some people with ASD possess TOM and, conversely, non-autistic individuals sometimes have problems with TOM (Frith, *Autism* 72; Happé, "An Advanced" 129). But, these researchers each tend to downplay the lack of true demarcation between autistic and non-autistic populations when interpreting their data. For example, Frith tempers the abilities of Aspergians, noting in medicalized language that "some *individuals with Asperger's* have written eloquently about their lives, *but their ability to talk about their emotions appears to be impaired (alexithymia)*" (Frith, "Emanuel Miller" 672; emphasis added). When Happé examines the autobiographies of three Aspergians, she admits that her data set is small, her method subjective, and her evaluation based on her own inability to evaluate what good writing or "normal" writing looks like ("Autobiographical" 221, 223). Despite these acknowledgements, she discusses the cases using inductive scientific language and finds the subjects lacking. For example, she frames her discussion with the following questions: "[J]ust how able are these people, or rather perhaps just how handicapped? What can we point to in their writings that deserve the label 'autistic'? And what is it about even the most able patients that lead us to say autism is a handicap that one does not grow out of?" ("Autobiographical" 207). Happé's reference to "handicaps" and "labels" reinforces representations of autistics as deficient. Elsewhere, she comments:

> Overall, the writing is remarkable and an achievement of which almost anyone would be proud. There can be no doubt that Temple Grandin is a capable and intelligent woman and a success story to encourage parents, teachers and those who themselves receive a diagnosis of autism. Her success lies, perhaps, in her lack of interest in social matters, and hence her lack of distress at her relative isolation. ("Autobiographical" 213)

Despite the compliment, Happé's language describes Grandin as isolated and impaired.

Other researchers report in more positive terms that some speaking autistic individuals prefer to communicate in writing and may indeed think complexly about their audiences. When Ian Hacking examines autistic autobiographies, Grandin's among them, his implicitly neurodiverse approach rejects TOM and the medical model and takes the writer's own thinking into account. Hacking observes, "These [writers] are often said to show autism from the 'inside'… instead they are developing ways to describe experience for which there is little preexisting language" (205). Similarly, Hacking suggests that many speaking autistic individuals understand the world around them, albeit in their own terms (205; cf. Baggs).[2] Similarly, Ann Marie Baines shows that ASD youth are well aware of their identity and of the labels imposed on them. They can actively "construct identities through social interactions to belong, compete, and participate" (Baines 547). She calls on readers not to assume that autistic people are "mindblind."

A growing body of life writing by autistic individuals supports this non-medical approach. Some writing appears in books (Grandin; Hughes; Igashida; Kedar; Mukopadhyay; Robison) and some on blogs and websites (Baggs; Grace; Monje). Life writing represents non-speaking (Igashida; Kedar; Mukopadhyay; Sequenzia) and speaking autistics (Grace; Grandin; Hughes; Monje; Robison; Wyatt). These examples of life writing show the ability of autistic individuals to write with many levels of audience awareness. The sheer number of publications by autistic individuals demonstrates these writers can connect with broad audiences (Hughes 31).

Although scholarship on disability and college writing is growing (Dunn; Lewiecki-Wilson and Brueggemann), relatively little addresses ASD. This shortage is especially unfortunate because of the link between ASD and communication issues, and the increasing, yet often unrecognized presence of individuals on the spectrum in postsecondary education. Within existing work on ASD and composition, medical and DS models, including neurodiversity, appear. But, these efforts consider few participants and rely too much on researchers' perspectives, to the exclusion of the participants' voices.

Given this research deficit, Val Gerstle and Lynda Walsh's anthology on ASD and writing is prescient. *Autism Spectrum Disorders in the College Composition Classroom* includes chapters that exhibit sensitivity to the stigma associated with ASD. Still, the collection suggests that students with ASD are likely to need remedial instruction.[3] As Walsh puts it, more and more students with ASD characteristics are participating in higher education for which they need good communication skills: "Unfortunately, the socially-intensive college composition classroom can be a particularly difficult environment for the student with ASD, who can have real problems working in groups, empathizing with potential audiences, and managing complex tasks such as constructing a lengthy research paper" (7). Although the issues Walsh describes exist, she suggests that students with ASD have many seemingly insurmountable problems and are always behind the "normal" students who do not experience such problems. Focusing on problems and cures, her characterization reveals the medical model and its attendant issues. Other chapters single out students who cannot handle the regular material, suggesting that writing issues (difficulty with thinking verbally rather than visually, with linear thinking and with collaboration, etc.) represent cognitive deficiencies (see chapters by Gerstle and Walsh 35; Mann; Wills).

Beyond Walsh's anthology, Ann Jurecic discusses her experience with a student, "Gregory," who did not identify as ASD, but, in her estimation, embodies the criteria. She states, "Gregory's problems were not different in kind from those of other students; rather they were different in degree and persistence" (427). Accordingly, she commits to using alternative embodied modes, genres, and class structures (e.g., 427, 434). Nonetheless, Jurecic stereotypes Gregory as a model of all individuals with autism (see Lewiecki-Wilson and Dolmage). She characterizes Gregory and others with ASD as people "who think and learn in ways that are substantially different from the norm" (427); she refers to how "our students with Asperger's may be active writers, even as they struggle to produce academic essays for a neurotypical audience" (427). When she observes that Gregory experiences "alienation associated with neurological difference," she evokes the notion of mindblindness—even if her goal is to reject such exclusionary teaching practices (422; cf. 427). By speaking for Gregory, she sometimes perpetuates the norms that she attempts to dismantle. Gregory stands alone against the class; he is not simply different but deficient.

Other relevant scholarship for this study includes two works that characterize disabilities in embodied terms of *mētis* (Dolmage, *Disability Rhetoric*; Walters; cf. Lindgren). *Mētis,* an ancient concept, is associated with cunning, fluidity, embodiment, and trickery, characteristics associated with a diverse range of ancient bodies, most notably, Odysseus (Detienne and Vernant 14-21). To link this notion with disability, Jay Dolmage focuses on Hesphaetus, god of the forge. Certainly, his lame limb disabled him; yet, his crab-like sideways movements assured him an embodied cunning that allowed him to succeed where other humans might not (*Disability Rhetoric* 154). For Dolmage, then, *mētis* is a rhetorical framework that focuses on "the craft of forging something practical out of these possibilities [which disability has], practicing an embodied rhetoric, changing the world as we move through it" (149).[5] Similarly, Shannon Walters looks at ASD through a *mētis*-like lens, linking ASD, women, writing, and animals to offer a plan for human actions. As she puts it, "the animal elements of *mētis* [are] a model for human behavior, also circulating among animal bodies, bring them together in ways that often trouble the accepted categories of ability and disability" (689). Keeping in mind this work that recognizes and values autistic individuals as part of the larger spectrum of humanity, we now turn to our study.

## Methods

We began our study by asking how self-identifying high functioning[6] autistic individuals interpret and manage writing tasks, particularly regarding their audiences. We sought to uncover whether participants had identified specific techniques that could serve as useful pedagogical tools for others who have a disability or who share a workplace with disabled individuals. By focusing on self-identified autistic adults, this research resists the tendency in Western societies to depict autism as "a disability of childhood," which disenfranchises and disempowers adult self-advocates (Stevenson, Harp, and Gernsbacher). Simultaneously, we recognize that the participants in our data set are one subgroup of autistics; the spectrum is quite broad and the ability to write is certainly not universal.

The survey (see appendix) was developed following the basic tenets of the Tailored Design Model (Dillman, Smyth, and Christian), which requires careful attention to design attributes throughout, as well as meticulous construction and ordering of questions. Following IRB approval, the survey was launched using Qualtrics survey software. Through six public disability listservs/discussion boards where we are members, we issued invitations to people over age 18 who self-identify as autistic to participate. The listservs and discussion boards are populated mainly by professionals, advocates, and academics interested in ASD. Thirty-two participants began the survey; 29 completed it. Participants represented a wide range of life roles, including instructors, students, professional writers, and others engaged in writing tasks outside the academy.

We organized the responses by question and independently completed thematic coding. The responses were broken into t-units and coded using Anselm Strauss's four coding paradigm components—condition, strategy, consequence, and interaction—as a framework for code identification (28). Following several rounds of independent open coding and memo writing, we compared our findings, and discussed and resolved discrepancies. The coding process uncovered themes across participants that organized our presentation of information. Data is often quoted at length so that participants might speak for themselves, opening spaces for rhetorical triangulation and self-advocacy (De Pew). We did not require participants to include their names in our survey; thus, participant words are cited anonymously below.

## Results

To begin, we turn to participants' overall impressions of writing. Following this big picture, we shift to writers' descriptions of their experiences within individual projects. Finally, the participants share writing techniques that they have found useful for helping them complete writing tasks and they offers several recommendations other instructors might try.

### The Participants' Overall Impressions about Writing

The survey first asked participants to discuss which aspects of writing were easiest and most difficult for them. Like non-ASD populations, participants' strengths and weaknesses varied greatly. Given this diversity, the participants provided insight into their identities as writers, particularly into how they frame their individual strengths and weaknesses. Several noted writing was by and large easy, whereas others hesitated to note a particular difficulty, stating instead that the entire writing process was a challenge. For instance, one participant commented, "I've made my living as a writer for 25 years. It's all easy." Yet, another noted, "writing in general is difficult for me." Another writer explained that having a personal investment in the writing eased the process: "The easiest part is writing about something I genuinely care about." Participants also referred to particular components of a text or the writing process as most or least approachable. Thus, four participants noted grammar as a strength or an aspect of writing that they particularly enjoyed. Other responses included references to composing introductions or conclusions, to editing, to researching, and to aspects of invention.

Regarding challenges, several participants commented on particular aspects of audience. For example, several struggled to understand how their writing would be evaluated by others and what they specifically needed to do to craft a successful "translation" for others. One contributor stated the greatest challenge was "finding the right words for the ideas that I want to say. I think in pictures, so writing is like translating my thoughts to a different language." While any act of writing involves translating ideas into text, this participant describes an extra layer of complexity. Another writer explained the greatest difficulty was "the actual writing! I can have a very clear idea of what I want to write, but the most difficult part is figuring out what words I want to use to connect my ideas. I usually spend hours with a thesaurus because I can't remember the word I wanted to use." Both participants describe distinct, troubling facets of addressing their audiences. Moreover, these two responses incidents characterize choosing words for self-expression as an act of translation from head to page or screen. While this is also a struggle for many who write professionally, whether they have ASD or not, these writers portray their struggle as prolonged because of the challenging work of managing translation and audiences.

Two participants noted different processes of audience adaptation: "The thing I hate about writing is I never know if what I wrote is 'right' or not. It is so subjective" and "[The greatest challenge is] providing information which neurotypicals consider relevant and linking paragraphs in a way that is coherent to neurotypicals." For these writers, the challenges lay in understanding the metric readers use for evaluation. These respondents understood the audience was sometimes challenging, but they met the challenge, and did not think only of themselves (cf. Baines; Frith).

## How the Writing Happens: Participants Describe Individual Projects

The survey asked participants to comment in detail about their work with one particular piece of writing. Participants wrote about several categories of texts: school, workplace texts, and web texts not directly connected to jobs or school. School texts included dissertations, theses, final exams, and papers; professional texts included novels, other fiction, and non-fiction articles. Web-texts included blog entries, emails, and public message board posts. The data set reflects the breadth of these participants' life roles; autistic individuals actively participate in varied workplaces and across academia, as both students and instructors.

As they reflected on the opening moments of composing, the participants tended to discuss how they picked specific arguments and appropriate audiences. They were also concerned with textual organization. For example, one respondent explained that the first things considered were "the order of what needed to be done and who would need to be involved to do it." For another writer, the concern was the "general concept and what I could argue most effectively." We also inquired whether they thought about someone specific while they were composing. Most often participants (54%) reported thinking about themselves. Other responses included current or former teachers (46%), the public (25%), co-workers or bosses (21%), friends (18%), a client (4%), or a significant other (4%). In six instances (21%) participants explained that they "did not think about anyone while writing the text."[7] These findings challenge the hypothesis that all autistic individuals struggle with TOM; in many cases, these individuals were actively considering varied audiences—even when they found it particularly challenging.

We also asked respondents how they dealt with composing their text. This participant describes his/her composition of a work-related text:

> First I wrote it like an outline and inserted the pictures, then I replaced the outline with the non technical business language explanation (for the non techy boss). For the tech details I didn't want to forget I put sentence fragments as placekeepers as I went along. Then I replaced the placekeepers and fleshed out the technical explanations with examples…Then I reread it to see if it was too long, repetitive or boring and cut out what repeated. Then I reread it one last time to see if it was too formal and replaced some long wordy phrases with shorter less formal language.

The writer analyzes the audience's needs and considers whether that audience might find it too technical, dull, or problematic in tone, and then goes on to describe a thoughtful, thorough approach to drafting, editing, and revising that appears to work well within this work environment.

Another participant describes his/her process as anxiety provoking until the writing gushes forth: "When I reach a point where needing to finish the writing makes me worry more than having to actually write in the first place, I just start furiously writing down words. During my anxiety portion, I am planning and mulling over what to say in the back of my mind." The respondent acknowledges a mental invention process that finds its way to page or screen after substantial incubation. This description suggests that s/he values having ample time to think through the topic, as opposed to being forced to write on demand. The discussions of particular projects revealed that each participant faced various issues, including anxiety and deadline pressures.

**Participants' Own Adaptive Techniques**

The participants provided substantial commentary on techniques they use when writing, which instructors and employers might use to create welcoming spaces for all writers. The first response category involved games the writers play. This grouping included mind games and organizational tools. One respondent suggested, "Play the 'So What?' game: Remove any comments which you cannot justify including in the text." Two noted particular ways of conceptualizing language: "think only in the language you are writing the text in," and "view writing for different audiences sort of like writing in various foreign languages." Two others suggested starting with the section that most interested them. Another writer described making "strips of paper with works [sic] or phrases that I can then shift to combine into sentences (sort of like magnetic poetry)." Other, more traditional organizational techniques included "writing an outline," following a rubric, and writing a "notecard of main ideas, points, and stories, and the format that is necessary for the writing." Several writers mentioned techniques or games they use to quiet inner critics. One reflected, "I can only think about the audience while revising: if I attempt it while actually writing I can't move forward." Similarly, another participant wrote, "To begin writing, I absolutely must make myself feel 'safe' by telling myself that it's only freewriting or brainstorming and that no one need ever see it. Before I learned to do that, often I was unable to write anything at all."

Often, participants wrote about the importance of having an appropriate physical space. They referred to supplies, such as computer equipment, as well as whiteboards, and color. Several prioritized freedom to move around within the writing environment. Four discussed auditory stimuli they found helpful—two listened to instrumental music, while two others either composed aloud or recorded themselves while writing.

Among their adaptive techniques, the writers frequently suggested how to structure writing sessions. Techniques varied widely, but several liked to begin with a plan for the ending already in place. For example, "I try to plan the end, if I possibly can, because I have written a lot of fiction but stopped before I finished because it's really hard to draw all the pieces of the story together in to one coherent, focused end." Several also commented on specific structural issues. To that end, one participant suggested seeing writing as conversation: "I find it useful to consider paragraphs as topics of conversation. In conversation, topics shift but not generally abruptly, there tends to be a link between the subjects discussed." Another suggested, "Keep the points you would like to make in mind, but don't worry about having a rigid structure." Twelve writers also argued for the importance of using spellcheck, reviewing their own writing, or having someone help with proofreading. Finally, eight writers described the importance of having ample time to compose. For several writers, breaks were necessary; they also suggested the need for mental time to process. In sum, respondents described numerous techniques they used to produce texts for varied writing situations, including classrooms and workplaces

## Participants' Suggestions for Writing Instructors

The final survey question asked respondents to share suggestions with writing instructors who might encounter autistic individuals in educational settings. The coded responses fit the following groupings: specific activities and accommodations to consider, with a subset of activities related to audience; provision of moral support; and recommendations about skills to target. Several participants cited the importance of providing examples. One wrote, "Sample essays helped me a lot—even if they were nothing to do with the subject matter, it took me a long time to learn a formal essay structure, and I don't think I truly understood it until I was at college." Regarding models, participants argued for reading other essays to encourage students to understand "how important it is to keep your audience in mind while writing." Another participant suggested it would be useful to "have them read an academic article and note aspects of that article they feel their neurotypical supervisors/markers may like them to use in their own assignment (the academic article can be one of their choice so they find it interesting)." Our participants also requested "extremely clear and detailed" instruction sheets to use as references while writing for their audiences.

Other audience-related comments included, "Let them get the ideas out in their own way of expressing it first, then edit it to their audience. If they spend focus on the audience first, they will lose the ideas." Like several other participants, this writer suggests that tasks, including understanding one's audience, are best accomplished when broken down into smaller pieces. Another writer encouraged overtly teaching students that "different audiences will require different writing styles." Participants recognized the importance of knowing their audiences, but also acknowledged the challenges that unpacking this complex concept may elicit for writers.

Respondents suggested several other specific activities, including engaging the writer's special interest: "perhaps ask them to write a few random paragraphs concerning aspects of their special interest and see if they can connect them (tenuous link game)." Finally, one participant suggested, "I think a lot of ASD people benefit from being told the instances where they SHOULD and SHOULDN'T tell the truth, for example I failed a few writing papers because I always felt I should write the truth in school, which wasn't always very interesting" (caps in original). While we cannot address how many or how often autistic individuals encounter this issue, this participant provides an insight worth considering, particularly during one-on-one sessions with a writer seeking adaptive techniques.

The participants also proposed accommodations instructors might consider like allowing computer use during class, reminding students about due dates, providing extra time when possible, breaking down tasks into smaller steps, and allowing "stims" (self-stimulating behavior—often a repetitive body movement, for instance, body rocking or finger flapping) as long as these are not too distracting to others. One participant explained the role of the stim, "if you notice a stim happening, we're just having trouble connecting to our thoughts probably due to a distraction in the environment. The stim kind of helps us disconnect to think because when we focus on the stim it helps block out the environment and lets us transition to thought." Reinforcing the neurodiversity perspective, this participant explained and justified the role of physical coping strategies in his/her writing process.

The writers surveyed, moreover, stressed the importance of moral support for autistic writers. Students should be "encouraged to realize that their writing style is not substandard, it is only different to the accepted norms of academia," suggested one participant. Similarly, another noted, "So many greats have/had AS or ASD, the students must understand that they can be an asset to universities, particularly once they find their passion." It is important to provide role models for students as well as to demonstrate perseverance. One participant provided a thoughtful response, characteristic of a neurodiverse perspective:

> Finally, if they have dyslexia or cross-over symptoms, they should embrace this difference, work with it rather than against it. It is only a difference, like left-handedness. Would they use left-handed scis-

sors if they were right-handed? Likely not, so why should they use black text on a white background if they are dyslexic and would benefit from a coloured/off-white background? Some of this is perhaps more psychological than academic but I believe it is important not to give students the impression that they are disabled, struggling or inferior to neurotypicals.

Writers should be encouraged to embrace the methods that work for them.

In addition, writers shared specific skills that they felt were useful for autistic students to learn. Although we do not wish to advocate a skills-driven approach to literacy or ASD, the participants' insights describe challenges they have faced when translating their perspectives into text for their audiences. The group's largest category of response dealt with taking a broader (as opposed to detail-oriented) view of the subject. In one respondent's words, "They need to practice being ok with not being 100% concise and comprehensive and to accept that the goal is to convey the main points, not to write the complete unabridged version." Another respondent explained, "We can get really lost in the details. We need to learn how to decide what details are important to include and what can be removed. We can learn this by writing it all down then editing. I have found several edits each with a specific goal works for me."

Several respondents noted the need for defining what constitutes high quality versus low quality texts. For example, one explained, "I think the rules and reasons of what makes a piece 'good' writing should be outlined much more clearly. . . . My writing style and process never change, but the subjectivity of evaluating my writing changes what grade I'm given in a particular situation." While standards for "good" writing are somewhat malleable depending on context and genre, this participant's observation deserves consideration—students may need greater clarification regarding standards within the given rhetorical situation. Finally, one respondent explained that s/he struggled to be "critical of texts—I could analyze the content of a text, but because I'm really incredibly literal, it was an uphill battle to convince myself that the text wasn't necessarily true, and that it was okay to look for flaws in reasoning or research." This response reiterates the importance of providing moral support for the writer, specifically, providing encouragement throughout the process, and empowering them to participate in argumentation with texts, other authors, and ideas.

In sum, the responses yielded numerous insights into how these writers operate within the classroom and workplace; and, although it is impossible to make broad generalizations, these writers generated plentiful starting points for discussion when engaging with autistic students/writers.

## Discussion

This study relies on the participants' voices, allowing readers to know them better as individual writers and to learn from their perspectives. While autism is a core attribute of their identities, being a writer and communicating with others is also highly important to many of these participants. These autistic writers describe challenges they face, but their varied responses also indicate that instructors should not make assumptions about how autistic students write. We also recognize that many autistic individuals are not able to write and face extensive challenges when communicating with neurotypical populations through both verbal and non-verbal means. With these caveats in place, we can, however, glean fragments of each student's or worker's identity, and ascertain certain "storylines" that allow us to better know each other, as Nancy Bagatell has suggested. Accordingly, in this section, we develop several storylines depicted across the data that lend support to the neurodiversity perspective.

First, our respondents showed that some autistics can and do employ many approaches to strategically communicating to audiences throughout their writing processes. Participants described the thought processes they used while composing and discussed their approaches to planning and organizing text. Participants also identified strengths and weaknesses within their writing, which varied significantly across their responses. What some described as a weakness (e.g., "grammar") others depicted as a strength. The label "ASD" does not necessarily define or delimit how the writer will cognitively approach all aspects of writing.

Second, the data does support a storyline about how some autistic individuals navigate the challenges of segmenting larger projects. To avoid becoming overwhelmed, several participants described their need to focus on one part of the text or one rhetorical concern at a time. As they explained, sometimes they were overwhelmed moving from the comfortable detail-oriented view to the broader audience-centered view required in many assignments. They noted the importance of considering a project as a series of small pieces.

A third storyline deals with mindblindness. The respondents help us identify several limitations regarding the broad applicability of this theory developed by Baron-Cohen, Leslie, and Frith. Within our data, many participants describe active audience analysis. They do not ignore the audience; rather, they actively consider how their audience thinks, although the task can be quite difficult. Nonetheless, several note challenges with translating their way of thinking into words that are meaningful for neurotypical populations. It is not that autistic individuals have their own language, but rather that some struggle with interpreting and expressing particular mainstream cultural values represented in certain genres. For instance, American business culture typically values brevity and succinctness. Some autistic individuals, the data suggests, may place a greater value on knowing a subject in great detail. These individuals face challenges when asked to fit that vast yet particular knowledge domain into an essay-shaped container of someone else's design. However, this particular challenge can also be viewed as a strength. For instance, many autistics participate in blogging and other forums, writing for and with each other (e.g., *Loud Hands* anthology; *Neurocosmopolitanism*; *Radical Neurodivergence Speaking*; *Shift Journal*). While these writers may be writing for neurotypical audiences, they have simultaneously engaged other autistics and created spaces, as both comments on their blog posts and the conversational back and forth established in *Loud Hands* indicate, where autistic community has the potential to flourish.

Understanding neurodiversity may also be helpful for writers as they navigate the process of translating a text from one system of textual values to another. Writers need to understand which ways of knowing are valued and expected in the workplace and academia. Yet, we should not dismiss the specialized kinds of knowledge that some autistic individuals may bring into the classroom and the workplace. For example, when writers are working as part of a team, the autistic writer might be encouraged to contribute in his/her greatest strengths, and might be viewed as a subject matter expert when his/her special interest is being addressed. As with all our students, we should acknowledge strengths to increase motivation and opportunities for success.

Finally, these writers described how important moral support was for them. They wanted to hear success stories from other autistics; they wanted others to think of them as different in their ways of knowing, not as disabled. We hope that the writers in this study will be thought of as autistics who represent success stories for others. These individuals are active writers; they can and do produce texts in schools and in the workplace. While the texts may sometimes differ from cultural norms, we should acknowledge and value the writers who craft those texts as well as the thinking that created them. ASD diagnosis does not preclude someone from becoming a productive, successful communicator.

## Conclusion

By asking autistics to respond to our questions, our study demonstrates that these individuals, like non-ASD students and writers, navigate challenging terrain when considering their audiences and preparing their texts. While our sample is a small subset of 29 autistic writers, and they do not claim to speak for all autistics, we do find value in their contributions. Many autistic individuals are aware of the writing process and they design writing to be shared with others. Their voices confirm that autistic people can possess TOM and hardly constitute a distinct and deficient group. Some, though not all, may communicate differently than people not on the spectrum, yet they also communicate in ways that they share with and are understood by non-autistics. These writers share many abilities and strategies with their readers, and they strive to communicate with their writing tasks in mind.

Our participants also tell us that composition pedagogy can be improved by including several adaptive techniques. For example, teaching the writing process helps writers deal with writer's block and/or tendencies toward perfectionism. But, not all people process and present information in the same way. To help students recognize and make the most out of their own composing, instructors should include varied assignment genres, deliver specific criteria for assignments, break up tasks into manageable units, respond to student writings in ways that are consistent with the criteria presented, and provide ample time and scaffolding. Their insights, quite simply, characterize good teaching for all students, those identifying as ASD or not.

In a broader sense, the teaching our participants describe involves flexible yet consistent pedagogy. To reach all writers while recognizing the embodied character of their practices, we encourage incorporating UDL into current composition pedagogy, thereby extending its primary use in the online classroom. Briefly, "UDL is a set of principles for curriculum development that give all individuals equal opportunities to learn" ("Building the Legacy"). Three primary principles guide UDL: providing multiple means of representation, of actions, and of engagement. In practice, these principles allow UDL to address affect, engagement, and motivation as well as executive function, organization, attention, and working memory; all of these principles speak to the kinds of difficulties encountered by some autistic students. UDI uses scaffolding, technology, and multiple media and modalities to address students' learning differences ("Building the Legacy"). UDL is also an embodied, spatial means of including the disabled student in the classroom (Dolmage, "Universal Design"). When we extend UDL's commitment to including spatial elements in pedagogy to embrace the flexible, embodied character of writing and teaching, we facilitate the erasure of stigma for *all* students. Especially when combined with the concept of *mētis*, UDL creates provision for integrating body and mind and place for all students—however they may be labelled—within a learning environment.

By demonstrating the continuity between all writers, our data also confronts the extremely influential *DSM-5* and offers another means of lessening its impact on autistic individuals. Because the *DSM*'s revised criteria locate characteristics of ASD on a continuum rather than identify a set of distinct types, as have past editions (APA, *DSM-5 Proposed Criteria*), the manual implicitly recognizes the continuity between all autistic individuals as well as those with non-ASD (e.g., people who have social anxiety or repetitive behaviors). Yet, this presumed continuity maintains its explicit diagnostic perspective and its basis in the medical model (APA, *DSM-5 Draft Criteria*).

We can take steps towards replacing the diagnostic perspective, even by degrees, with a neurodiverse, UD driven *mētis*-like approach in the writing classroom as a start. Using the notion of a spectrum, we can ground our pedagogy in principles that include the experiences of autistic individuals. Significantly, however, our data and our own experiences demonstrate that attempts to define ASD in the *DSM* fall far short of autistics' lived experiences. The participants' observations indicate that no criteria can fully capture what ASD is and that perhaps we should not even try. Potentially of greatest significance, oftentimes, our participants undermine the clinical theories surrounding TOM and confirm the underlying premise of neurodiversity—that autistic people want to be treated fairly and inclusively and are quite aware when they are not.

These principles and practices are consistent with the storylines we culled from the participants' observations, the strategies they offered, the needs of all composition students, and the fact that more students on the spectrum are attending college. We hope the voices of our participants will prompt educators to consider the potential of the neurodiversity perspective, which conceives autism as part of a whole, and we remind our readers that autistic individuals compose in ways that are just as valuable as the contributions of neurotypical writers.

## Notes

1. Writing studies scholars are increasingly adopting a DS perspective for examining what individuals with disabilities have to say, recognizing that academic discourse about disabilities dictates who is disabled and how this knowledge is represented (Vidali 617).

2. In Julia Bascom's *Loud Hands*, several non-speaking autistics share their experiences and demonstrate great insight into the world around them (e.g., Sequenzia 159). Bev Harp reminds us, "The most important thing to keep in mind is that speech is not the same thing as language, and that communication is a much larger concept still" (305).

3. Although remedial courses were designed to help students succeed, their underlying terminology of remedying diseases (Rose) supports the medical model and suggests that students are less able to function in higher education. Subsequent, alternative terminology, "basic" and "developmental," for instance, removes the explicit link with medicine and disease, but not the underlying association. Even in "normal" courses, students carry the deficit label.

4. Elsewhere, research evaluates particular aspects of autism and writing from DS perspectives. When Christopher Scott Wyatt considers the practical matter of ASD and online teaching, he finds that traditional approaches to accessibility are insufficient in online courseware platforms. In another theoretically based work, Carrie

Claudine Snow analyzes non-autistic students' engagement with "majoritarian" narratives as a means of diminishing labeling of autistic students. DS scholarship has also begun to probe the problems of faculty with disabilities in the academy (Price).

5. Karen Kopelson also addresses the writing classroom and *mētis*, but in terms of gender, race, and sexual orientation.

6. We acknowledge that the high-functioning/low-functioning binary is problematic (see Sequenzia; John Walker for discussions on this issue). Nonetheless, as we sought IRB approval for our research, we needed to use this common, flawed language to describe our participants. For the purpose of this study, "high functioning" means primarily that these individuals were capable of using writing to communicate and that they were capable of making informed decisions about whether to contribute their insights to our research project.

7. Participants were able to select multiple people whom they thought about while composing, thus the percentages do not sum to 100.

## Appendix: Survey

1. I have read and understood the above consent form and desire of my own free will to participate in this study. (Agree/Disagree)
2. In general, what part of writing a text is usually easiest for you?
3. In general, what do you find most difficult about writing a text?
4. When you are writing a text, how important is the audience to you? (Five item Likert Scale: Not at all Important to Extremely Important)
5. When you are writing a text, do you find it helpful to think in pictures or words? (Multiple choice: pictures, words, both, other)
6. Think back to a recent time when you had to write a text that was important to you on the computer or on paper. What was MOST important to you about writing that text?
7. The previous question asked you about a time when you were writing an important text. What kind of text were you writing? (Ex. a letter, a blog entry, a proposal, a memo, an essay, an email, something else)
8. What made this text important to you?
9. What did you think about first when you began developing that text?
10. Please continue thinking back to a recent time when you had to write a text that was important to you on the computer or on paper. While you were writing that text, who (if anyone) did you think about? (multiple choice: boss, co-worker/colleague, former teacher, current teacher, myself, friend, significant other, client, the public, I did not think about anyone, other-with space to fill in additional comments)
11. What did you most want to convey in that text?
12. Were there any problems that you had to solve when writing that text?
13. This question is very important for helping us understand your writing process. Please explain what steps you took in the process of writing that text.
14. Please provide any specific tips that you use to help yourself when you have to write a text.

15. Finally, please provide any suggestions you have for teaching high school and/or college students with AS or ASD how to write effectively. We appreciate your suggestions and advice.

## Works Cited

American Psychiatric Association. *Diagnostic Statistic Manual of Mental Disorders. (DSM-5)*. 5th ed. Rev. ed. Washington: APA, 2013. Print.

American Psychiatric Association. *DSM-5 Draft Criteria Open for Public Comment*. Release #24, 2 May 2012. Print.

American Psychiatric Association. *DSM-5 Proposed Criteria for Autism Spectrum Disorder Designed to Provide More Accurate Diagnosis and Treatment*. Release #12-03, 20 Jan. 2012. Print.

Bagatell, Nancy. *Constructing Identities in Social Worlds: Stories of Four Adults with Autism*. Diss. U of Southern California, 2004. Print.

Baggs, Amelia. "In My Language." Online video clip. *YouTube*. Youtube, 14 Jan. 2007. Web. 25 Oct. 2014. <http://www.youtube.com/watch?v=JnylM1hI2jc>.

Baines, Ann Marie D. "Positioning, Strategizing, and Charming: How Students with Autism Construct Identities in Relation to Disability." *Disability & Society* 27.4 (2012): 547-61. Print.

Baio, Jon. "Prevalence of Autism Spectrum Disorder among Children Aged 8 Years — Autism and Developmental Disabilities Monitoring Network, 11 Sites, United States, 2010." *Surveillance Summaries* 63.2 (2014): 1-21. Web. <http://www.cdc.gov/mmwr/pdf/ss/ss6302.pdf>.

Baron-Cohen, Simon. "Autism: A Specific Cognitive Disorder of 'Mind-Blindness'." *International Review of Psychiatry* 2 (1990): 81-90. Print.

---. *Mindblindness: An Essay on Autism and Theory of Mind*. Cambridge: MIT Press, 1995. Print.

Baron-Cohen, Simon, Alan M. Leslie, and Uta Frith. "Does the Autistic Child Have a 'Theory of Mind'?" *Cognition* 21.1 (1985): 37-46. Print.

Bascom, Julia, ed. *Loud Hands: Autistic People, Speaking*. New York: The Autistic Self-Advocacy Network, 2012. Print.

Brueggemann, Brenda Jo, Linda Feldmeier White, Patricia A. Dunn, Barbara A. Heifferon, and Johnson Cheu. "Becoming Visible: Lessons in Disability." *CCC* 52.3 (2001): 368-98. Print.

"Building the Legacy: IDEA 2004." *CAST. Transforming Education though Universal Design for Learning*. U.S. Department of Education, n.d. Web. 2 Apr. 2014. <http://idea.ed.gov>.

Couser, G. Thomas. *Signifying Bodies: Disability in Contemporary Life Writing*. Ann Arbor: U of Michigan P, 2009. Print.

Davis, Lennard J. "Introduction: The Need for Disability Studies." *The Disability Studies Reader*. Ed. Lennard J. Davis. New York: Routledge, 2006. 1-6. Print.

DePew, Kevin. "Through the Eyes of Researchers, Rhetors, and Audiences: Triangulating Data from the Digital Writing Situation." *Digital Writing Research: Technologies, Methodologies, and Ethical Issues* Ed. Heidi A. McKee and Dànielle Nicole DeVoss. Cresskill, NJ: Hampton Press, Inc. 2007. 49-70. Print.

Detienne, Marcel, and Jean-Pierre Vernant. *Cunning Intelligence in Greek Culture and Society*. Trans. Janet Lloyd. Chicago: U Chicago P, 1978. Print.

Dillman, Don A., Jolene D. Smyth, and Leah M. Christian. *Internet, Mail, and Mixed-Mode Surveys: The Tailored Design Method*. Hoboken: Wiley, 2009. Print.

Dolmage, Jay Timothy. *Disability Rhetoric*. Syracuse: Syracuse UP, 2014. Print.

---. "Mapping Composition: Inviting Disability in the Front Door." Lewiecki-Wilson and Brueggemann 14-28.

---. "Universal Design for Living: A Brief Annotated Bibliography on Online Resources." Lewiecki-Wilson and Brueggemann 171-74.

Dunn, Patricia A. *Learning Re-Abled: The Learning Disability Controversy and Composition Studies*. Portsmouth: Boynton/Cook, 1995. Print.

Frith, Uta. *Autism: A Very Short Introduction*. Oxford: Oxford UP, 2008. Print.

---. "Emanuel Miller Lecture: Confusions and Controversies about Asperger Syndrome." *Journal of Child Psychology and Psychiatry* 45.4 (2004): 672-86. Print.

Gerstle, Val, and Lynda Walsh, eds. *Autism Spectrum Disorders in the College Composition Classroom: Making Writing Instruction More Accessible for All Students*. Milwaukee: Marquette UP, 2011. Print.

Grace, Elizabeth J. *Tiny Grace Notes*. N.p., n.d. Web. 25 Oct. 2014. <www.tinygracenotes.blogspot.com>.

Grandin, Temple. *Thinking In Pictures: And Other Reports from My Life With Autism*. New York: Vintage Books, 1996. Print.

Hacking, Ian. "Autistic Autobiography." *Autism and Talent*. Ed. Francesca G.E Happé and Uta Frith. Oxford: Oxford UP, 2010. 195-209. Print.

Happé, Francesca G.E. "An Advanced Test of Theory of Minds: Feelings of Story Characters' Thoughts and Feelings by Able Autistic, Mentally Handicapped, and Normal Children and Adults." *Journal of Autism and Developmental Disorders* 24.2 (1994): 129-54. Print.

---. "The Autobiographical Writings of Three Asperger Syndrome Adults: Problems of Interpretation and Implications for Theory." *Autism and Asperger Syndrome*. Ed. Uta Frith. Cambridge: Cambridge UP, 1991. 207-43. Print.

Harp, Bev. "Are You Listening?" Bascom 305-308.

Hughes, Dawn Prince. *Songs of the Gorilla Nation: My Journey Through Autism*. New York: Harmony, 2004. Print.

Igashida, Naoki. *The Reason I Jump. The Inner Voice of a Thirteen-Year-Old Boy with Autism*. Trans. Y. A. Yoshida and David Mitchell. New York: Random House, 2013. Print.

Jurecic, Ann. "Neurodiversity." *College English* 69.5 (2007): 421-42. Print.

Kapp, Steven K., Kristen Gillespie-Lynch, Lauren E. Sherman, and Ted Hutman. "Deficit, Difference, or Both? Autism and Neurodiversity." *Developmental Psychology* 49.1 (2013): 59-71. Print.

Kedar, Ido. *Ido in Autismland: Climbing Out of Autism's Silent Prison*. Ido Ketar, 2012. Print.

Kopelson, Karen. "Rhetoric on the Edge of Cunning; Or, the Performance of Neutrality Considered as a Composition Pedagogy for Student Resistance." *CCC* 55.1 (2003): 115-46. Print.

Lewiecki-Wilson, Cynthia. "'Doing the Right Thing' versus Disability Rights: A Response to Ellen Barton." *JAC* 21.4 (2001): 870-81. Print.

Lewiecki-Wilson, Cynthia, and Brenda Jo Brueggemann, eds. *Disability and the Teaching of Writing: A Critical Sourcebook*. Boston: Bedford, 2008. Print.

Lewiecki-Wilson, Cynthia, and Jay Dolmage. "Two Comments on 'Neurodiversity'." *College English* 70.3 (2008): 314-19. Print.

Lindgren, Kristen. "Body Language: Disability Narratives and the Act of Writing." Lewiecki-Wilson and Brueggemann 96-109.

Linton, Simi. *Claiming Disability: Knowledge and Identity*. New York: NYU Press, 1998. Print.

Mann, April. "Structure and Accommodation: Autism and the Writing Center." Gerstle and Walsh 45-75.

Monje, Michael. "Not that Autistic. Monday." N.p., 21 January 2013. Web. 26 Oct. 2014. <www.mmonjejr.com>.

Mukopadhyay, Tito Rajarshi. *How Can I Talk If My Lips Don't Move? Inside My Autistic Mind*. New York: Arcade Publishing, 2008. Print.

Neurodivergent_K. *Radical Neurodivergence Speaking*. N.p., n.d. Web. 17 February 2015. <Timetolisten.blogspot.com>.

Newman, Sara. *Writing Disability: A Critical History*. Boulder: Lynne Rienner Publishers and FirstForum Press, 2012. Print.

Price, Margaret. *Mad at School. Rhetorics of Mental Disability and Academic Life*. Ann Arbor: U of Michigan P, 2011. Print.

Robison, John Elder. *Look Me in the Eye: My Life with Asperger's*. New York: Random House, 2007. Print.

Rose, Mike. "Narrowing the Mind and Base: Remedial Writers and Cognitive Reductionism." *CCC* 39 (1988): 267-98. Print.

Sequenzia, Amy. "Non-speaking, 'Low-functioning'." Bascom 159-161.

*Shift Journal of Alternatives: Neurodiversity and Social Change*. Mark Stairwalt, n.d. Web. 17 Feb. 2015. <www.shiftjournal.com>.

Snow, Carrie Claudine. *Interpreting Asperger Syndrome through an Analysis of Students' Engagement with "Majoritarian" Narrative*s. Diss. Teachers' College, Columbia University, 2010. Print.

Stevenson, Jennifer L., Bev Harp, and Ann Gernsbacher Morton. "Infantilizing Autism." *Disability Studies Quarterly* 31.3 (2011). Web. <http://dsq-sds.org/article/view/1675/1596>.

Strauss, Anselm. L. *Qualitative Analysis for Social Scientists*. Cambridge: Cambridge UP, 1987. Print.

Vidali, Amy. "Discourses of Disability and Basic Writing." Lewiecki-Wilson and Brueggemann 40-55.

Walker, John. "Throw Away the Master's Tool: Liberating Ourselves from the Pathology Paradigm." Bascom 225-237.

Walker, Nick. *Neurocosmopolitanism: Nick Walker's Notes on Neurodiversity, Autism, and Cognitive Liberty*. N.p., n.d. Web. 17 February 2015. <Neurocosmopolitanism.com>.

Walsh, Lynda. "Introduction: Autism Spectrum Disorders in College Composition." Gerstle and Walsh 7-15.
Walters, Shannon. "Animal Athena: The Interspecies *Mētis* of Women Writers with Autism." *JAC* 30 (2010): 683-711. Print.
Wills, Katherine V. "I Just Felt Kinda Invisible: Accommodations for Learning Disabled Students in the Composition Classroom." Gerstle and Walsh 45-75.
Worsham, Lynn, and Gary A. Olson. "Temple Grandin, Translator: Sounding Autism, Seeing Animals, Making a Difference." *JAC* 32 (2012): 11-56. Print.
Wyatt, Christopher Scott. *Online Pedagogy: Designing Writing Courses for Students with Autism Spectrum Disorders*. Diss. University of Minnesota, 2011. Print.

# Forget Formulas: Teaching Form through Function in Slow Writing and Reading as a Writer

*Michelle Tremmel*

> Arguing for teaching essay structure through slow writing and reading as a writer (RAAW), this article explains a measured-pace pedagogy. It offers a brief history of the concern about organization in writing instruction; defines slow writing and RAAW; details their components; offers a rationale for this guided workshop approach; and describes, with illustration, the basic process of working with short essays using RAAW.

---

> The population ages but never graduates.
> On hot afternoons they sweat the final in the park
> and when it's cold they shiver around stoves
> reading disorganized essays out loud.

In this passage from Billy Collins' poem "Schoolsville" (186), the speaker, a retired English teacher, bemoans disordered writing produced by his imaginary town's residents: former students. In such disappointment, he is not alone. For well over one hundred years of writing instruction, handwringing about the issue of organization in student writing has bordered on an obsession, probably second only to mechanical correctness, for teachers in college and secondary schools. This longstanding concern over disorganized student writing, particularly as manifest in essays, runs the gamut from Aristotle's delineating the proper parts of a classical oration in 4th century BCE (Cooper 220) to Kerri Smith in 2006 touting the five-paragraph theme as "a building block everyone should have" (17). It encompasses Barrett Wendell's worry in 1903 about the effect of "our poor muddled human heads" on form (136) and Victor Pudlowski's complaint in 1959 that "[a]ll [student] papers had one thing in common: they were thoroughly unorganized" (535). In 1929 Carroll Towle handed his so-called "Awkward Squad" (students at Yale struggling with English composition and placed into an extracurricular remedial course) "a possible outline by paragraph" to streamline these struggling students' in-class theme writing (674), and in 2012 University of Georgia–Athens instructor Josh Boldt claimed that the five-paragraph theme "works great as [an organizational] foundation." As the Smith and Boldt examples illustrate, many times the worry about structure has translated into quick-fix templates to check students' so-called unruly thinking; and efficiency approaches have been persistent and systemic, often with a time-saving emphasis.

A slower paced alternative to formulas, writing as self-exploration (Dornan, Rosen, and Wilson 228) emerged in the mid-1960s as a rebellion against the current-traditional paradigm and its grammar-, product-, and template-centered practices. To summarize briefly, this approach, sometimes known as expressivism,[1] first drew on the work of practitioner-scholars like James Britton, Jerome Bruner (*Process*), Peter Elbow, Ken Macrorie, James Moffett, and Donald Murray (*A Writer*). It championed the unique, idiosyncratic, and self-guided process of the individual and emphasized growth over time. This approach theorizes an organic "process"[2] in which writers first inquire into and make discoveries about a topic during "prewriting." From there, they compose by considering individual ideas, relationships among ideas, and connections between ideas and themselves. Once writers have gained satisfying insights into the topic and produced a piece of discourse they deem communicatively effective, they are done and move on to the next exploration (Dornan, Rosen, and Wilson 229). As envisioned by Elbow in *Writing without Teachers*, for example, self-exploration through writing is relatively unguided, individualized, open, recursive, and non-formulaic, allowing writers' freedom and written expression to drive instruction.

In the four and a half decades since self-exploration through writing began to influence composition teaching, both formulaic, current-traditional practices and student-directed, unguided workshops have appealed to teachers of writing. I would like to suggest that both approaches contain seeds of excess and, instead, propose a middle way, what I term "slow writing." Specifically, in this article I advocate for slow writing as an effective approach to teaching the short argument essay to first-year writers, who are transitioning from high school to college writing. My attention lies here especially because many first-year college writing programs and secondary English/writing classes use the essay as a starting point for academic discourse. A slow-writing pedagogy and one of its techniques, reading as a writer (RAAW), can help novice[3] writers in high school and college accomplish what "seasoned writers" do "naturally" with little direction: "pick up [key intellectual] moves unconsciously through their reading" (Graff, Birkenstein, and Durst xxv), as well as encourage them to organically discover essay structure (or other rhetorical techniques they need to learn).

## Slow Writing and RAAW

Slow writing signifies more than a set of techniques. It collapses a product-process duality and offers a different pace than either fast and efficient or "as long as it takes." Conceptualized as a way for novices and their teachers to be and become writers in the writing classroom, slow writing shares with other "slow" movements (like slow foods) a savoring of time and local context that allows students to practice as writers while they build proficiency. As in Thomas Newkirk's concept of "slow reading," slow writing questions a fast-food culture of speed and efficiency and believes, as Newkirk does, that "there is real pleasure in downshifting, in slowing down" ("The Case" 6).

This point about pace and pleasure is integral and important to slow writing and its intentional metacognition. Novices need time to find pleasure in the *activity* of writing since affect plays a powerful role in motivation and since the significant effort needed to build writing proficiency takes motivation. Building interest through a measured pace with time for writer-directed composing activities, slow writing involves the following: Writers keep a composer's notebook—less free than a daybook but less structured than Nancie Atwell's individualized "writing-reading handbook" (*In* 105). They move gradually and recursively through process to product. They examine and critique texts (their own and others') through RAAW. And they present their work for grading in a portfolio. Slow writing has two primary goals: to discover techniques in rhetorically real writing (i.e., that which is outside of school and responds to a "call to write," as John Trimbur puts it) and to try out techniques in pieces students compose for audiences and purposes that matter to them.

The RAAW method asks students to (1) become engaged with a genre (like the short essay), (2) study a particular essay feature (like structure), and (3) experiment with techniques for that feature in their composer's notebook. RAAW creates a reading-writing reciprocity in which each aspect of literacy enhances and develops the other through an intentionally textual interaction. In so doing, RAAW works within the guided process pedagogy of slow writing.

**How RAAW Works**

Although teachers can use slow writing and RAAW for any in-depth genre study, my discussion here focuses on the essay and the feature of structure because these have been most prone to pedagogies of formula or, in free-form workshops, abandonment. With that in mind, the essays I use in RAAW sessions are, whenever possible, home grown on the op-ed, feature, and sports pages of local newspapers. I have used opinion columns (for example, by Thomas Friedman on the value of a "quiet leader" and Harvey Mackay on advice-getting in business) and editorials like one celebrating the singer Andy Williams ("Andy Williams"). I find local periodicals useful sources for RAAW because they include relatively brief argument essays (often community-member written) of a length that early college students often write. There is no guarantee that using short essays will support RAAW; however, such essays are easily accessible, and, for my students, who are often repelled by long texts of any kind, they have proven less intimidating than textbook "reader" selections.

In starting with short, popular essays, teachers can gently ease first-year students, especially those accustomed to template-heavy secondary writing instruction, into the slow messiness of composing. These essays can build confidence, comfort, and trust before students tackle more demanding texts. Also, using short pieces can demonstrate that the essay genre is practical and ubiquitous and that people outside the academy write in it with sincere interest and passion. This, in turn, can demonstrate the pleasure in and worth of writing academic essays in unpressured conditions, in contrast to the ordered processes and testing environments in which students may have been required to perform formulaic essay writing.

Once they know what to look for, students and I search locally for high-interest essays (or go beyond the local to sources like National Public Radio's "This I Believe," "You Must Read This," "Three Books," and Youth Radio essays). We find topics that we care about and that tie into course texts or themes (e.g., diversity, technology, the environment), thereby incorporating RAAW into the established curriculum, as well as creating an essay bank for examining other essay features later.[4]

Sometimes we even study and apply strategies from visual texts like a *Non Sequitur* cartoon by Wiley Miller. This cartoon, which begins with an infant high above a swimming pool, demonstrates inductive thesis development. Seven vertical boxes, each depicting the person at various life stages, lead viewers to the essay's claim: "Life: It's not the size of the splash, but the joy you find along the way." In discussing the cartoon, we note how each panel communicates the central claim and how the overall cartoon works even while withholding that claim until the end. We also speculate about the effect of placing the claim above the visuals and then experiment with this organization and new content in our composers' notebooks.

Studying structure through a multimodal genre like this cartoon fits an expansive view of text appropriate to the twenty-first century. With the explosion of technology, teachers can bring written, oral, visual, and electronic texts "into productive conjunction" with each other in the service of literacy learning (Kress 468). Jody Shipka's "multimodal task-based framework," in which students compose using a wide variety of materials in multiple modes, is one example of textual expansiveness. Similarly, studying comics, websites, speeches, performed pieces, photos, drawings, paintings, and so on using RAAW can help novices develop a broad multimodal understanding of organization and other textual features.

## Underpinnings of Slow Writing and RAAW

One justification for RAAW and slow writing is that these methods not only follow the contours of mature writing practice and allow for multimodal study but also align with current standards. They encourage and develop, for instance, dispositions linked to "college readiness," as articulated in the *Framework for Success in Postsecondary Writing*: "*curiosity* . . . about the world; *openness* . . . to consider new ways of being and thinking in the world; a sense of *investment and involvement in learning*; the *ability to sustain interest* in and attention to short- and long-term projects; *flexibility* . . . to adapt to situations, expectations, or demands; and *metacognition*" (1, emphasis added). RAAW and slow writing especially value metacognition, intentional (self-)assessment that builds "rhetorical knowledge [and] critical thinking," and they nurture rhetorically savvy writers who can compose in "multiple environments" using many strategies (1).

Further, slow writing and RAAW intersect with the Common Core State Standards (CCSS)[5] because they follow an "integrated model of literacy" that recognizes a close connection between "reading, writing, speaking, listening, and language" ("Common Core" 4). The CCSS describe secondary students, in part, as "college and career ready" if they are independent learners who can "respond to the varying demands of audience, task, purpose, and discipline" and can "comprehend as well as critique" ("Common Core" 7). Slow writing, with RAAW as a primary method, promotes these qualities.

RAAW is also consistent with mentor-text practices used by others like Nancie Atwell and Kelly Gallagher. Since 1998, when Atwell argued in the second edition of *In the Middle* that minilessons and direct teaching should be as central to writing workshop as conferences (21), she has used mentor texts that push against "the school stereotype of essays—topic outlines, five paragraphs, [and] topic sentences to start each paragraph" (*Lessons* 30) to teach students about effective "leads" and concluding techniques (182-85), for example. Text mentoring for Gallagher means composing aloud in front of students and "closely examining writing from the real world [to see] how other writers compose [and] *how* . . . text is constructed" (20, emphasis in original). RAAW is part of this hands-on tradition of students learning to view texts (including essays and organization) through a writer's (rather than a reader's) eyes. It also aligns with George Hillocks' view of writing as "inquiry," which he defines as practices of "observation, interpreting, imagining, hypothesizing, testing, evaluating, and so forth" (13). Making meaning "in conjunction with other times, other people, other texts" in a "dialectical process" (Hillocks 8), RAAW helps novices develop into intentional, rhetorically sensitive composers by turning their attention to an examination of texts written by others, past and present, and then to a consideration of their own writing, in order to test how they might use the moves they see others making in developing and shaping their own ideas. In this way, students' texts participate in a larger textual conversation.

To build such sensitivity, RAAW as a method that supports slow writing emphasizes time, not speed and efficiency, unlike mentor-text approaches that privilege organization "over other qualities" (Calkins, Ehrenworth, and Lehman 148). Rather than teaching an efficient writing process designed to "promot[e] achievement" (157), the pace of RAAW allows students to engage their interest in mentor texts before examining structure. This is important because engaged reading and writing, which often do not move with lockstep efficiency toward "achievement," develop writing competence. RAAW uses mentor texts as malleable works-in-progress as close to students' environment and passions as possible, rather than as finalized products to emulate.

Also, in a purposeful shift from *like* to *as* in the common phrasing "reading like a writer," RAAW (reading *as* a writer) conceptualizes novice writers as equal to those whose texts they study. As such, novices interact with mentor texts as writers *already*, rather than occupying a subservient position from which they must model the behavior of someone they have yet to become. When I think of text and teacher mentoring in the slow writing context, I am thinking not as much about mentoring as a hierarchical, master-apprentice relationship—though that might be appropriate at times—but rather as *mutual* mentorship among students, teacher, texts produced in the classroom, and published texts, with all having equally legitimate ways to shape practice in a writer-among-writers space. RAAW's egalitarianism and the pace of slow writing allow novices time for self-direction and confidence building, the lack of which often causes them to give up on writing.

One way RAAW and slow writing build confidence is by debunking "mythrules" like "all paragraphs have topic and clincher sentences" embedded in the writing psyches of American culture (Lindblom 104). These "'rules' that rule no one—other than . . . hardened purists . . ." (qtd. in Lindblom 104) need challenging because they play a major role in "set" (Rose 393), an inflexible cognitive habit that Mike Rose showed impedes novice college writers' development. According to Rose's research, teaching writing via formula stymies development because it establishes set, a "'determining tendency' [or] habitual wa[y] of reacting [that has] dysfunctional effects" on problem solving (392-93). Set is different from a cognitive "plan," which establishes problem-solving hierarchies and creates a flexibly changeable "course of action with multiple paths that directs . . . response possibilities" (393). Instead, set is a rigid cognitive habit that creates "a limiting and narrowing of response alternatives with no inherent process to shift alternatives" (393).

Rose studied ten UCLA undergraduates (five "blocked" and five "unblocked") in order to understand what made writing easier or harder for them. He found that students who approached writing from the standpoint of set (e.g., "You must always have three points in an essay") were rhetorically stunted, unable to view a new writing task as a problem to solve rather than a container to fill and, thus, were "blocked." In contrast, writers who operated from the standpoint of plan had flexible rules (e.g., "*Try* to keep audience in mind" or "When stuck, write!")—or even anti-rule rules like "If a rule conflicts with what is sensible or with experience, reject it" (390, 394, 396-97). This way of thinking helped students in Rose's study generate ideas for substance, organization, and so on, rather than causing them to block.

What Rose's research suggests is that teaching by formula inculcates set rather than plan in students' cognitive processes and hampers an ability to address novel composing tasks. RAAW as a problem-solving component of slow writing with a critical eye for how (well) others' texts work in the world and a focus on time and substance promotes cognitive plan rather than set, encouraging writers to build a repository of composing techniques and flexible ways to think about writing.

Beyond Rose's findings on the connection between cognitive disposition and writer's block, Keith Hjortshoj's more recent research on blockage speaks to the importance of writing time for early college writers, something that the measured pace of slow writing and RAAW encourage. Hjortshoj found that limited writing time could be a blocking factor. For example, he describes sophomore Veronica's problems when lack of time intensified the "pressure to write well[,] . . . [taking] a toll on her concentration" because she could not "relax and think about what she was doing with greater composure" (67). Veronica's struggle shows that writers need time and space "[t]o make substantial progress . . . [like] blocks of time *actually writing* . . . linked in close sequence [, not] fragmented or sparse" (107). As Hjorshjoj argues,

> writing is . . . a real physical activity of letting language and thought converge in sentences on a page or screen, through motions of our arms, hands, and eyes, with our bodies present in a time and place. . . . Writing is . . . a little fire you tend regularly, with sustained attention, patience, and acceptance. It doesn't have to be so dramatic as a bonfire. . . . The main requirement is that you have to be there and keep it going: word after word, sentence after sentence, page after page. (110)

In subscribing to this line of thinking, a teacher engaging in slow writing and RAAW helps students build a continuing habit of reading, writing, thinking about, and figuring out text. Students become "[p]raxical writing-subjects . . . comfortable with and confident in their ability to immerse themselves in local situations and then use epistemic theory—for example, decontextualized strategies and processes—as a heuristic for determining how to proceed and make wise writerly decisions" (Rosinski and Peeples 14). With each other, their teacher, and essays approached using RAAW, novice writers build textual schema needed to tackle new composing problems.

Using such mutual mentoring, slow writing and RAAW guide novices without pre-packaged, short cut devices like the five-paragraph theme or other templates, which can promote dependence that stunts writing development. (For example, see Tina Kunkler-Laake's "Five Paragraph Essay Worksheet" or the Jane Schaffer "writing system," which prescribes not only the number of essay[6] paragraphs but also the exact moves and contents of each [cf. Gustke].) Even if instructors do not use templates in first-year college writing courses, though some do (see appendix), templates influence first-year students' composing practices because of their presence in secondary education. When used in precollege and early college writing instruction, templates create two problems, especially with students deemed remedial. The first, from a social justice perspective, is that container composing automatically assumes that novices are deficient "victims," to be "blam[ed] . . . and offered a quick fix" (Brannon et al. 17-18). Lil Brannon and her colleagues in the UNC Charlotte Writing Project Collaborative argue this point:

> When students are considered lacking—lacking organization, lacking ideas to write about, lacking understanding—writing in an arbitrary formula merely sustains the deficit perception. Students learn that writing means following a set of instructions, filling in the blanks. Such writing mirrors working-class life, which requires little individual thinking and creativity combined with lots of monotony and following orders. It's obvious what training the five-paragraph essay is really practice for. (18)

It is *not* practice for twenty-first century literacy or critical, innovative thinking but for continued deficiency and dependence.

A second problem with template teaching, as Bruce Pirie points out, is the negative developmental impact when students must go beyond the so-called basics. In teaching writing by container to novices, "we forget that early teaching has lasting impact. When students are first learning and struggling with a new practice, they take firm hold of anything that looks like help. Misconceptions introduced at the time of first teaching are appallingly persistent and hard to pry loose in later years" (Pirie 55). Novice college students expected to move on from templates often struggle because "skills-based literacy instruction and a deficit model of understanding of even the youngest children" begin early for them, even before teachers introduce essay templates, typically in middle school (Brannon et al. 18). Template reinforcement in many secondary programs, when teachers "believe that they [must] structure [and] scaffol[d] every aspect of the writing process" so that students will perform well on high-stakes tests (Brannon et al. 19), then intensifies student dependence on templates, and these templates become in effect, like Dumbo's crow-feather, essay talismans that are difficult for first-year college writers to set aside (Hilbert 78).

Scaffolding through slow writing and RAAW's measured pace and guided process builds student interest and investment in essay writing, which scaffolding by template does not, according to my own and other first-year college students (Gray 166). Instead, templates make the act of writing personally joyless and purposeless and cause resistance to writing from the start. Such resistance, learning theory suggests, does nothing to build the internal motivation and perseverance necessary to develop writing abilities. Indeed, formula in writing instruction may play a part in students' increasing disengagement from school. According to a 2012 Gallup Education poll, engagement levels drop from 8 in 10 students in elementary school to 4 in 10 in high school (Busteed). Although the poll does not address how writing in schools might intersect with this growing disengagement, my first-year students frequently report their waning interest in writing as they move from elementary to secondary schools and from writing they view as fun and creative to academic writing like the essay. The Gallup poll in concert with my students' self-reported experiences suggest that how we teach essay writing is important since disengagement impedes learning in general and learning to write in particular. Slow writing and RAAW can both scaffold student learning and engage student interest and involvement.

**Nuts and Bolts of RAAW**

When I initially use RAAW with first-year college writers to examine a genre (like the short essay) and a feature (like structure), we begin with a pre-reading and writing inventory in which students examine their knowledge, beliefs, and feelings about essays, using questions like "Why would someone choose this genre? What is its rhetorical job? Typically, how long is it? How do essayists decide on content placement and paragraphing? What are typical functions and makeup of paragraphs?" Such questions begin a collaborative conversation about essay writing by acknowledging students' experiences with the genre. More importantly, the questions help students explore why they should care about the essay (beyond an assignment or grade) and encourage them to think about the essay's value and functionality.

After globally considering a general "why" for essay writing, the next activity informed by RAAW asks students to talk about an essay's motivation and ideas—for example, Thomas Friedman's "Constructive Boys at Play Follow Quiet Leader"—before analyzing its structure. Engaging ideas first in RAAW's pre-feature-analysis stage helps novices recognize a writer's efforts to communicate something of worth and avoids instrumentalizing a text. As we discuss the essay, we consider questions like "What matters to Friedman and why?" "Why did he choose the essay to explore the idea of leading by example?" "What is his rhetorical situation?" "By what process did he 'invent' material?" "How did he make idea-placement decisions?" After interrogating the essay from this standpoint, students apply such questions to themselves (e.g., "What matters to me?" What idea could I express in an essay?"), slowly moving back and forth between their own and others' texts.

Next in RAAW's reading-writing cycle, we work with an essential question (EQ) related to structure: for example, "How does Friedman get the essay's ideas to cohere from beginning to end?" Then students pose sub-questions suggested by the EQ (e.g., "How many paragraph breaks does the essay have?" "What work does each paragraph do?" "Why does Friedman spend the first nine paragraphs on the Hot Wheels-track story?" "Where—if stated—or how—if implied—does he communicate his central point?" "What if he would begin with the small-business connection that comes later in the essay?").

From here, depending on students' analytical experience and skill (which vary widely in the first-year program in which I work), I think aloud through the essay to demonstrate RAAW in action, using the EQ and subquestions as a guide and sharing my discoveries about organization as I go. After examining writer strategies, we critique them (e.g., "In his closing, how could Friedman make a stronger connection between the Hot Wheels story and business leaders?") and speculate in our composer notebooks about how to apply what we are discovering to our own essays. Then we move to at least one whole-class, student-led RAAW session, during which we study a new essay, guided by critically analytical, student-generated questions about essay organization.

Following this activity, students work in relatively autonomous two- to four-person study groups on other published essays: discovering, critiquing their discoveries, and trying new techniques. For instance, they might have noticed how an essay's title, headings, extended images, parallelism, or repetition helped create idea coherence, and in their composer notebooks they would then discuss how they might use a particular technique or test the technique in drafting an idea of their own. In early RAAW study sessions, groups usually analyze the same essay so that we can compare individual findings and I can point out moves that students might have missed. Later, each group gets a different essay in order to increase our information pool for a feature like structure and to create a technique database with which students can experiment, forming some experiments into fully developed essays.

In preparing published essays for small-group study, I often follow Thomas Newkirk's annotation technique (c.f. "The Case" 9), pasting each essay onto poster paper (17.5" x 12") to give students a large space for annotating (circling, underlining, highlighting, labeling, making notes in the margins, etc.) as they develop their repertoire of close-reading strategies. Although I sometimes have to disrupt the original layout of the essay, I retain all material (e.g., photos, pulled quotes) for authenticity and context. As an electronic alternative, students work with PDFs of texts, marking them up with PDF reader tools.

Also, to facilitate students' study of published texts (depending on their proficiency with close reading and analysis), I usually provide guiding questions about common structuring techniques like those mentioned above or others like stock transitions, bulleted lists, or a narrative thread. We also establish unique collaborative roles for each group member—for example, team manager, oral reader, annotator—so that everyone is meaningfully engaged in the RAAW process.

At various points in our slow writing journey, I make explicit what we are learning about essay structure variability by posing a question like "Did the writer know the essay's organizational moves before writing?" Most often students indicate that, no, s/he probably had general ideas jotted down but probably not a script. Through such questioning, writers discover what one of my first-year students realized about her own writing processes: "You need to let the idea create the form, not necessarily . . . the form force the ideas." Admittedly, my students and I are engaging in a certain amount of speculation in trying to infer process from product (unless we find a writer discussing process for a particular text); nonetheless, such speculation is important for novice writers who often struggle to imagine composing approaches different from ones in which they have been trained. Although my students might speculate that an author followed a formulaic process (especially at first, since many are used to formulas), I am striving for them to imagine something else, something that might even turn the familiar on its head, like a writer who creates a detailed outline on paper but then discards it as s/he begins to draft. And I want to create openings to talk about writing in the service of inventing since many of my students have limited invention strategies and move prematurely to arrangement.

The key here in playing with process is that novices can explore the "possible worlds" of composing by creating process narratives, fictitious or not (cf. Bruner, *Actual*). Does it matter if a writer actually did what we imagine? Probably not. Important for novices is entertaining a spectrum of writerly processes, including those in which essayists write into structure and discover organization as they go. Although accepting that organization is an organic process may be common to experienced writers, novice college writers with whom I have worked find writing into structure difficult to comprehend, coming as they often do from template-heavy programs. When students do gain such insight into arrangement, they feel comfortable with uncertainty and can begin composing without first and foremost worrying about how pieces of a text will eventually fit together. RAAW's reading-writing reciprocity (study, critique, experiment, read again) reinforces messiness in a low-stakes composer's notebook that leads to polishing some, but not all, texts into essays for publication and evaluation.

## Benefits of RAAW and Slow Writing

Although standards-based education models imposed on elementary and secondary schools are now finding their way into post-secondary education,[7] the steady pace of RAAW and slow writing can save writing teachers from standardized pedagogies and offer students time both to invest in and develop an "interest *for* [essay] writing" (Lipstein and Renninger 85, emphasis added). In a slow writing environment, novices have time to build faith in form by *first* building faith in content, becoming confident and passionate about ideas that then guide composing decisions that are always subject to revision through interaction among peers, teacher, and other texts.

In terms of structural decisions, this openness might mean composing without paragraphs and inserting paragraph breaks later according to the principles of opening, development, and closing "moves." Or it might mean "reverse outlining" to examine the function and order of paragraphs and make organizational changes based on that analysis (Murray, *Craft* 125). Using such techniques, slow writing and RAAW commit to consistent in- and out-of-class opportunities for novice writers to practice the craft of writing, where everyone, every day, is expected to be a writer—including the teacher. In so doing, slow writing and RAAW can help early college-level writers escape an indictment of schooling sometimes attributed to Einstein: "Education is what remains after one has forgotten what one has learned in school" (O'Toole) and can, instead, motivate meaningful life-long composing of essays and other genres.

An educational and cultural entrenchment of current-traditional practices in writing instruction (in place since the late nineteenth century and still in existence in many composition classrooms) has turned the essay of Montaigne into a hollow vehicle for testing and correcting (Womack 44-45). And such practices have not substantially solved the problem of those "disorganized essays" of Billy Collins' poem. However, since slow writing and RAAW approach "text structure [as] a kind of meta knowledge [that] comes after a lot of experience with text," as Nancy Patterson puts it, they help novices build text fluency as a way into organizational knowledge. With slow writing we can forget formulas, which move too quickly to solving the problem of arrangement, and can attend to what really matters: students learning to direct their own composing processes, discovering composing tasks that engage them, and inventing and arranging material for rhetorically meaningful purposes on a path to mature writing development.

## Notes

1. Though commonly used to describe writing as self-exploration, I am avoiding the term "expressivism" because American classroom applications of expressivist theories have often reflected a superficial understanding of either the teacher's role in novice composing processes or the broader implications of James Britton's research in this area.

2. I hesitate to use "process" (though I do for succinctness) because it has become a too-diffuse term in the last forty years, signifying many different things to many different practitioners and ranging from rigid, linear, step-by-step procedures to highly recursive and expressive individual experiences, as in the work of Britton and Elbow.

3. A fluid term, "novice" can refer to writers of different ages with varying experience and writing and language abilities. As collaborative practices appropriate for accommodating difference, slow writing and RAAW are adaptable to elementary, secondary, and postsecondary writers in a variety of settings. In this article I focus on first-year college writers.

4. We return to our RAAW bank to study features beyond or intertwined with organization—for instance, how writers present evidence and develop ideas through reasoning; use anecdotes, facts and statistics, description, or narration in argument; or begin essays to immediately engage readers and set context for argument claims.

5. The CCSS were created in 2010 as a guide to college and career readiness in mathematics, English language arts, and literacy in history and social studies, science, and technical subjects. Since then, forty-two states, the District of Columbia, four territories, and the Department of Defense Education Activity have adopted them ("Standards"), often because the standards have been tied to federal education dollars in programs like "Race for the Top." Though controversial and, in my opinion, flawed conceptually in their details, the CCSS are relevant here because of their significant impact on students currently entering first-year college writing courses.

6. Others call short academic writing that adheres to the five-paragraph model or other templates an "essay." I avoid that term in favor of "theme" since container products participate neither in Montaigne's initial conception of the essay (Newkirk, *School*) nor in nonfiction essays published by expert writers in quality publications. For more on this distinction, see Thomas Newkirk's argument in *The School Essay Manifesto* as well as the history of education's conflating "essay" and "theme" in Peter Womack's "What Are Essays For?"

7. In 2013, legislation in Iowa mandated that large-enrollment college courses and programs with many sections of a single course (including first-year composition) standardize and create "continuous improvement plans" that "focus on student

learning outcomes . . . outlined on . . . course syllabi [, d]ata collection on the course and learning outcomes [, i]mplementation of changes based on data [, and c]ontinuous feedback and reassessment of data" ("Course-Level").

## Appendix

Outline for a rhetorical analysis of a written argument from a first-year college writing course

1. Part One: Introduction
   a. Identify the rhetorical situation.
      - Who is the speaker? What other work has he/she published?
      - What is the text? Where did you find this text (e.g., In what chapter of *Rereading America*? In what context?)? Where was this text originally published? Is it an excerpt? Is it a complete article?
      - When was this published? What was happening in the U.S.A that year?
      - Who is the speaker's intended audience? What is the audience's purpose (to enjoy, to examine, to criticize, etc.)?
   b. Identify the author's argument.
      - What type of argument is it? Use *Everything's an Argument* as one of your sources.
   c. Thesis Statement
      - What rhetorical strategies does this author employ? How? Why? For what purpose?
2. Part Two: Body Paragraphs

   *First Paragraph*: Summarize the text.

   *Second Paragraph*: Style—analyze the author's diction, syntax, details, tone, etc. How does the author's word choice affect her/his tone? How does his/her sentence structure affect her/his essay as a whole?

   *Third Paragraph*: Figurative language—analyze the author's use of metaphors, similes, symbolism, etc. How do these strategies work in the author's favor? Do they?

   *Fourth Paragraph*: Patterns of repetition—remember Patrick J. Buchanan's text. What patterns does your author employ? Why? How?

   *Fifth Paragraph*: Ethos—how does the author confirm her/his credibility? Does the writer use an ad hominem argument (does he/she undermine the ethos of a speaker in opposition?)? How does the author establish his/her authority?

   *Sixth Paragraph*: Logos—how does the author appeal to logic? How does the author use reason? How effective are the author's supporting arguments? Is her/his logic consistent? Does the author use facts/statistics in his/her favor?

   *Seventh Paragraph*: Pathos—how does the author appeal to the reader's emotions? Does the audience feel what the author feels? This can link back to sensory

details (touch, smell, see, taste), word choice, and/or tone. (You do not want to repeat your arguments; if your pathos paragraph has to link back to the figurative language paragraph, maybe those paragraphs should become one strong paragraph.)
3. Part Three: Conclusion
   a. Remind your readers of your introductory paragraph. What was the rhetorical situation? You do not need to restate it, but now that you've dissected the author's message, think about how the rhetorical strategies affect the rhetorical situation.
   b. Restate your thesis statement
4. Final thought: What do you want your readers to think about?

**Works Cited**

"Andy Williams Was One of Us." Editorial. *Des Moines Register* 27 Sept. 2012, metro ed.: 8a. Print.

Atwell, Nancie. *In the Middle: New Understandings about Writing, Reading, and Learning.* 2nd ed. Portsmouth: Boynton/Cook Heinemann, 1998. Print.

---. *Lessons that Change Writers.* Portsmouth: Heinemann, 2002. Print.

Boldt, Josh. "Should We Teach the Five-Paragraph Essay?" *Teacher in a Strange Land.* Education Week, 1 Oct. 2012. Web. 10 Oct. 2012. <http://blogs.edweek.org/teachers/teacher_in_a_strange_land/2012>.

Brannon, Lil, et al. "The Five-Paragraph Essay and the Deficit Model of Education." *EJ* 98.2 (2008): 16-21. Print.

Britton, James. *Language and Learning.* Baltimore: Penguin, 1972. Print.

Bruner, Jerome S. *Actual Minds, Possible Worlds.* Cambridge: Harvard UP, 1986. Print.

---. *The Process of Education.* Cambridge: Harvard UP, 1960. Print.

Busteed, Brandon. "The School Cliff: Student Engagement Drops with Each School Year," *The Gallup Blog*, Gallup, 7 Jan. 2013. Web. 11 Nov. 2013. <http://www.gallup.com/opinion/gallup/170525/school-cliff-student-engagement-drops-school-year.aspx>.

Calkins, Lucy, Mary Ehrenworth, and Christopher Lehman. *Pathways to the Common Core.* Portsmouth: Heinemann, 2012. Print.

Collins, Billy. "Schoolsville." *Learning by Heart: Contemporary American Poetry about School.* Ed. Maggie Anderson and David Hassler. Iowa City: U of Iowa P, 1999: 186-87. Print.

"Common Core State Standards for English Language Arts and Literacy in History/Social Studies, Science, and Technical Subjects." *Common Core State Standards Initiative.* Council of Chief State School Officers and the Natl. Governors Assn., 2010. PDF file. <www.corestandards.org>.

Cooper, Lane, trans. *The Rhetoric of Aristotle.* Englewood Cliffs: Prentice Hall, 1932. Print.

"Course-Level Continuous Improvement Plans." *Office of the Senior Vice President and Provost.* Iowa State U, 2012. Web. 7 Sept. 2015. <https://www-provost.

sws.iastate.edu/help/student-outcomes/course-level-continuous-improvement-plans>.

Dornan, Reade W., Lois Matz Rosen, and Marilyn Wilson. *Within and Beyond the Writing Process in the Secondary English Classroom*. Boston: Allyn and Bacon, 2003. Print.

Elbow, Peter. *Writing without Teachers*. New York: Oxford UP, 1973. Print.

*Framework for Success in Postsecondary Writing*. Council of Writing Program Administrators, NCTE, National Writing Project, 2011. PDF file. <http:wpacouncil.org/framework>.

Friedman, Thomas. "Constructive Boys at Play Follow Quiet Leader." *Ankeny Register and Press Citizen* 10 Sept. 2013: 10. Print.

Gallagher, Kelly. *Write Like This: Teaching Real-World Writing through Modeling & Mentor Texts*. Portland: Stenhouse, 2011. Print.

Graff, Gerald, Cathy Birkenstein, and Russel Durst. *They Say/I Say with Readings*. 2nd ed. New York: Norton, 2014. Print.

Gray, Jennifer P. "'You Can't Be Creative Anymore': Students Reflect on the Lingering Effects of the Five-Paragraph Essay." *Teaching/Writing: The Journal of Writing Teacher Education* 3.2 (2014): 152-67. ScholarWorks at Western Michigan U. Web. 28 May 2015. <http://scholarworks.wmich.edu/wte/vol3/iss2/>.

Gustke, Hollie. "Jane Schaffer Writing Strategy: How To Write an Effective Paragraph." *SchoolWorld*. Blackboard Engage, n.d. Web. 20 Apr. 2015. <http://teachersites.schoolworld.com/>.

Hilbert, Betsy. "It Was a Dark and Nasty Night It Was a Dark and You Would Not Believe How Dark It Was a Hard Beginning." *CCC* 43.1 (1992): 75-80. Print.

Hillocks, George, Jr. *Teaching Writing as Reflective Practice*. New York: Teachers College P, 1995. Print.

Hjortshoj, Keith. *Understanding Writing Blocks*. New York: Oxford UP, 2001. Print.

Kress, Gunther. "Genre and the Changing Contexts for English Language Arts." *Language Arts* 76.6 (1999): 461-69. Print.

Kunkler-Laake, Tina. "Re: Innovative Practices for Writing Centers?" *Teaching and Learning Forum*. NCTE, 11 Feb. 2012. Web. 1 Oct. 2012. <http://www.ncte.org/search?q=teaching+and+learning+forum>.

Lindblom, Kenneth. "Teaching English in the World: Writing for Real." *EJ* 94.1 (2004): 104-08. Print.

Lipstein, Rebecca, and K. Ann Renninger. "'Putting Things into Words': The Development of 12-15-Year-Old Students' Interest for Writing." *Writing and Motivation*. Ed. Pietro Boscolo and Suzanne Hidi. Oxford: Elsevier, 2007: 113-40. Print.

Mackay, Harvey. "How To Ask for Help." *Des Moines Register* 15 July 2013, metro ed.: 10a. Print.

Macrocrie, Ken. *Writing to Be Read*. New York: Hayden, 1970. Print.

Miller, Wiley. "Non Sequitur." Comic strip. *GoComics*. Universal Uclick. 14 Oct. 2012. Web. 23 Sept. 2013. <http://www.gocomics.com/>.

Moffett, James. *Teaching the Universe of Discourse*. Boston: Houghton Mifflin, 1968. Print.

Montaigne, Michel de. *The Complete Works of Montaigne*. Donald Frame, trans. Palo Alto: Stanford UP, 1957.

Murray, Donald M. *The Craft of Revision*. 5th ed. Boston: Thomson/Heinle, 2004. Print.

---. *A Writer Teaches Writing: A Practical Method of Teaching Composition*. Boston: Houghton Mifflin, 1968. Print.

Newkirk, Thomas. "The Case for Slow Reading." *Reading to Learn* 67.6 (2010): 6-11. Print.

---. *The School Essay Manifesto: Reclaiming the Essay for Students and Teachers*. Shoreham: Discover Writing, 2005. Print.

O'Toole, Garson. "Education is What Remains after You Have Forgotten Everything You Learned in School." *Quote Investigator*. N.p., 7 Sept. 2014. Web. 25 Jan. 2016. < http://quoteinvestigator.com/2014/09/07/forgotten/>.

Patterson, Nancy. "Re: 4th grade nonfiction text structure." *Teaching and Learning Forum Digest*. NCTE, 11 Jan. 2013. Web. 14 Jan. 2013. <http://www.ncte.org/search?q=teaching+and+learning+forum>.

Pirie, Bruce. *Teenage Boys and High School English*. Portsmouth: Boynton/Cook Heinemann, 2002. Print.

Pudlowski, Victor. "Compositions—Write 'Em Right." *EJ* 48.9 (1959): 535-37. Print.

Rose, Mike. "Rigid Rules, Inflexible Plans, and the Stifling of Language: A Cognitivist Analysis of Writer's Block." *CCC* 31.4 (1980): 389-401. Print.

Rosinski, Paula, and Tim Peeples. "Forging Rhetorical Subjects: Problem-Based Learning in the Writing Classroom." *Composition Studies* 40.2 (2012): 9-32. Print.

Shipka, Jody. "A Multimodal Task-Based Framework for Composing." *CCC* 57.2 (2005): 277-306. Print.

Smith, Kerri. "In Defense of the Five-Paragraph Theme." *EJ* 95.4 (2006): 16-17. Print.

"Standards in Your State." *Common Core State Standards Initiative*. Council of Chief State School Officers and the Natl. Governors Assn., 2016. Web. 25 Jan. 2016. <http://www.corestandards.org/standards-in-your-state/>.

Trimbur, John. *The Call to Write*. New York: Longman, 1999. Print.

Towle, Carroll S. "The Awkward Squad at Yale." *EJ* 18.8 (1929): 672-77. Print.

Wendell, Barrett. *English Composition*. New York: Scribner's, 1903. Print.

Womack, Peter. "What Are Essays For?" *English in Education* 27.2 (1993): 42-49. Print.

# The Linguistic Memory of Composition and the Rhetoric and Composition PhD: Forgetting (and Remembering) Language and Language Difference in Doctoral Curricula

*Carrie Byars Kilfoil*

This article analyzes the decline of linguistics in rhetoric and composition PhD programs in terms of the "linguistic memory" (Trimbur) of composition. Since the field of linguistics once offered the primary means for composition to address the structural, psychological, sociohistorical, and cultural dimensions of language in student writing, the loss of linguistics courses and requirements in graduate curricula can be interpreted as a "forgetting" that language issues are, and always have been, central to writing teaching and research in linguistically diverse institutions. To help composition remember its commitments to language in light of the multiple languages and language varieties spoken and written in U.S. universities, as well as in the increasingly global contexts of writing pedagogy and scholarship, this article suggests that graduate programs reincorporate insights from linguistics and take other steps to foreground matters of language and language difference in their curricula.

---

In her 2007 article "The Erasure of Language," Susan Peck MacDonald links a decline in CCCC topics and sessions focused on language since the 1950s to the more general decline of linguistics in composition research, and specifically, composition teacher education. MacDonald argues that over time, influential critiques of formal grammar instruction; reductive, binary approaches to language issues in composition; and potent "language-as-painful-remediation assumptions" (618) led to a "new generation of compositionists who lacked the background to sustain the intensive linguistic work of their predecessors, believed they should not do so, or found other rewards greater" (602). Subsequently, MacDonald argues, language-oriented composition pedagogies and scholarship, like sentence combining and bidialectal pedagogies, were largely abandoned in the late twentieth century.

However, if language was once "erased" from composition, it now appears to be in the process of reinscription. Recently, matters of language and language difference have resurfaced in disciplinary discourse, as evidenced by special issues of the field's journals as well as edited collections and themed conferences,[1] and, yes, growing numbers of CCCC sessions. In "It's the Wild

West Out There: A New Linguistic Frontier in U.S. College Composition," Paul Kei Matsuda attributes this renewed attention to language to efforts to address "the issue of language diversity for language minority students," "the globalization of U.S. college composition," and an "intellectual movement to see languages not as discrete entities but as situated, dynamic, and negotiated" (130). While he argues that this "linguistic turn" constitutes a "new frontier" for composition, he also cautions that it presents challenges, given the "huge void in the knowledge of language issues" (130) among the field members, which manifests in uncritical usage of terminology borrowed from linguistics in composition scholarship and narrow, perhaps ill-advised, pedagogical applications of this research. To be better positioned to address language issues in increasingly diverse, globalizing writing programs and institutions, Matsuda argues that composition needs to develop "a broader, more balanced framework for conceptualizing language" (132). Here, I believe, reconsideration of the place of linguistics in composition teacher education, and particularly, the pre-professional training that takes place in rhetoric and composition graduate programs, is key.

In this article, I analyze the erasure of linguistics, a broad field of study that addresses how language works as a formal system, a psychological process, a historical phenomenon, a cultural resource, and a social practice, from rhetoric and composition PhD programs through the 1990s and 2000s. I do so through the lens of what John Trimbur has called U.S. "linguistic memory," which has been characterized by the ritualized "forgetting" of the multiple languages spoken and written in the United States. I suggest that composition not only operates on English-only monolingual assumptions developed and advanced through U.S. linguistic memory, but that the curricular development of the field's graduate programs has re-enacted the historical process of forgetting that undergirds these assumptions to cement their dominance in the field. Since the field of linguistics once offered the primary means for compositionists to address the structural, psychological, sociohistorical, and cultural dimensions of language in student writing, its erasure from composition graduate curricula signifies a forgetting that language issues are, and always have been, central to composition's work in linguistically diverse institutions. In order to help the field remember its commitments to language in the context of a plurality of languages and language varieties spoken and written in U.S. higher education, as well as in the increasingly global contexts of writing pedagogy and scholarship, I suggest that composition graduate programs reincorporate insights from linguistics and take other steps to foreground matters of language and language difference in their curricula.

## Methodology

To examine the place of linguistics in composition graduate programs over time, I conducted a comparative analysis of the *Rhetoric Review* surveys of doctoral programs in the field (1987, 1994, 2000, 2008). Each of these surveys compile information about programs' missions, requirements, faculty, and recent graduates into individual profiles listed in alphabetical order. I reviewed the profiles in each survey and highlighted key terms relevant to linguistics in PhD curricula (e.g., "language," "linguistics," "grammar," "syntax," "discourse analysis," and "Teaching English as a Second Language" (TESL), etc.). I then organized the data I uncovered about linguistics courses, exams, and dissertations into searchable databases. Finally, I analyzed the data to determine how many programs in each survey reported that their students completed linguistics coursework, requirements, and scholarly projects. This analysis revealed a macro-level trend toward reducing and eliminating graduate linguistics courses and requirements through the 1990s and 2000s.

To evaluate how and why this curricular development took place, I then analyzed archival materials from two rhetoric and composition PhD programs in the Ohio River Valley. I selected these programs because they are relatively long-standing and robust: both were represented in every *Rhetoric Review* survey and have strong reputations in the field. Moreover, their physical proximity to me allowed me to work within material constraints on my research that made extended travel difficult. Although these two programs are less than two hundred miles apart, they offer very different pictures of the institutional concerns that shape the development of doctoral curricula. For this reason, I feel the profiles, though limited in scope and region, effectively illuminate the curricular trend I identify in institutional contexts.

While these methods allowed me to illustrate the decline of linguistics in composition graduate curricula, inconsistencies within the *Rhetoric Review* survey data and between it and the archival data indicate that my findings are far from incontrovertible. There is, for instance, a mismatch in every *Rhetoric Review* survey between programs that state an interest in language and linguistics in their program descriptions and those that actually provide for their study in course descriptions, and the numbers of programs stating this interest have held steady even as linguistics courses have disappeared. There was also some dissonance between program aims and curricula reported in the *Rhetoric Review* survey profiles and program descriptions and requirements drawn from archival materials. These discontinuities reflect the unreliability of graduate program texts as indicators of graduate program practices, which are embodied and emergent in the real-time behavior of faculty and students. That said, I believe the discursive representations of these practices in different texts (the *RR* surveys, course catalogs, graduate program guidelines, etc.) are worth considering, in the sense that they speak to the ways in which individual practices have sedimented over time to form "rules and resources" (Giddens 19) for coordinating faculty and student behavior in doctoral programs. Even if these texts cannot offer a clear picture of the work that takes place in the rhetoric and composition PhD, they can provide a sense of the ways in which faculty and students imagine this work to subsequently carry it out in response to disciplinary and institutional expectations.

## The Erasure of Linguistics in Composition Graduate Education

The first *Rhetoric Review* survey (1987) indicates that linguistics was an important part of early composition graduate curricula, with 89% (n=34) of the thirty-eight programs profiled reporting core and elective linguistics coursework. These courses were, for the most part, general "Introduction to Linguistics" courses and courses on the structure and history of the English language (e.g., "English Linguistics," "Modern English Grammar," and "History of the English Language"), though courses in sociolinguistics, psycholinguistics, and various areas of applied linguistics (e.g., stylistics, semantics, discourse analysis, contrastive analysis, and TESL) were also represented. Roughly one third (34%; n=13) of programs listed "linguistics" as an area of their comprehensive exams, and 38% (n=10) listed dissertation projects concerned with linguistics, basic writing[2], or TESL among their "recent dissertations."

However, the importance of linguistics in the rhetoric and composition PhD appears to have been short-lived (see table 1). In the 1994 survey, only 36% (n=26) of the seventy-two programs profiled reported having core and elective linguistics courses. This percentage held relatively steady for the 2000 survey, where 37% (n=24) of the sixty-five programs profiled reported such coursework. In the 2008 survey, 25% (n=14) of the fifty-five programs profiled reported having linguistics core and elective courses. Of these programs, only 7% (n=4) reported having linguistics requirements and only 5% (n=3) listing linguistics as an area of comprehensive exams.

Table 1
Programs with and without Linguistics Courses in the *Rhetoric Review* Surveys (1987-2008)

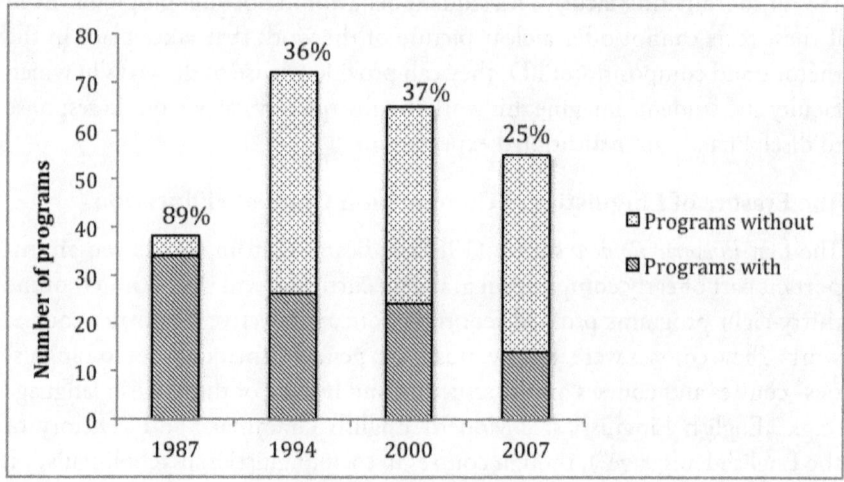

Source: David W. Chapman and Gary Tate, "A Survey of Doctoral Programs in Rhetoric and Composition," *Rhetoric Review* 5.2 (1987), p. 124-86; Stuart C. Brown, Paul R. Meyer, and Theresa Enos, "Doctoral Programs in Rhetoric and Composition: A Catalog of the Profession," *Rhetoric Review* 12.2 (1994), p. 240-389; Stuart C. Brown, Rebecca Jackson, and Theresa Enos, "The Arrival of Rhetoric in the Twenty-First Century: The 1999 Survey of Doctoral Programs in Rhetoric," *Rhetoric Review* 18.2 (2000), p. 233-373; Stuart C. Brown, Theresa Enos, David Reamer, and Jason Thompson, "Portrait of the Profession: The 2007 Survey of Doctoral Programs in Rhetoric and Composition," *Rhetoric Review* 27.4 (2008), Web, 13 April 2017, <http://www.u.arizona.edu/~enos/>

Of course, the four *Rhetoric Review* surveys vary in terms of the total number of programs profiled, making percentages to illustrate historical trends suspect. To determine if individual programs were actually eliminating their linguistics requirements over time, I compared the profiles of programs that reported core linguistics course requirements in the 1987 survey with their profiles in later surveys. The University of Alabama, Purdue University, the University of South Carolina, Texas Tech University, the University of Wisconsin at Milwaukee, and the University of Iowa all reported linguistics requirements in the 1987 survey, but did not list these requirements in the 1994 survey or any survey thereafter, even though their programs were represented in these surveys. Bowling Green State University, the University of Nebraska-Lincoln, Texas Christian University, Wayne State University, and Texas A&M University reported core linguistics requirements in the 1987 and 1994 surveys, but not in the 2000 survey. Of the twenty-five programs that reported core linguistics requirements in the original 1987 survey, only six—Arizona State University, The Catholic University of America,[3] The Ohio State University, Indiana University of Pennsylvania, the University of New Mexico, and the University of Washington—were still reporting linguistics requirements in 2000, and only one—the University of Washington—was still reporting this requirement in 2008.

Comparative analysis of the above programs' survey profiles indicates these programs were replacing their linguistics courses and requirements with others in rhetorical history, research methods, composition theory, and critical and cultural theory. This trend is most clearly illustrated through analysis of the 2000 survey in relationship to the 1987 survey (see table 2). Between 1987 and 2000, these programs' average number of rhetoric courses increased from 1.52 to 2.45, their average number of research methods courses increased from .47 to 1, their average number of composition theory courses increased from 1 to 1.75, and their average number of critical and cultural theory courses increased from 0 to .55.

Table 2
Average Number of Rhetoric, Research, and "Theory" courses in the 1987 and 2000 Surveys Listed by Programs that Lost Linguistics Requirements between 1987 and 2008

|  | 1987 Survey | 2000 Survey |
|---|---|---|
| **Rhetorical History and Theory** | 1.52 | 2.45 |
| **Research in Rhetoric and Composition** | .47 | 1 |
| **Composition Theory** | 1 | 1.75 |
| **Critical and Cultural Theory** | 0 | .55 |

Source: David W. Chapman and Gary Tate, "A Survey of Doctoral Programs in Rhetoric and Composition," *Rhetoric Review* 5.2 (1987), p. 124-86; Stuart C. Brown, Rebecca Jackson, and Theresa Enos, "The Arrival of Rhetoric in the Twenty-First Century: The 1999 Survey of Doctoral Programs in Rhetoric," *Rhetoric Review* 18.2 (2000), p. 233-373.

This shift in curricula is perhaps unsurprising, given the forces at work distancing composition from linguistics at the end of the twentieth century. By the late 1970s, as both Lester Faigley and Sharon Crowley have described, compositionists had become increasingly wary of the structuralist tradition in modern linguistics, which, insofar as it focused on small units of text (phonemes, morphemes, clauses, sentences), seemed inadequate to address the larger semantic, discourse-level issues in student writing. At the same time, the growing influence of generative grammar, with its focus on language as abstract, formal, and intuitive, implicitly suggested that linguistics had little to do with actual language practices (as they take place in composition classes and student writing) and that language study was inessential to composition teachers, given that students (assumed to be English native speakers) already had an intrinsic language competence. As MacDonald has described, composition's tendency to conflate the dominant structuralist and generative traditions with *all* linguistic approaches eclipsed relevant work in descriptive and functional linguistics to promote the sense that language study was far afield of composition.

By the 1990s, the interdisciplinary field of second language writing had grown to develop its own journals and graduate programs, and its continued development, coupled with composition's longstanding "disciplinary division of labor" with ESL (Matsuda, "Composition" 700), likely furthered the sense that language was not the purview of mainstream composition or its graduate programs. In addition, public opposition to remediation in college teaching, often signaled by concerns with "language" and "grammar," may have made it politically expedient for some programs to distance themselves from language study and align their curricula with other areas of English studies less likely to be associated with language teaching, like Western rhetoric and critical and cultural theory, in the 1990s and early 2000s.

Though the choice to eliminate linguistics courses and requirements may have seemed necessary (and even common sense) at the time, I want to consider its practical impact on the field. Linguistics courses provided officially sanctioned curricular spaces for considering language and, by extension, language diversity in writing programs, and I believe their loss has made it more difficult to imagine, propose, and see the need for graduate courses focused on language and language differences in composition teaching and research. In this way, the disappearance of these courses can be linked to what Matsuda has called the "myth of linguistic homogeneity" in composition: the false sense that a privileged variety of English acts a neutral, transparent medium of communication in U.S. universities, their writing programs, and FYC classes ("Myth" 638). In what follows, I interpret the loss of linguistics in graduate curricula as part of a larger "systematic (and systematically incomplete) forgetting" (Trimbur 579) of composition's (and its graduate programs') historical concerns with language and linguistic heterogeneity in U.S. higher education.

### Surrogation and Forgetting in Doctoral Curricula

In "Linguistic Memory and the Politics of U.S. English," Trimbur argues that U.S. culture has worked to forget its multilingual past through surrogation: "a substitution for the missing original" that imperfectly defers its memory

(579). Following Joseph Roach, Trimbur suggests that late colonial and early national efforts to define and codify "American English," as a "free born" and linguistically superior alternative to British English, resulted in "an incomplete substitution and systematic forgetting" (580) of the multiple languages spoken and written in the U.S., including French, German, Spanish, and, of course, the many Native American languages. Because, like all surrogates, American English is an "inexact fit" for the multiple languages it has replaced, it has been "a source of ambivalence" about multilingualism in the United States "rather than a resolution to the anxiety of displacement" (579). This anxiety lingers despite the assumption of unidirectional English monolingualism in U.S. society and its institutions, and specifically, U.S. colleges and universities' English departments and writing programs.

While Trimbur critiques U.S. college composition as a largely English monolingual enterprise, currently and historically, composition and its graduate programs, like the U.S. generally, can be read as having a "multilingual"[4] past, insofar as without the reality of patterns of speech and writing associated with multiple languages and varieties of English in American higher education, neither would exist. As Matsuda, following Robert J. Connors and Susan Miller, has observed, the college composition course was developed in the late nineteenth century as means to address language differences among students identified primarily as English "native speakers," but whose "errors" in spelling, punctuation, and syntax marked them as academic outsiders in need of socialization to dominant academic (English) language norms ("Myth" 638; cf. Fox). With open admissions and other academic inclusion measures in the 1960s and 1970s, language differences in U.S. higher education became both more widespread and pronounced, as growing numbers of socioculturally and linguistically diverse students enrolled in U.S. colleges and universities. In response, English departments accepted more graduate students to serve as teaching assistants (TAs) and set up "mass management procedures" and "in-service teacher training programs," which, as Richard Lloyd-Jones has described, emerged as the first "*de facto* doctoral programs in composition" (491).

Insofar as many of these early composition graduate programs were specifically concerned with language teaching to language minority students enrolled in "basic writing" and other introductory writing courses, the heavy emphasis on language (in the form of linguistics) in the first *Rhetoric Review* survey makes sense. While it is dangerous to assume that survey data (and official curricula generally) speak directly to the lived experiences in any given program, the trend reflected in the subsequent *Rhetoric Review* surveys toward replacing linguistics courses with various "surrogate" courses suggests that, over time, many programs moved away from an emphasis on language and toward new conceptions of composition, its students, and its work. Of course, classes in rhetoric, research, and "theory" are valuable to aspiring composition teacher-scholars and frequently, in their own ways, address diversity in writing and writing instruction. As MacDonald notes in her historical analysis of CCCC topics and sessions, the growing "lack of an emphasis on language" at CCCC annual conventions could simply be attributed to "a shift in terminology" (50) used to discuss practical matters of difference in writing teaching, through, for instance, terms associated with critical and cultural theory. It could be argued that rhetoric and composition PhD programs did away with their linguistics courses and requirements in order to embrace new terms to discuss differences in student writing in accordance with general trends in the field and U.S. institutions. However, as MacDonald suggests, such terminological shifts do not come without a cost. In the case of CCCC topics and sessions, MacDonald argues that the erasure of the terms "language," "linguistics" and "ESL" masks the complexities associated with language differences in writing, and ultimately, the interests of growing numbers of students who use English as a second language in composition classes.

In order to illustrate this process of surrogation and forgetting in doctoral curricula, I will now consider the curricular history of two doctoral programs: The University of Louisville's PhD in Rhetoric and Composition and Miami University's PhD in English (composition and rhetoric specialization). My intent in sketching these case studies is not to write conclusive histories of these programs, but rather to provide brief narratives of curricular development set within particular institutional contexts. These narratives were developed using archival resources that were somewhat random and incomplete, and, as a result, lack the nuance and complexity that could be attained from reviewing a wider swath of written and oral resources. However, I believe the available documents can begin to suggest how surrogation and the subsequent forgetting of each program's history in linguistics, and relatedly, issues of language and language difference, was enacted in relationship to institutional conditions and the pressures they create.

## A Graduate Program to Support an "Urban Mission": The University of Louisville PhD in Rhetoric and Composition

In 1977, the University of Louisville (U of L) English department formed their rhetoric and composition PhD program in the context of changing institutional demographics and, specifically, a growing population of multidialectal undergraduate students. Over the course of the late 1960s and through the 1970s, tuition at Louisville was halved and scholarships were added to dramatically expand its enrollment. By 1979, U of L had more African American students than any other university in Kentucky (including Kentucky State, a historically black institution), and had amassed a "less affluent white student population" ("English PhD"). Public outcry about declining standards at U of L coalesced into a discussion about the language education of these students in the local media. As one *Louisville Times* reporter described them, these students "from low income and culturally deprived homes... come from areas such as sections of southern Jefferson county or black inner-city neighborhoods where a dialect is spoken. For such students...standard, written English must almost be taught as a foreign language" (Raymond). In response, U of L expanded its basic writing program under director of composition Joseph Comprone, hired in 1976. Comprone spearheaded the rhetoric and composition emphasis in the pre-existing English PhD program and, later, argued to make the emphasis the sole focus of the program when the state proposed eliminating it on the grounds it duplicated the English PhD (in literature) at the University of Kentucky (cf. Strain). Comprone argued that the PhD program in rhetoric and composition was a course of study in teacher training that, as he emphasized to one reporter, met the university's "urban mission," the changing demographics of higher education nationally, and the needs of those undergraduate students who "can't write a sentence" (Aprile B2).

As Comprone describes in his 1981 article "Graduate Programs for Teachers of Basic Writing: The University of Louisville's PhD in Rhetoric and Composition," the Louisville program was designed to reflect "the specific needs of our institution" by providing "a foundation for the training of basic writing teachers" (24). He argues that this foundation necessarily requires a working knowledge of "applied linguistics"—"theories and methods of analyzing syntax"—and other areas of linguistics deemed relevant to the teaching of open admissions students who either "speak English as a second language" or come from "oral cultures" (29). He writes:

> Training in English as a second language, in contrastive linguistics and error analysis, and in sociolinguistics provides a basic writing teacher with both the cultural-linguistic understanding and the empirical-analytical skills to develop more effective writing programs for such students. . . . Courses in sociolinguistics, history of the English language, and teaching English as a second language will prepare teachers for the cross-cultural and dialect-interference problems their students have when they write academic English . . . (30)

The concern with language and language differences Comprone describes is apparent in the curriculum outlined in the 1977-1978 "Graduate Program Guidelines" (the first year of the rhetoric and composition concentration). Applicants to the program were required to "show evidence of having taken college level courses in the history of the English language [and] general approaches to grammar," and in the absence of having taken such courses, were required to complete the department's ENG 523 History of the English Language and ENG 522 Structure of American English before matriculating into the program (1). Once matriculated, all students had to complete at least two courses in "Linguistics and Reading," a core area of study that included descriptive linguistics, sociolinguistics, and TESL courses under the "ENG" prefix. "Linguistics and Composition" was an area of the qualifying exam (until that exam was eliminated in 1985), and "Linguistics, Composition, and Pedagogy" was one of three options for the comprehensive exam.

In the late 1980s and through the 1990s, the role of linguistics was reduced in the program while the role of rhetoric was expanded. In 1987, the year David Chapman and Gary Tate published the first *Rhetoric Review* survey, the comprehensive exam was redrawn, and the "Linguistics, Composition, and Pedagogy" exam was eliminated. Under the new exam structure, linguistics was one of five options for the "Interdisciplinary Studies and Composition Exam," and "History of Rhetoric" was elevated to having its own, required exam ("Guidelines" 1987). In 1989, the number of linguistics courses students were required to take was reduced from two to one, and the number of linguistics courses available to doctoral students for credit was reduced from nine to five ("Guidelines" 1989). At the same time, available courses in rhetoric doubled from three to six ("Guidelines" 1989).

In 1991, the comprehensive exam was restructured again, and this time linguistics was no longer a stated component of any of the three required exams in Contemporary Rhetorical Theory, a Specified Research Area, and a Literary Period ("Guidelines" 1991). During the same year, there was a subtle change in admissions guidelines. Every previous version of the "Graduate Program Guidelines" stated that applicants were expected to show coursework "in the history of the English language," but this was changed in the 1991 "Guidelines," which stipulated that students were expected to "have taken advanced college-level coursework in the history of *criticism*" (my emphasis), even though the program remained, as it had been since 1980, solely in rhetoric and composition, and not in English literature. Though the expectation that prospective students had taken coursework in English grammar remained, the concern with English language had been effectively removed from the material social history that has shaped and given meaning to dominant English grammar conventions. In place of language study, a concern with historical knowledge of a particular interpretative tradition associated with the study and teaching of literature was inserted, signaling the privileging of traditional structures of academic study in English and the beginning of the end of the program's focus on language, the initial emphasis of which brought basic writers to the fore.

The 1996-1997 "Graduate Program Guidelines" is the last to list the single three-credit linguistics course requirement. The following year, U of L President John Shumaker announced that U of L was "getting out of the remedial education business," ("U of L to Drop Remedial Ed" 2K), and U of L's basic writing program, which had been under scrutiny for some time from both the department and other institutional entities (Roskelly), was eliminated. Since the inception of the rhetoric and composition PhD program, its faculty had expanded to include individuals with diverse interests and areas of expertise, and it is likely that by this point, it had already lost much of its identity as a graduate program specifically designed for teachers of basic writing. However, the decision to relocate basic writing to the local community college no doubt contributed to the program's ongoing restructuring of scholarly and pedagogical priorities. The language differences of undergraduate students who would be remediated at Jefferson Community College in Louisville were no longer a pressing concern for the department, its TAs, or the faculty charged with training them, and those students who would be mainstreamed into FYC courses were, perhaps, not to be dwelled upon, given the prevailing wisdom that these students, as English "native speakers" (Matsuda, "Myth"), brought to their writing an innate language competence.

In the years that followed, linguistics courses were relocated to the humanities department as part of the formation of a humanities MA concentration in linguistics in 2001. Faculty specializing in linguistics retired from the English department (Robert Miller, Karen Mullen) or were moved to new departments (Robert St. Clair) and new hires were made in rhetoric and composition, literature, and creative writing. Although the three-credit linguistics requirement was still listed in the 2001-2003 U of L "Graduate Catalog," (51) the program did not report a linguistics requirement in the 2000 *Rhetoric Review* survey, which perhaps reflected a sense amongst graduate program faculty that the requirement was unnecessary or undesirable. By 2008, linguistics was neither required nor offered in the program ("Guidelines" 2008). Students who wished to take linguistics courses had to exercise their option for one elective course outside the field to count toward their degrees.

This policy is still in effect, even though the program description in the current University of Louisville "Graduate Catalog" still mentions graduate training in linguistics as one aspect of the program (2013-2014). That this relic of the past curriculum is preserved in the program's description could simply be attributed to the low priority of revising the program statement in relationship to other more pressing administrative tasks. However, it might also point, at least in part, to an anxiety rooted in the recognition that the issues of language and language difference signaled by linguistics training are indeed still relevant to the work of graduate students and faculty in the department.

## A Graduate Program to Prepare Students for Jobs: The Miami University PhD in English, Composition and Rhetoric Specialization

Unlike the U of L program, Miami University's composition and rhetoric PhD specialization did not arise in response to institutional demographic change. Rather, archival materials suggest the program developed in response to a changing job market in English studies brought about by shifting demographics in higher education nationally. Department memos from 1978 show that the department's graduate committee was considering drastically reducing or even eliminating the PhD in English Literature and Language due to concerns about "the terrible plight of young, highly qualified PhD's [sic] who cannot find tenure-track positions" (Harwood). In a letter to recent graduates dated 26 September 1978, Director of Graduate Study Donald Fritz requested feedback on whether the program should continue, and if so, how it might better prepare future faculty for jobs. He received a number of responses, in which several alumni urged the program to capitalize on Donald A. Daiker, Max Morenberg, and Andrew Kerek's sentence combining research as well as Paul Anderson's research in technical writing given, as one alumnus wrote, the undeniable "trend toward hiring people with preparation in technical writing or linguistics and sentence combining" (Anderson). Citing this faculty expertise, alumnus Jack Selzer, in a letter dated 20 October 1978, suggested that "composition be elevated to a status equal to the eight literary 'fields' that students may choose to concentrate in." These recommendations, in conjunction with a Miami University English Graduate Organization (EGO) position paper arguing for the need for more professional training in composition ("Ego Position Paper"), likely influenced the establishment of the composition and rhetoric specialization in 1980.

The beginnings of the Miami specialization in faculty research at the intersection of structural linguistics and writing (in the form of sentence combining and technical writing) speaks to the importance of linguistics in English studies and the rapidly professionalizing field of composition in the 1970s. The early composition graduate curriculum at Miami reflects this state of affairs, as the 1980-81 Miami "Graduate Bulletin" shows that students in all graduate tracks were required to take a general linguistics course, English 601 Introduction to Language and Linguistics, in addition to four other required courses: English 602 Introduction to Rhetoric, English 603 Introduction to Literary Criticism, and English 604 Introduction to Research. However, the 1985-87 "Graduate Bulletin" reveals a curriculum change, so that students had a choice between English 601 and English 603, linguistics or criticism. The introduction of this choice coincided with an expansion of course offerings in composition theory (English 731 The Theory and Practice of Teaching Composition, a new required course for TAs) and research (English 730 Studies in Composition Research and Pedagogy). It also corresponded with the creation of the graduate "double-major," which required students to choose primary and secondary specializations from nine fields (seven literary historical periods, literary theory, and composition and rhetoric) or create a devised field.

Available documents suggest that through the 1990s, the role of linguistics in the curriculum was reduced while course offerings in other areas expanded. In the 1995-1997 "Graduate Bulletin," English 601 Introduction to Language and Linguistics was no longer included among course requirements, which were listed as English 603 Introduction to Literary Criticism and English 605 Historiography and other Issues in the Profession, a new course. The apparent reconstitution of the formerly required linguistics course as an elective coincided with the creation of several other new courses: English 732 Studies in Composition Theory, English 733 Studies in Rhetoric, English 734 Issues in Composition Pedagogy, and English 735 Research Methods in Composition. While a 1995 department self-study includes linguistics as one of five areas in which "all doctoral candidates in the field should have proficiency," the study offers a more detailed account of how students might make use of available resources (in the form of new coursework and faculty specializations) in literary and cultural theory in order to complete scholarly projects that reflect the department's interest in "unifying composition and literary studies" (Powell et al. 12).

It may be significant that the Ohio Board of Regents' review of Miami's English doctoral program in 1995, for which the 1995 self-study was conducted, expressed "concern…for the intellectual rigor and academic viability of all English doctoral programs in the state" given "the sudden growth of Rhetoric and Composition programs" (Walters). As James Slevin has described, the "graduate courses designed to prepare teachers" that rhetoric and composition graduate programs grew out of were traditionally seen as "lacking the rigor and breadth of other graduate offerings" in English (14). That said, the Ohio Regents found the Miami program to be "of high quality and academically rigorous" (Walters). By aligning the program with literary studies and particularly literary and cultural theory, and not with linguistics or technical communication (and the focus on language pedagogy an alliance with these fields might imply), the department may have been working strategically to affirm that the program met the Ohio Regents' intellectual standards of viability. In the process, the department kept the program firmly ensconced within its own academic unit, avoiding potentially complicated interdisciplinary relationships with other departments offering linguistics courses (i.e., psychology and various modern language departments) as part of an interdisciplinary undergraduate major in the subject.

By the next department self-study, conducted in October 2000, linguistics was not mentioned as an area of focus in the Miami curriculum. Sociolinguistics is cited as a "well established devised field" for students creating what the department referred to as their graduate program "majors," but the document also notes the trend toward new devised fields in "postcolonial literature and theory, women's rhetoric, feminist theory and rhetoric, and performance studies," suggesting that self-designed majors in sociolinguistics could be becoming passé (Sadoff et al. 26).

While this self-study, in conjunction with the 1995-97, 1997-1999, and 1999-2001 Miami University "Graduate Bulletins," indicates that the program had largely moved away from a focus on linguistics by the turn of the twenty-first century, other documents suggest otherwise. A copy of the "Miami University English Graduate Program Handbook" from the 2000-2001 academic year lists ENG 601 Introduction to Language and Linguistics as a "foundation course" for the composition and rhetoric major. Moreover, the Miami program, in both the 1994 and 2000 *Rhetoric Review* surveys, represents itself as having core linguistics requirements (described as "Linguistics and Writing" in the 1994 survey and "Introduction to Linguistics" in the 2000 survey), which contradicts the information about its curriculum in the 1993-5 and 1999-2001 Miami "Graduate Bulletins." As with U of L, I suggest that these inconsistencies may speak to a lingering sentiment, or in Trimbur's terms, "anxiety," that language study is indeed still relevant to writing teaching and research.

## Conclusion: Remembering Language and Language Difference in Rhetoric and Composition Graduate Education

While Matsuda ("Wild West") attributes composition's recent attention to language to exigencies brought on by its current material and intellectual moment, I suggest the "linguistic frontier" is an area composition has, at least in some sense, visited before, and if it remembers its past sojourns there, it may be better positioned to address the challenges a renewed focus on language poses for its future. Specifically, recalling the history of linguistics in composition graduate education can help graduate faculty design curricula to address Matsuda's concern that composition lacks "a developed and socially shared theoretical framework for discussing language issues" in writing pedagogy and research ("Wild West" 32).

For instance, if we remember that composition graduate programs have traditionally addressed matters of language and language difference through separate, supplemental linguistic courses, we can see the limitations of this approach. Separate courses suggest that language issues are distinct from mainstream composition, and this sense of separateness can contribute to the marginalization and elimination of linguistics training as institutional conditions change over time. While I believe many programs should consider adding more specialized linguistics courses to their curricula for students to take for credit toward their degrees, I also think they should consider ways to incorporate insights from linguistics into pre-existing "core" courses, like rhetorical history, composition theory, and the composition teaching practicum. In so doing, programs could ensure that they are providing future teacher-scholars with a broad, research-based set of terms and practices to address language issues in their teaching and scholarship.

Rhetorical history courses, which often focus exclusively on the Western, Anglo-American rhetorical tradition, could be modified to include discussions of rhetorics associated with other contexts and languages (see Silva, Leki, and Carson) as well as contrastive rhetoric and critical approaches to this field of study. Required courses in composition theory, which, following the structure of readers like *Cross-Talk in Comp Theory* (Villanueva and Arola), are often surveys of disciplinary theory beginning around 1980, could pay greater attention to linguistic approaches to writing teaching developed by compositionists during the 1960s and 1970s to address the language differences of open admissions students. These courses could also cover theory *outside* the field of U.S. composition studies relevant to the teaching of linguistically diverse writers, including work from sociolinguistics, second language acquisition (SLA), bilingualism, Teaching English as a Second or Other Language (TESOL), and other branches of applied linguistics. Finally, required composition practicum courses could draw greater attention to the English L2 and multidialectal writing that takes place in mainstream composition courses and make more efforts to inform new college writing instructors about strategies for teaching these writers through, for instance, instruction in pedagogical grammar and best practices for corrective feedback (Matsuda, "WPA"; Ferris et al.).

Composition graduate faculty can take other steps to foreground matters of language and language difference in their work with students. For instance, they can encourage students to consider how their own language backgrounds affect their writing and teaching, facilitate their development of additional language knowledge through assigning international scholarship in languages other than English, and lead discussions on the ways in which language works structurally, psychologically, and sociohistorically to shape meaning in particular contexts of disciplinary work. While such graduate pedagogical practices may diverge from the norm, they can help future compositionists, and composition itself, to remember that language issues are, and always have been, central to writing and teaching writing. This fact, if not always recognized, has influenced the development of the field, in no small part through graduate programs.

## Acknowledgements

I would like to thank editor Laura Micciche, two anonymous reviewers, and Bruce Horner, Lisa Arnold, and Vanessa Kraemer Sohan for helpful feedback on previous versions of this article.

## Notes

1. See "Cross-Language Relations in Composition" in *College English* (Horner, Lu, Matsuda); "Working English in Rhetoric and Composition" in *JAC* (Horner, Lu, NeCamp, Nordquist, and Sohan); and "Second Language Writers and Writing Program Administrators" in *WPA* (Matsuda, Fruit, Lamm). See also edited collections *Language Diversity in the Classroom* (Smitherman and Villanueva), *ALT DIS: Alternative Discourses and the Academy* (Bizzell, Schroeder, and Fox), *Cross-Language Relations in Composition* (Horner, Lu, and Matsuda), *Writing in Multicultural Settings* (Guerra, Severino, and Butler), *Generation 1.5 Meets College Composition: Issues in the Teaching of Writing to U.S.-Educated Learners of ESL* (Harklau, Losey, and Siegal), and *Code-Meshing as World English: Pedagogy, Policy, Performance* (Young and Martinez). Finally, see the 2010 Thomas R. Watson Conference in Rhetoric and Composition (theme: Working English in Rhetoric and Composition) and the 2011 Penn State Conference on Rhetoric and Composition (theme: Rhetoric and Writing Across Language Boundaries).

2. I link basic writing pedagogy dissertations to linguistics insofar as early basic writing scholarship relied on theories and approaches developed in modern linguistics, including structural and transformative grammar, syntax-as-heuristic and sentence combining, and error analysis.

3. The Catholic University of America and the University of Wisconsin at Milwaukee were not represented in the 2007 survey.

4. I use this term not in the traditional fashion to reference the presence of multiple, discrete (national) languages, but as it has been more recently applied (along with terms like translingual, plurilingual, and heteroglossic) in second language studies to denote dynamic multilingual practices that cross traditional boundaries of language, culture, and modality (see De Korne 482).

## Works Cited

Anderson. "Letter to Donald Fritz: October 10, 1978." TS. Miami University Archives, Oxford, OH.

Aprile, Dianne. "U of L's Doctoral Program in English May Change or Die." *The Louisville Times* 17 July 1979: B1-B2. Print.

Bizzell, Patricia, Chris L. Schroeder, and Helen Fox, eds. *ALT DIS: Alternative Discourses and the Academy*. Portsmouth: Boynton/Cook, 2002. Print.

Brown, Stuart C., Theresa Enos, David Reamer, and Jason Thompson. "Portrait of the Profession: The 2007 Survey of Doctoral Programs in Rhetoric and Composition." *Rhetoric Review* 27.4 (2008). Web. 13 April 2017, <http://www.u.arizona.edu/~enos/>

Brown, Stuart C., Rebecca Jackson, and Theresa Enos. "The Arrival of Rhetoric in the Twenty-First Century: The 1999 Survey of Doctoral Programs in Rhetoric." *Rhetoric Review* 18.2 (2000): 233-42. Print.

Brown, Stuart C., Paul R. Meyer, and Theresa Enos. "Doctoral Programs in Rhetoric and Composition: A Catalog of the Profession." *Rhetoric Review* 12.2 (1994): 240-389. Print.

Chapman, David W., and Gary Tate. "A Survey of Doctoral Programs in Rhetoric and Composition." *Rhetoric Review* 5.2 (1987): 124-86. Print.

Comprone, Joseph. "Graduate Programs for Teachers of Basic Writing: The University of Louisville's PhD in Rhetoric and Composition." *Journal of Basic Writing* 3.2 (1981): 23-45. Print.

Connors, Robert J. "The Erasure of the Sentence." *CCC* 52.1 (2000): 96-128. Print.

Crowley, Sharon. "Linguistics and Composition Instruction: 1950-1980." *Written Communication* 6.4 (1989): 480-505. Print.

DeKorne, Haley. "Towards New Ideologies and Pedagogies of Multilingualism: Innovations in Interdisciplinary Language Education in Luxembourg." *Language and Education* 26.6 (2012): 479-500. Print.

Faigley, Lester. "The Study of Writing and the Study of Language." *Rhetoric Review* 7.2 (1989): 240-56. Print.

Ferris, Dana, et al. "Responding to L2 Students in College Writing Classes: Teacher Perspectives." *TESOL Quarterly* 45.2 (2012): 207-34. Print.

Fox, Tom. *Defending Access: A Critique of Standards in Higher Education*. Portsmouth: Heinemann, 1999. Print.

Giddens, Anthony. *The Constitution of Society: Outline of the Theory of Structuration*. Berkley: U of California P, 1986. Print.

Guerra, Juan C., Carol Severino, and Johnnella E. Butler, ed. *Writing in Multicultural Settings*. New York: MLA, 1997. Print.

Harklau, Linda, Kay M. Losey, and Meryl Siegal. *Generation 1.5 Meets College Composition: Issues in the Teaching of Writing to U.S.-Educated Learners of ESL*. Mahwah: Lawrence Erlbaum, 1999.

Harwood, Britton J. "Graduate Committee on Future of Miami University English PhD" Interoffice Memorandum, 5 June 1978. Miami University English Department. TS. Miami University Archives, Oxford, OH.

Horner, Bruce, Min-Zhan Lu, and Paul Kei Matsuda, eds. *Cross-Language Relations in Composition*. Carbondale: SIUP, 2010. Print.

Horner, Bruce, Min-Zhan Lu, Paul Kei Matsuda, eds. *Cross-Language Relations in Composition*. Spec. issue of *College English* 68.6 (2009). Print.

Horner, Bruce, Min-Zhan Lu, Samantha NeCamp, Brice Nordquist, and Vanessa Kraemer Sohan, eds. *Watson Conference Keynote Articles*. Spec. issue of *JAC* 29.1/2 (2009). Print.

Kerry, et al. "Miami University Graduate School Report Review of the PhD Degree Program in English." 1995. TS. Miami University Archives, Oxford, OH.

Lloyd-Jones, Richard. "Who We Were, Who We Should Become." *CCC* 43.4 (1992): 486-96. Print.

MacDonald, Susan Peck. "The Erasure of Language." *CCC* 58.4 (2007): 585-625. Print.

Matsuda, Paul Kei. "Composition Studies and ESL Writing: A Disciplinary Division of Labor." *CCC* 50.4 (1999): 699-721. Print.

---. "It's the Wild West Out There: A New Linguistic Frontier in U.S. College Composition." *Literacy as Translingual Practice*. Ed. A. Suresh Canagarajah. New York: Routledge, 2013. 128-38. Print.

---. "Let's Face It: Language Issues and the Writing Program Administrator." *WPA: Writing Program Administration* 36.1 (2012): 141-63. Print.

---. "The Myth of Linguistic Homogeneity in U.S. College Composition." *College English* 68.6 (2006): 637-51. Print.

Matsuda, Paul Kei, Maria Fruit, and Tamara Lee Burton Lamm, eds. *Second Language Writers and Writing Program Administration*. Spec. issue of *WPA: Writing Program Administration* 30.1/2 (2006). Print.

Miami University Department of English. "Handbook for Graduate Students 2000-2001." TS. Miami University Archives, Oxford, OH.

Miami University English Graduate Student Organization. "The PhD Program in English: An EGO Position Paper." 1978. TS. Miami University Archives, Oxford, OH.

Miami University Graduate School. "Graduate Bulletin 1980-1." Miami University. 127-31. Print. Miami University Archives, Oxford, OH.

---. "Graduate Bulletin 1985-87." Miami University, 65-67. Print. Miami University Archives, Oxford, OH.

---. "Graduate Bulletin 1991-3." Miami University. 45-6, 70-71. Print. Miami University Archives, Oxford, OH.

---. "Graduate Bulletin 1993-5." Miami University. 49, 76-77. Print. Miami University Archives, Oxford, OH.

---. "Graduate Bulletin 1995-1997." Miami University. 45, 73-76. Print. Miami University Archives, Oxford, OH.

---. "Graduate Bulletin 1997-1999." Miami University. 47-47, 77-79. Print. Miami University Archives, Oxford, OH.

---. "Graduate Bulletin 1999-2001." Miami University. 50, 79-80. Print. Miami University Archives, Oxford, OH.

Miller, Susan. *Textual Carnivals: The Politics of Composition*. Carbondale: SIUP, 1991. Print.

*Penn State Conference on Rhetoric and Composition: Rhetoric and Writing Across Language Boundaries*. July 10-12, 2011. Penn State University, State College, PA

Raymond, Linda. "Not-So Mighty Pens." *The Louisville Times* 22 Nov. 1975. Print. University of Louisville Archives, Louisville, KY.

Roach, Joseph. *Cities of the Dead: Circum-Atlantic Performance*. New York: Columbia UP, 1996.

Roskelly, Hephzibah. "Survival of the Fittest: Ten Years in a Basic Writing Program." *Journal of Basic Writing* 7.1 (1988): 13-29. Print.

Sadoff, Dianne, et al. "Department of English Academic Program Review." 2000. TS. Miami University Archives, Oxford, OH.

Selzer, Jack. "Letter to Donald Fritz." October 20, 1978. MS. Miami University Archives, Oxford, OH.

Silva, Tony, Ilona Leki, and Joan Carson. "Broadening the Perspective of Mainstream Composition Studies: Some Thoughts from the Disciplinary Margins." *Written Communication* 14.3 (1997): 398-428. Print.

Slevin, James. "Depoliticizing and Politicizing Composition Studies." *The Politics of Writing Instruction: Post-Secondary*. Ed. Richard H. Bullock, John Trimbur, and Charles I. Schuster. Portsmouth: Boynton/Cook, 1991. 1-21. Print.

Smitherman, Geneva, and Victor Villanueva, eds. *Language Diversity in the Classroom: From Intention to Practice*. Carbondale: SIUP, 2003. Print.

Strain, Margaret M. "Local Histories, Rhetorical Negotiations: The Development of Doctoral Programs in Rhetoric and Composition." *Rhetoric Society Quarterly* 30.2 (2000): 57-76. Print.

Thomas R. Watson Conference in Rhetoric and Composition: Working English *In Rhetoric and Composition*. October 14-17, 2010. University of Louisville, Louisville, KY.

"Times Opinion: English PhD Would Fit U of L's Urban Mission." *The Louisville Times* 29 June 1979. Print. University of Louisville Archives, Louisville, KY.

Trimbur, John. "Linguistic Memory and the Politics of U.S. English." *College English* 68.6 (2006): 575-88. Print.

University of Louisville English Department. "English Department Graduate Program Guidelines." 1985. TS. English Department, University of Louisville, Louisville KY.

---. "Graduate Program Guidelines." 1987. TS. English Department, University of Louisville, Louisville KY.

---. "Graduate Program Guidelines." 1989. TS. English Department, University of Louisville, Louisville KY.

---. "Graduate Program Guidelines." 1991. TS. English Department, University of Louisville, Louisville KY.

---. "Graduate Program Guidelines." 1996. TS. English Department, University of Louisville, Louisville KY.

---. "Graduate Program Guidelines." 2008. TS. English Department, University of Louisville, Louisville KY.

---. "Graduate Program Guidelines." *University of Louisville Department of English*. University of Louisville English Department, 2013. Web. 8 August 2013. <http://louisville.edu/english/graduate/graduate-program-guidelines-2>.

---. "PhD in English with Concentration in Rhetoric and Composition Guidelines1977-78." 1977. TS. English Department, University of Louisville, Louisville KY.

University of Louisville Graduate School. "Graduate Catalog 2001-2003." *University of Louisville Graduate Catalog Archive*. University of Louisville Graduate School, 2001. Web. 5 March 2017. <http://louisville.edu/graduatecatalog/archive/pdf/Graduate%20Catalog%202005-2007.pdf>

University of Louisville School of Interdisciplinary and Graduate Studies. "Graduate Catalog 2013-2014." *University of Louisville Graduate Catalog Archive*. Web 5

March 2017. <http://louisville.edu/graduatecatalog/archive/pdf/graduate-catalog-2013-2014>

"U of L to Drop Remedial Ed." *The Kentucky Post*. 30 April 1997: 2K. Print.

Villanueva, Victor, and Kristin L. Arola, eds. *Cross-Talk in Comp Theory: A Reader*. 3rd ed. Urbana: NCTE, 2011. Print.

Walters, E. Garrison. "Letter to Anne Hopkins Re: Ohio Board of Regents Review of English at Miami University." October 4, 1995. TS. Miami University Archives, Oxford, OH.

Young, Vershawn Ashanti, and Aja Y. Martinez, eds. *Code-Meshing as World English: Pedagogy, Policy, and Performance*. Urbana: NCTE, 2011. Print.

# Course Designs

## Taco Literacy: Public Advocacy and Mexican Food in the U.S. Nuevo South

*Steven Alvarez*

"You can now study tacos at the University of Kentucky," read the January 2016 headline on *Munchies*, a website and video channel from Vice media "dedicated to food and its global purpose" (Cabral). In a matter of minutes, the interview about Writing, Rhetoric, and Digital Studies (WRD) 422: Taco Literacy, a course I designed and piloted days before the story appeared, went viral. For a brief moment the University of Kentucky (UK) became the national focus of conversations around food literacies for a writing class about tacos in the U.S. South. However, taco literacy goes beyond an appreciation of tacos. As I explained to *Munchies* writer Javier Cabral, I envisioned taco literacy as a course engaging qualitative research studying foodways and the social, cultural, economic, and symbolic practices of producing and consuming food as a prism for understanding demographic change and social issues facing Mexican immigrants in their new home of Lexington, Kentucky.

As a term, foodways comprise approaching culinary practices and eating habits as social research that intersects with public advocacy. Taco literacies took a foodways approach connected to languages and literacies. In terms of organizing the course, I established four goals: students would (1) write about their personal connections to Mexican food and their sense of Mexican food as part of Southern and global cuisines, (2) engage with food politics by researching the production of ingredients in a particular dish of their preference, (3) further research local variances of their chosen dish and its movement to different locations, and (4) explore foodways social movements and both Southern and transnational food activist voices. WRD 422 students also used digital platforms to publish their research and contributed to a class archive of original ethnographic research into the foodways of Mexican Kentucky, housed at http://tacoliteracy.com. These digital archives became public records of the growing Latinx communities of the South and the issues these communities face.

### Institutional Context

UK is a large public land-grant university with a combined undergraduate and graduate population of over 30,000 students and growing. WRD 422 is one of the upper-division electives for the WRD undergraduate major and minor—one of the newest major and minor programs offered in the College of Arts and Sciences, UK's largest college. According to the WRD catalogue, "the course is designed to connect the study of persuasion in specific social movements, campaigns, and genres with opportunities for students to create texts and campaigns. This course may offer a historical or contemporary focus, and may examine local, regional, national, or transnational movements" ("Course Descriptions"). Students may take WRD 422 more than once, as the focus will change depending upon instructors' different approaches to teaching and learning about public writing.

WRD was initially a division within the Department of English at the University of Kentucky. In 2014, WRD became a stand-alone department. Since then, WRD has also added a minor in Professional and Technical Writing. The dynamic flexibility of WRD appeals to students who choose to earn either a Bachelor of Arts or a Bachelor of Science in WRD depending on their track: professional writing and editing, rhetorical theory and practice, and digital studies. The first track is geared toward students interested in editing and publishing or writing for the non-profit or business sectors. The second track is for students interested in community advocacy, government, or law. The third track is for students who want to write, design, and produce content for online spaces; for this track, students learn digital literacies by making multimodal projects. Regardless of track, students choose from a range of electives that connect to their interests and through which they produce work toward a senior portfolio. WRD students are required to complete 27 elective credit hours for the major and 18 for the minor. The variety of department courses on public writing, like WRD 422, address local literacy practices as social action. In the realm of public advocacy, WRD 422 largely attracts students enrolled as majors and minors in the rhetorical theory and practice track, but it also bears significance for students interested in how local groups use digital tools to communicate transnationally. WRD 422 prepares students for senior thesis portfolio projects by introducing a range of particularized topics, tools, and research to build upon for extended study. WRD 422: Taco Literacy in this respect is an upper-division course that extends public conversations beyond the classroom into communities with stakeholders. This focus on community entails ethnographic research into local lived experiences expressed through foodways literacies.

## Theoretical Rationale

In recent years, there has been a steady increase in the number of trade publications and cookbooks on Mexican food. Popular interests in the transnational migrations of Mexican food connected to multilingual, transnational, and cross-cultural issues in the humanities, including representations of Mexican cooking in film and literature (Soler and Abarca), food memoirs

(Chávez), and culinary histories (Arellano; Morton; Pilcher). In addition, scholarly works about Mexican food across disciplines range from important social justice issues in regards to food activism (Counihan and Siniscalchi), migrant labor (Purcell-Gates), targeted marketing (Carr Salas and Abarca), and the translation of indigenous cuisine for corporate consumption in different contexts (Calvo and Esquibel). Indeed, the influence of food across the U.S.-Mexico border is deeply connected to local experiences of global migration. Global migration connected to the history and networks of Mexican and Mexican American food in the United States demonstrates how transnational community literacies sustain emotional connections and local relationships among individuals building publics across borders and languages.

The turn to foodways in WRD 422 for me was an extension of a previous WRD first-year composition course in which I focused student attention on the demographic changes of "Mexington, Kentucky." In that class, I took students on a tour of one of the *barrios* of Kentucky to explore a local bakery, a western wear store, a family-owned grocery store, a bilingual library, and a local *taquería*. Needless to say, the tacos were a hit with the students. As it were, students were familiar with the local prestige of some of Lexington's Mexican restaurants thanks to media coverage from national outlets such as *FiveThirtyEight*, which ranked Lexington's Tortillería y Taquería Ramírez burrito as one of the best in the nation (Barry-Jester). With the success of the food unit, I decided to design an entire class exploring the foodways of Mexican migration in the South that would engage ethnographic methods.

Foodways literacy research requires students to conduct fieldwork in communities, and to learn by listening and recording the stories of local lived experiences around food. In *Writing Instruction in the Culturally Relevant Classroom*, Maisha T. Winn and Latrise P. Johnson write, "students can be involved in participatory action projects such as examining 'spatial location and demographic trends' in their community [. . .] and study the linguistic practices of others through close listening" (71). Winn and Johnson's ideas about students becoming ethnographers also apply to students conducting writing projects about foodways that explore social advocacy and neighborhood inequalities. WRD 422 prepares student researchers to pose arguments and compose reflective writing about foodways as well as pose critiques about sociopolitical issues affecting the public. As ethnographers, students compose a great deal of writing, such as field notes and reflective observations, interview transcriptions, tables, concept maps, and literature reviews of primary and secondary sources. With a broad array of ethnographic tools, students' assignments write about cultures through lived experiences.

Qualitative research also contributes to students' increasing awareness of social and cultural contexts and builds academic writing strategies like community collaboration, description, revision, analysis, and investigative writing. For the course, students created WordPress websites where they archived their research, which covered topics stretching from the links between Kentucky burgoo and Mexican *birria* stews to Mexican food restaurant franchises across the South, gendered family roles connected to food, organic produce available in *barrio* markets, and city policies regarding street food vendors. The topics students pursued allowed them to explore public advocacy within communities, learning by listening to the wisdom of local stakeholders. In *Del Otro Lado: Literacy and Migration Across the U.S.-Mexico Border*, Susan V. Meyers argues that an activist methodology requires the "ethical responsibility of adding to or giving back" to local communities (14). Meyers theorizes that a "reflexive critical ethnography" has the potential to rewrite the impact of researchers in their own studies. I extend this notion of reflexive critical ethnography to a social justice orientation for ethnographers as public advocates, mediating between community audiences, participants, and competing representations and stories, while being attuned to diverse voices advocating for change. Within this social justice orientation, I agree with Meyers that writing instructors must reinforce the importance of ethical responsibilities with regards to local communities and on whose behalf researchers can claim to speak.

The public advocacy in the course, from my view, comes from my own critical reflexive research among Latinx activist communities in the South. Over my four years of living and teaching in the South, my research into the literacy practices of Latinxs and Latin American immigrants has led me to link foodways, community activism, citizenship, and literacy. Through my research, I have come to discover the deep emotional connections to food shared transnationally among Mexican immigrants across the nation, including the *barrios* of Kentucky. Yes, the *barrios* of Kentucky.

According to U.S. Census data, the Latin American-origin population of Kentucky nearly tripled between 1990 and 2015, with nearly 90% of Latin American migration in Kentucky coming from Mexico. Research has demonstrated that stiff border policing criminalized Latin American migrants crossing borders without visas or overstaying visas (Mohl; Rich and Miranda). The heightened levels of border security compelled formerly transnational migrants to settle in Kentucky rather than risk the inability to leave. During interviews over tacos and coffee, I also met several families who moved to Kentucky when anti-immigrant sentiment toward Latin Americans in Georgia and North Carolina increased. In those states, an increasingly hateful and dehumanizing rhetoric connected to xenophobic policy became emotionally distressing. Sharing food with community members when discussing lived struggles became a humanizing opportunity for coming together to learn from and share with one another.

Despite those experiences with food and ethnography, I think it was in my classrooms where I realized I needed to teach a WRD class focused exclusively on Mexican foodways in Kentucky. When teaching WRD courses that have examined rhetorics of citizenship and the literacy practices of immigrants, I began observing how students in courses looked to these issues via social media. I use the verb "look" because our platform of choice has been Instagram. On Instagram, students from different classes used the hashtag #MexKy to archive their required Instagram posts exploring issues in the local Mexican community. As students contributed to this archive, I noticed that, without prompting, students would explore images and repost their findings to share with classmates and with their audiences of followers.

Building on the success of Instagram in the previous course, I included the platform for Taco Literacy. What I learned from this, and what I learned from teaching about the complexities of immigration to largely white students at a Southern university, is that people in Kentucky love Mexican food. You can peruse #tacoliteracy on Instagram to see for yourself. Students constantly posted pictures of themselves eating Mexican food or documenting memories they had of special events at Mexican restaurants. Several students uploaded images of restaurants where they worked. A few students even uploaded posts of themselves preparing Mexican food. Students used the opportunity to explore and publish their images and stories of Mexican foodways, offering advice, writing reviews, and interacting with one another. I found students' uses of Instagram for engaging audiences involved with farm labor activism in Mexico especially insightful. By exploring geotags and hashtags, students were able to research and communicate with farm labor activists advocating for wage increases and boycotts. Connected to these political uses of Instagram, students realized that the platform was not only a space for sharing about a culture's cuisine but also for engaging both local and transnational publics and social movements around migration. Foodways, in other words, became a point to explore further, and with that I realized the tremendous potential for blending the study of digital literacies, foodways, and—one of my special interests—tacos in Mexican Kentucky.

## Critical Reflection

Taco Literacies taught me a great deal about how WRD students approach the emotional connections between food, literacies, and narratives. Students explored personal stories that connected people through food, piecing together narratives that are part of the foodways of communities. Foodways narratives intersect with languages and literacies, and in the case of Mexican food in the Nuevo South, with bilingual communication, community building, migration, and transnational lives. Education also becomes a theme, both in about foodways and traditions, but also in learning about culture through the languages and social situations with food at the center. In different contexts, I can imagine the shape of this class moving into more political issues that affect food production in the United States, including farm labor. Indeed, the wealth of Kentucky also has transnational agricultural significance and depends upon immigrant labor. An approach to foodways in the manner of Gabriela Raquel Ríos's "Cultivating Land-Based Literacies and Rhetorics" points to how taco literacies could turn to deeper political forms of persuasion in the hands of activists close to the means of production. The wealth of immigrant labor in Kentucky and in so many parts of the United States is a potential fund of knowledge to explore further, and also to connect to academic content linked to local literacy practices. The intersections of foodways, literacy, photography, social justice, and emergent bilingualism are rich material for writing projects at all levels.

The voices of the South are indeed multilingual, representing the growing awareness of a Latinx presence in the region. Over the last twenty years the South has seen the largest growth of Latin American and Latinx populations in the United States. Kentucky, along with South Carolina, Arkansas, and Tennessee, are four of the five states with a current population growth of over 100% over the last decade (Stepler and Brown). The prism of food helps students to better understand the cultural significance of food, language, literacy, and identity for Kentucky in the twenty-first century. Through the prism of food, for example, instructors can probe issues related to immigration and citizenship in ways that are welcoming, significant, and human.

As this was my first time teaching the class, I would change some things for the future. I would incorporate more social media into the course in order for students to engage further with "foodies" across the nation who share interests in Mexican food. The #tacoliteracy hashtag found fans across the globe who added to the archive and followed students and commented on posts. This aspect of directly building and engaging audience was something completely new for students who found viewers of their blogs and Instagram accounts as a real audience that shaped their academic compositions. Indeed, using Instagram for multimodal foodways research was a good start, but I would incorporate the photo-sharing platform's potential for cultivating an audience even more. The popularity of the class meant students had an instant audience, and how they approached this offered much to think about in terms of digital rhetoric. This aspect of cultivating a public audience via social media is an aspect I intend to explore further. I also intend to try a turn to Twitter to tweet photographs as students would share their work and build an audience on that platform. On Twitter, students could also share direct links to their blog posts, as well as share articles related to their research, while building a following. No doubt, the *Munchies* article put Taco Literacy in the public spotlight and this led students to closely consider their public voices as they shared their research.

I encourage all writing instructors to learn more about foodways literacies and to look deeper into how food relates to activism and local communities. Let me assure you, when tacos on fresh corn tortillas are distributed among *gente*, dialogues about daily aspects of community living across spaces and languages happen enjoyably.

**Works Cited**

Arellano, Gustavo. *Taco USA: How Mexican Food Conquered America*. New York: Scribner, 2013. Print.

Barry-Jester, Anna Maria. "Some Restaurants in the South Stretch the Definition of Burrito." *FiveThirtyEight*. ESPN, 13 Jun. 2014. Web. 13 Jan. 2016. <http://fivethirtyeight.com/features/some-restaurants-in-the-south-stretch-the-definition-of-burrito/>.

Cabral, Javier. "You Can Now Study Tacos at the University of Kentucky." *Munchies*. Vice, 27 Jan. 2016. Web. 20 June 2016. <https://munchies.vice.com/en/articles/you-can-now-study-tacos-at-the-university-of-kentucky>.

Calvo, Luz, and Catriona Rueda Esquibel. *Decolonize Your Diet: Plant-Based Mexican-American Recipes for Health and Healing*. Vancouver: Arsenal, 2015. Print.

Carr Salas, Consuelo, and Meredith E. Abarca. "Food Marketing Industry: Cultural Attitudes Made Visible." *Latin@s' Presence in the Food Industry: Changing How We Think About Food*. Ed. Consuelo Carr Salas and Meredith E. Abarca. Fayetteville: U of Arkansas P, 2015. 203-22. Print.

Chávez, Denise. *A Taco Testimony: Meditations on Family, Food and Culture*. Tucson: Rio Nuevo, 2006. Print.

Counihan, Carole, and Valeria Siniscalchi, eds. *Food Activism: Agency, Democracy and Economy*. London: Bloomsbury, 2014. Print.

"Course Descriptions." *Department of Writing, Rhetoric, and Digital Studies*. University of Kentucky, n.d. Web. 13 Jan. 2016. <https://wrd.as.uky.edu/wrd-course-descriptions>.

Meyers, Susan V. *Del Otro Lado: Literacy and Migration Across the U.S.-Mexico Border*. Carbondale: SIUP, 2014. Print.

Mohl, Raymond A. "Globalization, Latinization, and the Nuevo New South." *Journal of American Ethnic History* 22.4 (2003): 31-66. Print.

Morton, Paula E. *Tortillas: A Cultural History*. Albuquerque: U of New Mexico P, 2014. Print.

Pilcher, Jeffrey M. *Planet Taco: A Global History of Mexican Food*. New York: Oxford UP, 2012. Print.

Purcell-Gates, Victoria. "Literacy Worlds of Children of Migrant Farmworker Communities Participating in a Migrant Head Start Program." *Research in the Teaching of English* 48. 1 (2013): 68-97. Print.

Rich, Brian, and Marta Miranda. "The Sociopolitical Dynamics of Mexican Immigration in Lexington, Kentucky, 1997-2002: An Ambivalent Community Responds." *New Destinations: Mexican Migration in the United States*. Ed. Victor Zuñiga and Rubén Hernández-León. New York: Russell Sage, 2005. 187-219. Print.

Ríos, Gabriela Raquel. "Cultivating Land-Based Literacies and Rhetorics." *Literacy in Composition Studies* 3.1 (2015): 60-70. Print.

Soler, Nieves Pascual, and Meredith E. Abarca, eds. *Rethinking Chicana/o Literature Through Food: Postcolonial Appetites*. New York: Palgrave Macmillan, 2013. Print.

Stepler, Renee, and Anna Brown. "Statistical Portrait of Hispanics in the United States." *Hispanic Trends*. Pew Research Center, 19 Apr. 2016. Web. 20 June 2016. <http://www.pewhispanic.org/2016/04/19/statistical-portrait-of-hispanics-in-the-united-states-key-charts/>.

Winn, Maisha T., and Latrise P. Johnson. *Writing Instruction in the Culturally Relevant Classroom*. Urbana: NCTE, 2011. Print.

Villamizar, Monica. "The Fruits of Mexico's Cheap Labor." YouTube. YouTube, 13 Aug. 2015. Web. 16 Jan. 2017. https://www.youtube.com/watch?v=YT6AvAhDx8Q.

# Syllabus

WRD 422: Taco Literacy: Public Advocacy and Mexican Food in the Nuevo South

*Course Description:*

In recent years, there has been a steady increase of interest in the transnational migrations of Mexican food popularized by television food shows and travel journalism. In addition to the immense number of trade publications and cookbooks devoted to Mexican food, important social justice issues in regards to multilingualism, migrant labor, and digital activism, as well as representations of Mexican cooking in film and literature and the translation of indigenous cuisine for corporate consumption in different contexts, have also become topical. This course will examine transnational community food literacies and how these connect stories of people and build publics across borders of all kinds. Students will explore Mexican and Mexican American food in the United States and their links to rhetorics of authenticity, local and regional variations, and how food literacies situate different spaces, identities, and forms of knowledge.

*Course Texts:*

Arellano, Gustavo. "Bluegrass and Birria." Southern Foodways Alliance Oral Histories, Center for the Study of Southern Culture at U of Mississippi, 2015, http://www.southernfoodways.org/oral-history/bluegrass-and-burria/. Accessed 10 Jan. 2017.

---. "Sombreros Over the South." *Gravy Quarterly*, no. 58, 2016, http://www.southernfoodways.org/sombreros-over-the-south/. Accessed 10 Jan. 2017.

---. *Taco USA: How Mexican Food Conquered America.* Gustavo Arellano, Scribner, 2013.

Barry-Jester, Anna Maria. "Burrito Heads to the Land of Sweet Tea." *FiveThirtyEight*, 9 Jun. 2014, https://fivethirtyeight.com/features/the-search-for-americas-best-burrito-heads-to-the-land-of-sweet-tea/. Accessed 10 Jan. 2017.

---. "Some Restaurants in the South Stretch the Definition of Burrito" *FiveThirtyEight*, 13 Jun. 2014, http://fivethirtyeight.com/features/some-restaurants-in-the-south-stretch-the-definition-of-burrito/. Accessed 10 Jan. 2017.

Duncan, Samantha. Appraising Tacos: Unraveling Value-Imbuing Processes and Narratives of Authenticity. Undergraduate Honors Thesis, Northwestern University, 2015.

Dura, et al. "De Aquí y de Allá: Changing Perceptions of Literacy Through Food Pedagogy." *Community Literacy Journal*, vol. 10, no. 1, 2015, pp. 21-39.

*East of Salinas.* Directed by Laura Pacheco and Jackie Mow, PBS Independent Lens, 2015, http://www.pbs.org/independentlens/films/east-of-salinas/.

Hernández, Daniel. "The Best Place for Food In Mexico: MUNCHIES Guide to Oaxaca (Part 1)," *YouTube*, uploaded by MUNCHIES, 5 May 2014, https://www.youtube.com/watch?v=ZEeU4c2G7sc.

"Mexican People Try Taco Bell for the First Time," *YouTube*, uploaded by BuzzFeed-Video, 8 Mar. 2015, https://www.youtube.com/watch?v=TWSOiZrs3oA.

Pilcher, Jeffey M. *Planet Taco: A Global History of Mexican Food.* Oxford UP, 2012.

*Southern Foodways Alliance.* Center for the Study of Southern Culture at U of Mississippi, 2017, http://www.southernfoodways.org. Accessed 10 Jan. 2017.

---. "Hot Tamale Trail." Southern Foodways Alliance Oral Histories, Center for the Study of Southern Culture at U of Mississippi, 2005, http://www.southernfoodways.org/oral-history/hot-tamale-trail/. Accessed 10 Jan. 2017.

---. "Gravy Podcast." Southern Foodways Alliance Oral Histories, Center for the Study of Southern Culture at U of Mississippi, 2017, http://www.southernfoodways.org/gravy-format/gravy-podcast/. Accessed 10 Jan. 2017.

*Tacopedia.* Deborah Holtz and Juan Carlos Mena, Phaidon P, 2015.

*Tortillas: A Cultural History.* Paula E. Morton, U of New Mexico P, 2014.

"The Sushi Chef: Culichi Town." *YouTube*, uploaded by MUNCHIES, 31 Aug. 2015, https://www.youtube.com/watch?v=htDtGc1SPlc.

"Traditional Mexican Cuisine: Ancestral, Ongoing Community culture: The Michoacán Paradigm." *UNESCO Intangible Cultural Heritage*, 18 Nov. 2010, http://www.unesco.org/culture/ich/en/RL/traditional-mexican-cuisine-ancestral-ongoing-community-culture-the-michoacan-paradigm-00400.

*Un Buen Carnicero.* Directed by Victoria Bouloubasis, Southern Foodways Alliance Films, 2014, https://www.southernfoodways.org/film/un-buen-carnicero/. Accessed 10 Jan. 2017.

Villamizar, Monica. "The Fruits of Mexico's Cheap Labor," *YouTube*, uploaded by VICE News, 13 Aug. 2015, https://www.youtube.com/watch?v=YT6AvAhDx8Q.

*Course Goals:*

1. Students will begin by writing about their personal connections to Mexican food, their preferences, and their sense of what Mexican food means culturally, as part of American and global cuisine.

2. Students will engage with the history of a particular dish of their preference and further research regional differences and the movement of the dish to different locations.
3. Students will engage the global perspective of Pilcher's *Planet Taco* with the national context of Arellano's *Taco USA*, which is tied to local, Kentucky responses and varieties of Mexican food.
4. Students will contribute to a digital platform to blog reactions to texts and to publish their fieldwork and research about local Mexican restaurants.
5. Students will research social movements and advocacy relating to Mexican food in the Nuevo South and transnationally.

*Platforms and Assignments:*

*WordPress and Instagram*
You will compose 20 Instagram and 20 WordPress posts for the semester. Consider these posts as informal journal entries where you can record your fieldwork and early drafts of assignments. These posts will generate material for you to use for your formal assignments, as well as serve as a space for you to experiment with archiving your research. The dates for the sets of 5 posts are listed below.

*Major Assignments*

The research project is term-long, and will be completed in 5 assignments—all published on your WordPress website. Your assignments will focus on issues discussed in class, or your reflections responding to readings, documentaries, writing from the course, and direct community research. In all, the five major assignments will form the core of your ethnographic study of foodways literacies in Kentucky. All Instagram photos/videos will appear on the WordPress site to meet the multimodal requirements for each assignment.

In *Assignment 1* you will write about your personal connections to Mexican food and your sense of Mexican food as part of Southern and global cuisines. For this assignment, you will compose a photo-essay reviewing a local Mexican restaurant, following a particular dish you have researched. Using the models of reviews we have read in class, you must also engage the global perspective of Pilcher's *Planet Taco* with the national context of Arellano's *Taco USA*, which is tied to local responses and varieties of Mexican food. Your piece must tell a story and capture aspects of taste and emotion connected to food literacies and the location. The foodways narratives of the Southern Foodways Alliance archive are demonstrative in this respect and models to emulate. Your photos should also tell a story that gives voice to flavors. You must also include five translations of words from Spanish, and describe the roots of words, making note of indigenous loanwords. The text should include 6-8 photographs embedded within the body of the blog page, as well as captions. The text must be 1,200 words and include correct MLA works cited and hyperlinked sources.

In *Assignment 2* you will engage with food politics by researching the production of ingredients in a second dish, as well as the history of this dish. You are to research into variances, local varieties, and the movement of the dish to different locations across Mexico and the United States. In addition, you must also research the production of ingredients and preparation of the dish. Your text must include 10 photographs/images that depict the dish as well as preparation and migration maps. The text must be 1,500 words and include correct MLA works cited and hyperlinked sources.

In *Assignment 3* you will conduct a literature review of a topic related to your research interests. You will research 5 articles related to your interests and include reviews for each article you uncover. For each article, you must summarize key points or ideas that connect to your previous two assignments. You will be evaluated on the quality of your sources as well as how you engage with them. For each source, you must include quotes with which you practice close-reading analysis of both culinary research methods and key findings. The text must be 2,000 words and include correct MLA works cited and hyperlinked sources.

In *Assignment 4* you will explore local foodways through community voices by conducting team interviews with a classmate. (I will assign individuals for pairs to interview.) You and your classmate will interview an individual with deep connections to Mexican food and culture. You and your partner will conduct an interview, and you will use it to compose a written profile. Your profile must quote directly from the interview, while also engaging five sources from your literature review and two quotes from either or both *Taco USA* and *Planet Taco*. Your portrait should focus on your interviewee's lived experience connected to culture, history, geography, and migration. You must also include 4 photographs from the interview and 4 relevant videos or maps that connect to what you uncover. The text must be 2,000 words and include correct MLA works cited and hyperlinked sources. You must also provide me the signed interview release form distributed in class.

In *Assignment 5* you will review your previous research and fieldwork as you compose a critical reflection that engages a scholarly argument concerning a topic or topics from your previous assignments. This text will be the capstone writing for your semester-long portfolio where you offer insight into each assignment and where your research has travelled up to this point, as well as potential directions for future research. You must include 10 photographs/images from your semester-long research that best encapsulate themes you present in your reflection. This text will be 750 words and include correct MLA works cited and hyperlinked sources.

Included in this assignment, you are to finalize the visual preferences for your WordPress site, including (1) updating your header image and background colors and personalizing your website title, (2) updating your "About" page to include your contact information as well as your Instagram username, 3) updating the sequential order of blog pages, and 3) creating a single references page where you will house all the sources from your previous assignments.

Assignments will be published on a site that will become an extended single text archived online. The revised larger project will develop with the additional information and insights you gain through your fieldwork as you become more familiar with and knowledgeable about Mexican food, literacies, and local issues. Use the readings in class and your instincts to guide your topics for all five assignments.

You will depend on your classmates, tutors in the Writing Center, and me as readers who will help you make decisions about how to present material and how best to interest your audience, but ultimately you will be the expert on your chosen topic. If you spend a lot of time developing, revising, and working on certain aspects of your writing, all of this effort and expertise will be reflected in your final project and your grade. That means that your attention to revision and your awareness of your own work habits, strengths, and weaknesses will become a very important element of your writing process. Your final course grade will be based primarily on your participation, active blogging, and your community engagement.

*Assessment Criteria Grading Breakdown*

| Assignments | 100% total |
|---|---|
| Assignment 1, Personal Narrative | 10% |
| Assignment 2, Foodways Politics Interview | 10% |
| Assignment 3, Foodways Literature Review | 15% |
| Assignment 4, Community Voices and Foodways | 15% |

| Assignment 5, Final Portfolio | 20% |
|---|---|
| WordPress Journal Posts | 10% |
| Instagram Journal Posts | 10% |
| Participation | 10% |

## Class Calendar

| Week 1 | <ul><li>Freewrite about Mexican food.</li><li>Create your URL, username, and password for the class blog.</li><li>Create your Instagram account for class. Find images to upload for your free-write.</li><li>Read "Sombreros Over the South" by Gustavo Arellano.</li></ul> |
|---|---|
| Week 2 | <ul><li>Discuss "Sombreros Over the South": search for images and review food experiences.</li><li>Search Google Maps for Mexican restaurants in Lexington and Greater Kentucky.</li><li>Overview of the Southern Foodways Alliance website and *Gravy* podcasts. Look for more research for your first writing assignment.</li><li>Read the Southern Foodways Alliance oral history project "Bluegrass and Birria."</li><li>Read the Hot Tamale Trail. Choose two locations for conducting your research; next week we will create a list of locations from everyone.</li></ul> |
| Week 3 | *Post 5 images on Instagram and 5 journal posts on WordPress.<ul><li>Discuss the Hot Tamale Trail and discuss *Tacopedia*'s design and images.</li><li>Watch the documentary, *Un Buen Carnicero*.</li><li>Collect images using *Tacopedia*.</li><li>Draft of Assignment 1 due on your blog, published as a page (not a post).</li><li>Read *FiveThirtyEight*'s Best Burrito tournament, "Burrito Heads to the Land of Sweet Tea."</li><li>Review locations for mapping *taquerías* via Instagram. You should also include five images for your WordPress blog that you will use for Assignment 1.</li><li>Your first five WordPress posts are also due. The posts should offer compliments to the images you collect, whether they are images you published on Instagram or not.</li><li>Read "Some Restaurants in the South Stretch the Definition of Burrito."</li></ul> |

| Week 4 | *Assignment 1 due. <br><br>• Read *Taco USA*, Introduction, Chapter 1, Chapter 3, and Chapter 4. Search for quotes from the book to speak about in class, and also post key quotes from each chapter on your blog. We will use these for class discussion.<br>• Discuss *Taco USA*, analyzing quotes, and citing sources in MLA format.<br>• Watch *The Sushi Chef: Culichi Town*.<br>• Read *Taco USA*, Chapter 8, Chapter 9, Chapter 10, and Chapter 11. For two of these chapters, find key quotes to post to your WordPress blog. |
|---|---|
| Week 5 | • Discuss *Taco USA*, preparing issues to discuss with author Gustavo Arellano via Skype. We will draw up a set of class questions, but also bring three individual questions for Arellano about Mexican food.<br>• Continue with *Taco USA*, Chapter 13, and Conclusion<br>• Upload five images to your blog that will be included in your next project.<br>• Your next set of blog posts and Instagram posts are due next class. |
| Week 6 | *Assignment 2 due.<br>*Post 5 images on Instagram and 5 journal posts on WordPress.<br><br>• Debrief on interview session with Arellano and finish discussing *Taco USA*.<br>• Read *Planet Taco*, Introduction and Chapter 1. |
| Week 7 | • Discuss *Planet Taco* Introduction and Chapter 1.<br>• Read *Planet Taco*, Chapters 2 and 3. Add three quotes from the reading to a blog post, give the page numbers, and provide a three-sentence close reading of each quote. Pay attention to the language in the quotes and use it to help you read the passage.<br>• Guest visitor and class tasting.<br>• Read *Planet Taco*, Chapters 4 and 5. |
| Week 8 | • Continue discussion of *Planet Taco*; research further themes from the book online.<br>• Read *Planet Taco*, Chapters 6 and 7. Add four more key quotes, from any chapter in the book you found relevant, to your WordPress blog. Again, add page numbers and offer a reflection of each quote.<br>• Prepare materials for both portions of the Assignment 3, due next week.<br><br>*Saturday Class: Barrio Taco Tour, 1-3:30 pm. We will meet in front of the Main Building if you need a ride; otherwise, we can carpool. |

| Week 9 | *Assignment 3 due.<br>*Post 5 images on Instagram and 5 journal posts on WordPress.<br><br>• Return to *Taco USA* and *Planet Taco* for reviewing research topics. You will choose two of the sources cited in each book to summarize, review, and present to the class.<br>• Review *Taco USA* and *Planet Taco* for organization models, arguments, and research. |
|---|---|
| Week 10 | • Continue discussion with *Taco USA* and *Planet Taco*.<br>• Read "Appraising Tacos" by Samantha Duncan and find two key passages to quote on your WordPress blog. Also note that this text was composed as an undergraduate senior thesis: review the text's sources for further ideas for research. |
| Week 11 | • Review of outing.<br>• Read reviews of local *taquerías* and write reviews.<br>• Review the food studies works cited of "Appraising Tacos."<br>• Read "De Aquí y de Allá" by Dura, et al. |
| Week 12 | *Assignment 4 due.<br>*Post 5 images on Instagram and 5 journal posts on WordPress.<br><br>• Read UNESCO report on Mexican cuisine.<br>• Read *Tortillas*, Prologue, Chapter 1, and Chapter 2. |
| Week 13 | • Class visitor who will speak about tortilla production in Kentucky.<br>• Discuss UNESCO report and connect to *Tortillas* (discuss the history of wheat and corn in Mexico, popular foods, elite cuisines, and class distinctions in Mexican food).<br>• Read *Tortillas*, Chapter 3, Chapter 4, Chapter 5, and Chapter 6.<br>• Watch *The Fruits of Mexico's Cheap Labor*, a film about transnational labor. |
| Week 14 | • Discuss *Tortillas*.<br>• Watch *East of Salinas*.<br>• We will also contribute individually to the film's discussion thread, leaving links to sources for readers.<br>• Finish your second restaurant visit if you haven't done so already. |
| Week 15 | *Assignment 5 due.<br><br>• Share projects with classmates, and revising blogs.<br>• Review materials for your final project.<br>• Watch *The Best Place for Food in Mexico*.<br>• Watch "Mexican People Try Taco Bell for the First Time." |

# Stretch and Studio Composition Practicum: Creating a Culture of Support and Success for Developing Writers at a Hispanic-Serving Institution

*Cristyn L. Elder and Bethany Davila[1]*

This course design describes a 3-credit, two-week intensive Stretch and Studio Practicum course at the University of New Mexico (UNM). Because the Stretch and Studio composition curriculum is designed to help students who may be at greater risk of not succeeding, instructors are required to complete the practicum before teaching in the program. The learning outcomes for the practicum ask instructors to (1) become familiar with the theory and pedagogy of basic writing[2], multilingual writers, metacognition, and reading instruction; (2) develop best practices in writing instruction for students who traditionally have been marginalized in higher education; (3) recognize students' existing skills and literacies as resources and strengths that can be built upon; and (4) develop activities and assignments to help Stretch and Studio students progress toward and reflect on the learning outcomes for first-year composition (fyc).

## Institutional Context

UNM is a Hispanic-Serving institution designated as "Highest Research Activity" by the Carnegie classification system. Due to Legislative Lottery Scholarships[3], UNM sees large numbers of first-generation students and significant economic diversity among its students. Additionally, UNM's access-oriented mission is visible, in part, in incoming student test scores. Until fall 2014, 35% to 45% of incoming first-year UNM students placed into one or more "Introductory Studies" (IS) courses, which were taught on UNM's campus by local community college faculty and did not count toward graduation credit. However, like many other universities, UNM is making concerted efforts to move away from "remedial" education. Leading this effort within the writing curriculum, the authors of this article piloted a two-semester Stretch program (which stretches the curriculum of our fyc course across two semesters) in the summer of 2013 and a Studio composition program (an fyc course with an additional weekly hour of lab time) in the fall of 2013. As of fall 2014, these courses have replaced all IS writing courses at UNM. To prepare instructors to teach the new Stretch and Studio curriculum, we developed an accompanying two-week Stretch and Studio composition practicum course, described in this article. The following section provides our theoretical rationale for the

Stretch and Studio composition practicum curriculum. The critical reflection later in the article shares the instructor feedback that motivated some of our choices when revising the practicum as well as considerations for the course moving forward.

**Theoretical Rationale**

The two-week Stretch and Studio composition practicum curriculum builds on a one-semester (3-credit) teaching composition practicum that all new TAs take. The initial one-semester practicum course aims to offer just enough theoretical background to support the best practices that we ask TAs to enact in their classrooms. Specifically, we provide graduate students with a theoretical and practical overview of the rhetorical situation (Bean), teaching critical genre awareness (Bean; Devitt et al.; Dirk) and student reflection (Yancey). The course also covers topics such as creating assignment prompts, rubrics, and lesson plans; grading and responding to student papers; scaffolding activities and assignments; and incorporating the program's student learning outcomes into every aspect of the course design (Bean).

The Stretch and Studio composition practicum curriculum builds on this more general practicum course, providing additional training so that our instructors (TAs and lecturers) will be prepared to meet the needs of the Stretch and Studio students. As Greg Glau notes in his description of stretch courses, by stretching an FYC curricula across two semesters, the additional time allows instructors to "acclimat[e] students, particularly nontraditional or first-generation college students, to the unfamiliar expectations, workload, and discourse conventions of the university" (1). The Studio model, with its extra hour per week of small group meetings with the instructor, presumably has similar potential. The extra time the Stretch and Studio courses provide allow for additional "revision" and "discussion" (Glau 1) and a focus on "grammatical and rhetorical issues" (Lalicker). However, we questioned whether our instructors would know how to make the best use of this additional time in order to meet these goals. Therefore, when designing the Stretch and Studio Practicum, we sought to build upon the theoretical overview instructors received in the first semester practicum by emphasizing the following areas: language attitudes, teaching grammar, teaching reading, and metacognition. In the subsections that follow, we describe the assumptions that informed our curricular choices and example readings that help us to address these areas with instructors. We then describe the course assignments, which work to develop positive instructor dispositions toward linguistic diversity and nontraditional learners and provide instructors with best practices to use in their courses.

*Language Attitudes*

Like many in our field (Canagarajah; Horner et al.; Perryman-Clark, Kirkland, and Jackson; Smitherman and Villanueva), we believe our students' linguistic diversity is an asset that can enrich composition courses and curricula. As such, we emphatically disagree with a deficit model of thinking that positions students' "nonstandard" languages and/or dialects as a disadvantage or barrier that must be "dealt with." One of our goals for the Stretch and Studio practicum is to make sure our instructors understand and share this theoretical positioning. Therefore, our curriculum is designed, in part, to help instructors shift their perspectives about our students through readings and discussions that allow us to confront language attitudes that position "standard" English as a singular and intrinsically superior language variety.

As a way to introduce and uncover attitudes about students who have been labeled "remedial" because of their "nonstandard" language use, we assign the introduction to Mina Shaughnessy's *Errors and Expectations*. In the introduction to this iconic text, Shaughnessy describes a group of students who have grown up in "racial enclaves" where they spoke "other languages or dialects at home and never successfully reconciled the worlds of home and school" (388). Most significantly, as Shaughnessy notes, CUNY (City University of New York) teachers at the time declared this group of students, after only one week of instruction, as "irremediable" and likely to fail (389). Certainly there has been significant progress in basic writing and composition studies scholarship over the past 30 years in regards to reframing developing writers. Nevertheless, we find that the faculty attitudes and perspectives that Shaughnessy describes persist today. With this in mind, by assigning Shaughnessy's introduction and the accompanying discussion board prompts (described later), and through the resulting class discussions, we give our instructors an opportunity to reflect on assumptions they might make about students' identities and intelligence based on their language use and writing strategies. Instructors are then able to challenge and reframe these assumptions, reconceiving developing writers as beginners rather than as deficient.

Linguistic diversity at our institution includes international and domestic nonnative English speakers as well as students whose language is influenced by the significant linguistic diversity within our state and students' homes, even if those students themselves are native speakers of English. Because our students may not have audible accents, there is a risk that our instructors might assume a predominantly monolingual student population. To counter this risk and to help instructors broaden their understandings of multilingualism, we assign Paul K. Matsuda's "The Myth of Linguistic Homogeneity." As Matsuda explains, this myth refers to "the tacit and widespread acceptance of the dominant image of composition students as native speakers of a privileged variety of English" (638). Through this reading and accompanying reading questions, we encourage instructors to think past the binary of native versus nonnative speaker in order to acknowledge the linguistic diversity of the region and our students' lives when considering the linguistic difference they might encounter in the classroom.

Finally, in addition to recognizing the linguistic diversity of their students, we want instructors to value difference in their students' writing. This requires a direct confrontation of common language ideologies, particularly standard language ideologies that position any language that is not "standard" as substandard. To uncover and address these ideologies, we ask instructors to read "The Educational System: Fixing the Message in Stone," a chapter from Rosina Lippi-Green's *English with an Accent*, which shows how a traditional classroom approach to teaching "standard" grammar can subordinate other language varieties. This reading describes the role of language ideologies in positioning one language variety as better than all others and questions the logic that suggests that, because some nonstandard language varieties are negatively valued by employers and other teachers, we should only teach students or value "standard" English. The focus on language ideologies allows us to challenge this privileging of a "standard" English as well as foster discussion on the easy slippage between judgments about language and judgments about language users—or, more specifically, the ways that writing ability and intelligence have been conflated and the assumptions that surround perceived errors in student writing. In order to fully support our teachers in valuing students and their language(s), we provide them with a mix of theoretical and practical support regarding language pedagogy.

*Teaching Grammar*

One of the struggles our instructors often face when working with students whose language use is considered nonstandard in some way is how to grade their work, particularly in relation to students more proficient in "standard" English. In "Let's Face It: Language Issues and the Writing Program Administrator," Matsuda shares a narrative in which a TA at his institution faces a similar challenge. To address the student's concerns, he uses S. Alan Cohen's concept of "instructional alignment," in which "'intended outcomes, instructional processes, and instructional assessment' correspond with one another" (Matsuda, "Let's" 143). Like Matsuda, we encourage instructors to evaluate their students according to what is covered in class and the program's student learning outcomes.

Additionally, rather than instructors taking a "norm-referenced assessment" approach in which they compare the writing of native and nonnative writers or more and less proficient students as they grade, we emphasize "criterion-referenced writing assessment, which assesses what individual writers can do in reference to the predetermined set of outcomes" (Matsuda, "Let's" 144). In this way, our instructors are able to recognize where their students are at the beginning of the semester and how they are progressing in relation to the program outcomes rather than where they are in comparison to their peers.

In addition, recognizing the expectation that institutional stakeholders have in terms of our students' ability to write "correctly," we ask instructors to reflectively address grammar in their courses. In fact, scholarship on second language writers, basic writers, and the role of "standard" English in composition courses convincingly argues that composition instructors should provide explicit grammar instruction as a way to facilitate second language acquisition or to help traditionally underrepresented students gain access to mainstream power through mastery of "standard" English. Therefore, we emphasize for instructors that—as with all writing instruction—grammar instruction should be contextualized (see Nunan). In line with Dana R. Ferris and John S. Hedgcock's idea that a writing class is not a grammar class, grammar instruction should be limited in scope and begin with an awareness of students' needs. We encourage instructors to use students' anonymized writing as examples of what can be improved and what is working well, when appropriate. Moreover, we explicitly discourage a "kill and drill" approach in which students complete fill-in-the-blank exercises that have no application to the writing students are doing in class. We also require instructors to make grammar worth no more than 5% of a student's assignment grade (or to treat grammar and usage as "ethos points" that can add onto or detract from an assignment grade), and only when explicit grammar instruction has been incorporated into the class. Finally, we dedicate class time to discussing effective grammar instruction and ask instructors to create and share their own lessons that incorporate these best practices, as described in greater detail below.

*Teaching Reading*

Similar to the ways we attempt to reframe instructors' assumptions about developmental writers and challenge deficit models of thinking, we also want our instructors to shift their perspectives about our students as readers. In "Reading Value: Student Choice in Reading Strategies," Karen Manarin reports on faculty's negative evaluations of students' reading practices and abilities. She states, for example, that faculty "complain that students can't or won't do the reading required for a course (Brost and Bradley 2006) and that they don't comprehend what they do read" (282). Then, in describing her own research regarding students' reading strategies, Manarin shows that, while students might not always choose effective strategies for approaching texts, they do read and engage with the material. We assign Manarin's essay to our instructors as a way of opening up conversations about common assumptions related to students as readers and to help instructors develop strategies for talking about reading with their students—including assigning a reading journal similar to the one Manarin describes.

In order to help instructors understand the benefit of explicit reading instruction, we assign Michael Bunn's "Motivation and Connection: Teaching Reading (and Writing) in the Composition Classroom," which argues that students' motivation to read increases when they understand how the reading relates to their writing assignments. Then, we allocate class discussion time to inform instructors that—much like best practices in writing instruction—the scholarship on teaching reading calls for a contextualized approach that acknowledges reading as an umbrella term for many related practices that vary by context, purpose, medium, and so on. By helping instructors to recognize these similarities, we help them to see that the approaches they use for teaching writing can help them teach reading as well.

*Metacognition*

In addition to asking instructors to reframe their beliefs about our students as language users, we also want our instructors to consider assumptions they might make based on certain kinds of student choices or attitudes. Like Susan A. Ambrose et al., we believe that "[educators] must recognize that students are not only intellectual but also social and emotional beings, and that these dimensions interact within the classroom climate to influence learning and performance" (156). In other words, students' prior experiences—and their responses to those experiences—influence their learning and behavior in our classrooms. Again and again, we find that our entering writing students do not like writing, in part, because they are afraid of writing and/or because they have been told they are not good writers. Therefore, we discuss with Stretch and Studio instructors how to help students build confidence as writers and readers by, for example, supporting students in their developing ability to reflect, self assess, and identify strategies for improvement. Finally, we devote the beginning of every class period to ice breakers and community-building activities in order to expand our instructors' resources for creating trust among their students and for identifying the many resources students bring to our writing classes.

*Course Assignments*

The course readings we assign for the Stretch and Studio Practicum provide the necessary theoretical context for the methods that instructors will employ with their students and, as Catherine Latterell notes, give instructors "a language for talking about teaching" (15). We further attempt to engage instructors in an uncovering of composition pedagogy (Reid) or in a "constructive interrogation" of teaching methods (Swyt 26) by asking instructors to respond to the course readings in two ways: (1) through written discussion board posts that inform class discussion and (2) by creating and presenting lesson plans or activities that enact the theory found in the readings.

The prompts for instructors' written discussion board posts are divided into three parts. First, under "before reading," we activate instructors' schemata by asking them to reflect on what knowledge and/or experience with the topic they bring to the reading. So, for example, in response to the reading by Ferris and Hedgcock cited above, we would pose the following example questions to instructors: "What is your feeling about how/whether grammar instruction should be included in the composition classroom? For example, how much instruction should be included? How often? What should the focus of this instruction be? What are you satisfied with in your approach to teaching grammar or how you have been taught grammar? What are you dissatisfied with?" Next, under "during reading," we ask instructors to highlight, annotate, or make note of any new understandings they come to as a result of the reading. Finally, for the "after reading" questions, we ask instructors to think of ways that their approach to teaching writing (or, in this example, approach to grammar instruction) in the Stretch and Studio classroom might be newly influenced by, changed, or reinforced by the reading. Instructors are then asked to respond to a peer's discussion post, so as to learn from each other's responses to the readings. The practicum participants' engagement with the course readings in this way aligns with the "CCCC Position Statement on the Preparation and Professional Development of Teachers of Writing," in which prospective and active teachers are encouraged to "write," "read and respond to the writings of [others]," "experience writing as a way of learning," "study research and other scholarly work in the humanistic discipline of the teaching of writing," and, in the case of L2 composition and metacognition, "study writing in relation to other disciplines." Additionally, through the format and design of these discussion posts, we model for instructors how they might engage their own students in the readings they assign for class.

In addition to the above posts, we also ask instructors to make connections between class readings and teaching in the Stretch and Studio program through the creation and presentation of original lesson plans for class activities that reflect their learning from the readings. The assigned lesson plans work to both develop instructors' pedagogical toolkits and capitalize on the diversity of our instructors (who come from a range of disciplines in the College of Arts and Sciences, with only a minority enrolled in the Rhetoric and Writing program). The largest assignments for the practicum (in terms of length and percentage of course grade) are the revision of first-year composition course materials (e.g., instructor and student calendars, assignment prompts and rubrics, reading selections and guiding questions, handouts, etc.) specifically for use in a Stretch or Studio course. By the end of the two-week practicum, all instructors create detailed materials for an entire semester of teaching either Stretch or Studio composition along with written reflections that explain how the class readings and discussions influenced their decisions when revising existing teaching materials to use in the Stretch or Studio course they are designing. We provide feedback on all of these materials, offering advice about how instructors can continue to tailor their materials for use in our program and praising instructors' thoughtful revisions and development as writing teachers.

## Critical Reflection

### Assessing the Stretch and Studio Practicum

After piloting the intensive, two-week Stretch and Studio Practicum in May 2013, and as we prepared to teach the course a second time in May 2014, we relied on a number of (IRB-approved) feedback measurements in order to assess the strengths of the practicum course. Our assessment was based on the following: (1) post-practicum anonymous online course evaluations, (2) post-practicum participant surveys, and (3) anonymous, online instructor surveys and face-to-face interviews following the practicum participants' first semester teaching.

It is clear from the data we collected from practicum participants in the summer and fall of 2013, following their first semester teaching in the Stretch and Studio program, that they were, overall, very pleased with the practicum course and how well it prepared them to teach specific areas of the curriculum. A common theme across all instructors' answers was that they had great success in creating a positive learning environment for their students and that they and their students felt a strong sense of community. Instructors additionally reported seeing increased fluency in their students' discussion of the rhetorical situation and discourse communities, as well as students' ability to reflect on how these concepts applied to their lives beyond the classroom. Finally, instructors noted improvement in their students' writing as well as increased student confidence, as college students and as writers. From this feedback, we could see, for example, that instructors understood from the readings on noncognitive factors the importance of creating a safe and engaging learning environment for students. And we saw this understanding put into practice when we observed these instructors' classes.

However, additional feedback revealed that some instructors were still struggling with the practical implications of the theory that informed the

Stretch and Studio Composition curriculum. In the 2013 post-practicum course evaluations and surveys, instructors noted that they would have liked more support with in-class language and writing activities, more information about the students they would be teaching, and guidance regarding better meeting this student population's diverse needs. These comments demonstrated for us that, on the one hand, following the practicum, instructors had philosophically moved away from deficit models of understanding Stretch and Studio students in order to (1) value students' linguistic diversity, (2) understand their students as not just intellectual but also as social and emotional beings whose class performance is influenced by factors beyond the classroom, and (3) recognize that these "nontraditional" or "at-risk" students may require more patience and guidance. On the other hand, what these comments also told us is that we needed to do a better job of helping our instructors put these newfound perspectives into practice in the classroom. Indeed, the most common feedback we received was participants' desire to have more practical support for teaching. This revealed to us the major tension underlying the teaching of this practicum course: How do we strike the right balance between theory and practice?

*Balancing Theory and Practice*

To better balance theory and practice, we revised the assignment that asks instructors to create and present original lesson plans. During our first time teaching the Stretch and Studio practicum, we did not allow enough time for this activity and treated it as a largely informal part of class discussion. Because the feedback we received specifically noted that instructors would have liked even more time devoted to this activity, we revised the curriculum to devote nearly 50% of class time to this endeavor and formalized our expectations for the lesson plans that instructors would create and share. The result of this change was phenomenal: Instructors took the assignment seriously and developed and shared creative lesson plans that thoughtfully engaged the readings for the day. For example, in response to Matsuda's "The Myth of Linguistic Homogeneity," one instructor designed a mini-profile assignment that asks students to investigate the diverse literacy practices and language attitudes of their peers. Used as an icebreaker at the beginning of a new semester, each student uses a set of questions to interview a peer in the class about their past experiences with language, reading, and writing, including how many languages or dialects they speak, what their first memories are in relation to reading and writing, and what their greatest challenges and hopes are related to language, reading and writing. The interviewer then reflects on how their peer's experiences are similar to and different from their own and then introduces their peer to the rest of the class through the mini profile they've written. This assignment serves to build community while also recognizing and valuing the diverse language and literacy backgrounds of the students in the class.

To further support instructor practice we added readings (e.g., Bunn "How to Read"; Fondas; Giles) to the course that instructors could assign to their own students in order to talk about reading, grammar, and reflection. Even if instructors choose not to use these readings in their Stretch or Studio courses, the readings provide instructors with model language they might use to make these topics meaningful and understandable to students.

*Understanding and Addressing Stretch and Studio Students' Needs*

In addition to requesting more practical support for teaching, instructors also indicated that they wanted to know more and earlier on about the student population they would be teaching in the Stretch program. Our instructors also voiced an interest in learning how to help their students develop "successful college habits" while also being responsive to students' individual needs. Instructors were particularly concerned about students' increasingly busy schedules. As one instructor noted, "[My students] work a lot. One student works 35 hours per week and is taking 15 credit hours. They're all taking a minimum of 12 credit hours while working. They're extremely busy." Additionally, student absences (sometimes due, for example, to Native American funeral rites) and late assignments (sometimes due to a lack of internet access in rural locations) were a concern. From these examples, it is clear that students' diverse needs can often challenge a writing program's more traditional classroom policies.

To address instructor feedback, the second time we taught the practicum we invited a number of partners from across campus whom we thought could help our instructors learn more about the demographics and needs of our students in our institutional context and the services available to support them. These campus partners include our Associate Vice President of Enrollment; the director of the College Enrichment and Outreach Programs, whose mission is to "ensure students an equal access to education and foster excellence through a collaboration of support services"; support staff from our campus Writing and Language Center, El Centro de la Raza, and the LGBTQ Resource Center; and academic support staff from the Lobo Center for Student-Athlete Success. These guest speakers offer important insights about our students' lives and experiences—many students are first-generation, from low-socioeconomic backgrounds, and/or students of color—and provide instructors with suggestions for using their services to help address students' needs. Inviting these speakers into our practicum also helps us emphasize to instructors that they are not alone in supporting Stretch and Studio students on the road to academic success. Moreover, we have adjusted our practicum curriculum to allow more time for talking with our instructors about how to be responsive to their students' needs, which may mean adopting or adjusting flexible classroom policies on tardiness, absences, and late work, for example. Although there are no magic solutions to the challenges identified by our instructors, we have welcomed these conversations into the practicum so we can all learn from one another and acknowledge the demands our instructors and their students face.

In conclusion, instructors' most recent comments on the May 2014 practicum participant survey and final course evaluation illustrate their positive responses to the curriculum changes we made as described above. Comments ranged from this being the "best graduate course" the participant had taken to appreciating the "deeper understanding of the community [they] teach in." Additionally, instructors valued the strong emphasis on "creative lesson planning skills" and "the level of creative and practical output" that they said helped them to "create a strong Stretch course." Instructors also used the post-stretch-instruction survey as a chance to express how much they appreciated their students and valued teaching in the program. As one instructor wrote, "I don't know if there are words to express what a joy it is to teach Stretch. It's an honor and a pleasure to work with these amazing students and, more than anything, to reassure them that their voice is heard." Frankly, we couldn't agree more.

## Notes

1. The authors contributed equally in the writing of this article.
2. While we use the term "basic writing" when referencing the scholarship on beginning or developing writers, we prefer the term "developing writers" to refer to our students.
3. The New Mexico Legislative Lottery Scholarships, funded by the state lottery, cover a percentage of tuition at any public college within the state for students who graduated from a New Mexico high school or received a GED.

## Works Cited

Ambrose, Susan A., et al. *How Learning Works: Seven Research-Based Principles for Smart Teaching*. Hoboken: Wiley, 2010. 153-87. Print.

Bean, John C. *Engaging Ideas: The Professor's Guide to Integrating Writing, Critical Thinking, and Active Learning in the Classroom*. 2nd ed. Hoboken: Jossey-Bass, 2011. Print.

Bunn, Michael. "How to Read Like a Writer." *Writing Spaces: Readings on Writing*. Ed. Charles Lowe and Pavel Zemliansky. Vol. 2. Anderson: Parlor, 2011. 71-86. Web. 20 Jan. 2015. <http://writingspaces.org/bunn--how-to-read-like-a-writer>.

---. "Motivation and Connection: Teaching Reading (and Writing) in the Composition Classroom." *CCC* 64.3 (2013): 496-516. *NCTE*. Web. 12 Feb. 2015.

Canagarajah, A. Suresh. "The Place of World Englishes in Composition: Pluralization Continued." *CCC* 57.4 (2006): 586-619. *JSTOR*. Web. 1 Apr. 2015.

"CCCC Position Statement on the Preparation and Professional Development of Teachers of Writing." *NCTE.org*. NCTE, 2015. Web. 1 Apr. 2015. <http://www.ncte.org/cccc/resources/positions/statementonprep>.

Devitt, Amy J., et al. "Materiality and Genre in the Study of Discourse Communities." *College English* 65.5 (2003): 541-58. *JSTOR*. Web. 1 Apr. 2015.

Dirk, Kerry. "Navigating Genres." *Writing Spaces: Readings on Writing*. Ed. Charles Lowe and Pavel Zemliansky. Vol. 1. Anderson: Parlor, 2010. 249-62. Web. 1 Apr. 2015. <http://writingspaces.org/essays/navigating-genres>.

Ferris, Dana R., and John S. Hedgcock. "Chapter 8: Improving Accuracy in Student Writing: Error Treatment in the Composition Class." *Teaching L2 Composition: Purpose, Process, And Practice*. 3rd ed. New York: Routledge, 2014. 279-308. Print.

Fondas, Nanette. "Study: You Really Can 'Work Smarter, Not Harder.'" *The Atlantic*. Atlantic Monthly Group, 18 May 2014. Web. 19 May 2014. <https://www.theatlantic.com/education/archive/2014/05/study-you-really-can-work-smarter-not-harder/370819/>.

Giles, Sandra L. "Reflective Writing and the Revision Process: What Were You Thinking?" *Writing Spaces: Readings on Writing*. Ed. Charles Lowe and Pavel Zemliansky. Vol. 1. Anderson: Parlor, 2010. 191-204. Web. 1 Apr. 2015. <http://writingspaces.org/essays/reflective-writing-and-the-revision>.

Glau, Gregory R. "Stretch Courses, WPA-CompPile Research Bibliographies, No. 2." *WPA-CompPile Research Bibliographies* (2010): 1-4. Web. 12 Feb. 2015. <http://comppile.org/wpa/bibliographies/Glau.pdf>.

Horner, Bruce, et al. "Opinion: Language Difference in Writing: Toward a Translingual Approach." *College English* 73.3 (2011): 303-21. <http://ir.library.louisville.edu/cgi/viewcontent.cgi?article=1065&context=faculty>.

Lalicker, William B. "A Basic Introduction to Basic Writing Program Structures: A Baseline and Five Alternatives." *BWe: Basic Writing e-Journal* 1.2 (1999): n. pag. Web. 15 Feb. 2015. <https://bwe.ccny.cuny.edu/Issue%201.2.html>.

Latterell, Catherine. "Training the Workforce: An Overview of GTA Education Curricula." *WPA: Writing Program Administration* 19.3 (1996): 7-23. <http://wpacouncil.org/archives/19n3/19n3latterell.pdf>.

Lippi-Green, Rosina. "The Educational System: Fixing the Message in Stone." *English with an Accent: Language, Ideology, and Discrimination in the United States*. 2nd ed. New York: Routledge, 2012. 78-100. Print.

Manarin, Karen. "Reading Value: Student Choice in Reading Strategies." *Pedagogy* 12.2 (2012): 281-97. Web. 1 Apr. 2015. <https://provost.uni.edu/sites/default/files/documents/reading_value_0.pdf>.

Matsuda, Paul Kei. "Let's Face It: Language Issues and the Writing Program Administrator." *WPA: Writing Program Administration* 36.1 (2012): 141-63. Print.

---. "The Myth Of Linguistic Homogeneity in U.S. College Composition." *College English* 68.6 (2006): 637-51. *JSTOR*. Web. 20 Jan. 2015.

Nunan, David. "Teaching Grammar in Context." *ELT Journal* 52.2 (1998): 101-09. *ERIC*. Web. 1 Apr 2015.

Perryman-Clark, Staci M., David Kirkland, and Austin Jackson, eds. *Students' Right to Their Own Language: A Critical Sourcebook*. Boston: Bedford/St. Martins, 2015. Print.

Reid, E. Shelley. "Uncoverage in Composition Pedagogy." *Composition Studies* 32.1 (2004): 15-34. Web. 1 Apr. 2015. <https://www.uc.edu/content/dam/uc/journals/composition-studies/docs/backissues/32-1/Reid.pdf>.

Shaughnessy, Mina P. "Introduction to Errors and Expectations: A Guide for the Teachers of Basic Writing." *The Norton Book of Composition Studies*. Ed. Susan Miller. New York: Norton, 2009. 387-96. Print.

Smitherman, Geneva, and Victor Villanueva, eds. *Language Diversity in the Classroom: From Intention to Practice*. Urbana: NCTE, 2003. Print.

Swyt, Wendy. "Teacher Training in the Contact Zone." *WPA: Writing Program Administration* 19.3 (1996): 24-35. <http://wpacouncil.org/archives/19n3/19n3swyt.pdf>.

Yancey, Kathleen Blake. *Reflection in the Writing Classroom*. Logan: Utah State UP, 1998. Print.

# English 540: Teaching Stretch and Studio Composition Practicum

Dr. Beth Davila and Dr. Cristyn L. Elder
University of New Mexico
(Offered during the two-week May Intersession,
between spring and summer semesters)

*Course Overview*

This course will prepare you to teach Stretch and Studio Composition at UNM by introducing you to relevant theory and pedagogy in the areas of basic writing, multilingual writing, metacognition, and reading instruction.

While the English 537: Teaching Composition Practicum aims to give you a broad understanding of teaching composition using a genre approach, this course asks you to consider how to tailor your pedagogy for students who may require additional layers of support. We will encourage you to, above all else, view your students' existing skills and literacies as resources that can be built upon in your class. And, of course, we will support you in developing a course that will promote your students' progress toward our student learning outcomes.

*Student Learning Outcomes (SLOs)*

In this course you will:
- become familiar with the theory and pedagogy of basic writing, multilingual writers, metacognition, and reading instruction;
- develop best practices in writing instruction for students who have been traditionally marginalized in higher education;
- recognize students' existing skills and literacies as resources and strengths that can be built upon; and
- develop activities and assignments to help Stretch and Studio students progress toward and reflect on the learning outcomes for first year composition.

*Required Texts and Materials*

Ambrose, Susan A., et al. "Chapter 6: Why Do Student Development and Course Climate Matter for Student Learning?" *How Learning Works: Seven Research-Based Principles for Smart Teaching*. Hoboken: Wiley, 2010. 153-87. Print.

---. "Chapter 7: How Do Students Become Self-Directed Learners?" *How Learning Works: Seven Research-Based Principles for Smart Teaching*. Hoboken: Wiley, 2010. 188-216. Print.

Bishop, Wendy. "Helping Peer Writing Groups Succeed." *Teaching Lives: Essays and Stories*. Logan: Utah State UP, 1997. 14-24. Print.

Bunn, Michael. "How to Read Like a Writer." *Writing Spaces: Reading on Writing.* Ed. Charles Lowe and Pavel Zemliansky. Vol. 2. Anderson: Parlor, 2011. 71-86. Web. 20 Jan. 2015. <https://www.saylor.org/site/wp-content/uploads/2013/08/K12ELA006-2.1.1-HowToRead.pdf>.

---. "Motivation And Connection: Teaching Reading (and Writing) in the Composition Classroom." *CCC* 64.3 (2013): 496-516. Web. 20 Jan. 2015. <https://www.wilfridlaurier.ca/documents/55209/Reading_and_writing_-_Bunn_2013_CCC_Feb.pdf>.

Ferris, Dana R. and John S. Hedgcock. J. S. "Chapter 7: Response to Student Writing: Issues and Options for Giving and Facilitating Feedback." *Teaching L2 Composition: Purpose, Process, And Practice.* 3rd ed. New York: Routledge, 2014. 237-78. Print.

---"Chapter 8: Improving Accuracy in Student Writing: Error Treatment in the Composition Class." *Teaching L2 Composition: Purpose, Process, And Practice.* 3rd ed. New York: Routledge, 2014. 279-308. Print.

Fondas, Nanette. "Study: You Really Can 'Work Smarter, Not Harder.'" *The Atlantic.* Atlantic Monthly Group, 18 May 2014. Web. 19 May 2014. <https://www.theatlantic.com/education/archive/2014/05/study-you-really-can-work-smarter-not-harder/370819/>.

Glau, Greg. "Stretch at 10: A Progress Report on Arizona State University's Stretch Program." *Journal of Basic Writing* 26.2 (2007): 30-48. *JSTOR.* Web. 20 Jan. 2015.

Goldstein, Lynn. "Questions and Answers about Teacher Written Commentary and Student Revision: Teachers and Students Working Together." *Journal of Second Language Writing* 13 (2004): 63-80. *SCIENCEDIRECT.* Web. 20 Jan. 2015.

Grego, Rhonda, and Nancy Thompson. "Repositioning Remediation: Renegotiating Composition's Work in the Academy." *CCC* 47.1 (1996): 62-84. *JSTOR.* Web. 20 Jan. 2015.

Hess, Mickey. "Ch 3: Composing Multimodal Assignments." *Multimodal Composition.* Ed. Cynthia L. Selfe. New York: Hampton, 2007. 29-37. Print.

Holschuh, Jodi Patrick, and Eric J. Paulson. "The Terrain of College Developmental Reading." *CRLA.net.* The Coll. Reading and Learning Assoc., July 2013. Web. 20 Jan. 2015. <http://fliphtml5.com/acng/gads>.

Hull, Glynda, et al. "Remediation as Social Construct: Perspectives From an Analysis of Classroom Discourse." *CCC* 42.3 (1991): 299-329. Web. 20 Jan. 2015. <http://www.hullresearchgroup.info/wp-content/uploads/2011/12/Remediation-as-Social-Construct.pdf>.

Humes, Edward. "Introduction." *Garbology: Our Dirty Love Affair with Trash.* New York: Penguin, 2012. Print.

Kerschbaum, Stephanie. L. "Avoiding the Difference Fixation: Identity Categories, Markers of Difference, and the Teaching of Writing." *CCC* 63.4 (2012): 616-44. Web. 20 Jan. 2015. <http://www.spelman.edu/docs/teachingrrc/avoiding-the-difference-fixation-.pdf>.

Lippi-Green, Rosina. "The Educational System: Fixing the Message in Stone." *English with an Accent: Language, Ideology, and Discrimination in the United States*. 2nd ed. New York: Routledge, 2012. 78-100. Print.

Manarin, Karen. "Reading Value: Student Choice in Reading Strategies." *Pedagogy* 12.2 (2012): 281-97. Web. 20 Jan. 2015. <https://provost.uni.edu/sites/default/files/documents/reading_value_0.pdf>.

Matsuda, Paul Kei. "The Myth Of Linguistic Homogeneity in U.S. College Composition." *College English* 68.6 (2006): 637-51. *JSTOR*. Web. 20 Jan. 2015.

Myhill, Debra A., Susan M. Jones, Helen Lines, and Annabel Watson. "Re-thinking Grammar: The Impact of Embedded Grammar Teaching on Students' Writing and Students' Metalinguistic Understanding." *Research Papers in Education* 27.2 (2012): 139-66. Web. 20 Jan. 2015. <https://ore.exeter.ac.uk/repository/bitstream/handle/10036/4479/2012Re-thinkingGrammarRPiE.pdf?sequence=5&isAllowed=y>.

Navarre Cleary, Michelle. "The Wrong Way to Teach Grammar." *The Atlantic*. Atlantic Monthly Group, 25 Feb. 2014. Web. 20 Jan. 2015. <https://www.theatlantic.com/education/archive/2014/02/the-wrong-way-to-teach-grammar/284014/ >.

Rose, Mike. "The Language of Exclusion: Writing Instruction at the University." *College English* 47.4 (1985): 341-59. Web. 20 Jan. 2015. <https://vaia110spring11.qwriting.qc.cuny.edu/files/2011/01/Mike-Rose_The-Language-of-Exclusion.pdf>.

Shaughnessy, Mina P. "Introduction to Errors and Expectations: A Guide for the Teachers of Basic Writing." *The Norton Book of Composition Studies*. Ed. Susan Miller. New York: Norton, 2009. 387-96. Print.

Takayoshi, Pamela, and Cynthia L. Selfe. "Ch 1: Thinking about Multimodality." *Multimodal Composition*. Ed. Cynthia L. Selfe. New York: Hampton, 2007. 1-12. Print.

Yancey, Kathleen Blake. "Getting beyond Exhaustion: Reflection, Self-Assessment, and Learning." *The Clearing House* 72.1 (1998): 13-17. Print.

*Course Requirements*

The assignments for this course are designed to set you up for teaching Stretch and Studio Composition. As such you will

- Write assignments, rubrics, lesson plans, and activities.
- Adapt three first-year composition sequences (or units) for use in Stretch and Studio classes and write reflective letters to describe the revisions you make.
- Present mini-lessons to your peers on daily activities you may use in your Stretch or Studio class, based on our class readings.

## Grades

You will be graded on the following:

| Assignments | % | Description |
|---|---|---|
| Readings/Class Discussions | 10 | You will post your reading responses to Blackboard Learn. As this is a two-week intersession course, it will be very fast-paced. You are expected to complete daily reading assignments and activities and come to class prepared. |
| Sequence 1*<br>Sequence 2<br>Sequence 3 | 20<br>20<br>20 | Rhetorical Situation: The Core Writing program at the University of New Mexico has just launched the new Stretch and Studio Composition courses and wants to provide instructors with model sequences that fully integrate the SLOs while attending to the unique needs of Stretch and Studio students. As one of the first instructors of these courses, you have been asked to make your materials as detailed and developed as possible so other instructors can use them without much adaptation.<br><br>Task: Adapt a calendar and materials for the first sequence of your Stretch and/or Studio course. Your sequence should include the following elements: (1) a reflective letter, (2) writing prompts (two write-to-learn prompts and one formal writing prompt) and corresponding rubrics, and (3) calendar of writing assignments and other activities (including summary of mini-lecture, class discussion, group work, peer review, presentations, etc.).<br><br>Evaluation: Each of the three sequences will be evaluated according to the following: (1) the clear articulation in your reflective letter of the choices you made in designing/adapting each course sequence and how well the sequence is likely to address and support students' needs as they work toward the Stretch and Studio SLOs, (2) the inclusion of all required elements of the sequence listed in the Sequence assignment prompt, (3) an explanation of how the Stretch and Studio SLOs will be addressed in each sequence, and (4) bonus ethos points for the professional presentation of your materials. |

| Assignments | % | Description |
|---|---|---|
| Mini Lesson 1*  Mini Lesson 2 | 15  15 | Rhetorical Situation: You are enrolled in the 540 Stretch and Studio Composition Practicum at UNM with other instructors from a range of disciplines who have varying levels of teaching experience. One aspect you have in common is that all of you will be teaching Stretch and/or Studio for the first time. Thus, you will create two lesson plans (each worth 15%) over the course of the two weeks to share with your colleagues that relate to that day's course readings. In 15 minutes, you will give an overview of the lesson plan and model an activity from that lesson plan for your peers. You should prepare an activity that is related to the readings you have done for the day's class (i.e., grammar, multilingual students, metacognition, reflection, and/or reading). Then, you should plan on leading the activity for the class, allowing time for a couple of minutes of questions.  Task: On Blackboard Learn, post to the Discussion Board (for your peers) and under Assignments (to receive a grade) a detailed description of the activity, including the materials needed, step-by-step instructions for the teacher (and students) on how to facilitate the activity, a timeline that shows how long each step is expected to take, and the student learning outcomes addressed by the activity.  Evaluation: This assignment will be evaluated according to the level of detail you have provided in order to allow an instructor to lead the activity in her own class without additional work as well as how effective and engaging the activity is in working towards the student learning outcomes for Stretch and Studio composition. |
| Total | 100 | |

*You will be given a separate handout that explains in detail the expectations for each of these assignments.

## Course Calendar

| | Date | In-class Topic | Reading Due | Assignments Due |
|---|---|---|---|---|
| Week #1 | M | Instructor and student introductions<br>Review of course syllabus<br>College Enrichment and Outreach Programs (ceop.unm.edu)<br>Writing and Language Center (caps.unm.edu/programs/writing-and-language-center/)<br>Student demographics presentation by Vice President of Enrollment | All read:<br>UNM Core Writing SLO Handbook<br>Glau (2007)<br>Grego and Thompson (1996) | |
| | T | Basic writing | All read:<br>Shaughnessy (2009)<br><br>One article per group:<br>Rose (1985)<br>Kerschbaum (2012)<br>Hull et al. (1991)<br>Bishop (1997) | Group lesson plan or activity posted to Learn |
| | W | Multilingual writers | All read:<br>Matsuda (2006)<br>Goldstein (2004)<br>Ferris and Hedgcock (2014): Ch. 7 and 8 | Reading questions posted to Learn<br><br>Mini Lessons |
| | Th | Grammar<br>Language attitudes | All read:<br>Lippi-Green (2012)<br>Myhill et al. (2012)<br>Navarre Cleary (2014) | Mini Lessons |
| | F | No class. Work due online. | | Adapted Sequence #1 plus reflective cover letter; due at 11:59pm |

|  | Date | In-class Topic | Reading Due | Assignments Due |
|---|---|---|---|---|
| Week #2 | M | No class. Memorial Day. | | |
| | T | Multimodal composition<br>Lobo Common Reading Experience<br>Celebration of Student Writing | All read:<br>Takayoshi & Selfe (2007)<br>Hess (2007)<br>Humes (2012) | Adapted Sequence #2 plus reflective cover letter due online at 11:59pm |
| | W | Metacognition/reflection | All read:<br>Ambrose et al. (2010) Ch. 6 & 7<br>Yancey (1998)<br>Fondas (2014) | Mini Lessons |
| | Th | Reading | All read:<br>Manarin (2012)<br>Bunn (2013)<br>Bunn (2011)<br>Holschuh & Paulson (2013) | Reading questions posted to Learn<br><br>Mini Lessons |
| | F | Representatives from athletics<br>Sequence #3 | | Adapted Sequence #3 plus reflective cover letter due online at 11:59pm |

# Spies Like Us: Gamifying the Composition Classroom and Breaking the Academic Code

Jessica E. Slentz, Kristin E. Kondrlik, and Michelle Lyons-McFarland

## Course Description

English 150: Expository Writing is an undergraduate course in expository and research writing offered by special partnership to both the students of Case Western Reserve University (CWRU) and the students of the Cleveland Institute of Music (CIM). English instructors from CWRU provide writing instruction to CIM students as a part of their school's general curriculum, and CWRU students may also enroll in the course as an elective. The course provides student writers experience in the critical reading and writing practices required for engaging with and producing well-researched, well-organized, well-argued, and stylistically complex academic prose. The CWRU course catalog describes English 150 as "requir[ing] substantial drafting and revising of written work." The overall topics, readings, and writing assignments vary from semester to semester, based on the discretion of the instructor. English 150 is a requirement for CIM students who have not previously completed either an Advanced Placement (AP) requirement or college equivalent course. It is not part of a first year writing sequence, but may be preceded by English 148, a foundational English writing course, depending on a student's TOEFL scores upon admission. For CWRU students who have their writing requirements fulfilled in interdisciplinary general education seminar courses through the SAGES program, English 150 is an elective offering more focused attention on expository writing and can be taken at any time in their undergraduate career.

The course we describe here arose from a composition bridge course we designed and collaboratively taught as part of CWRU's Emerging Scholars Program, a six-week intensive summer program in academic writing, calculus, and study skills offered to select first-year students matriculating from under-performing high schools in the surrounding area. At the conclusion of that summer course, we, all three graduate instructors in the English Department at the time, were awarded an Enriching Curricula Grant from CWRU's Baker-Nord Center for the Humanities to turn this course into a semester-long composition course for a multilingual classroom. We then received permission from the English department to teach this section of English 150 collaboratively.

## Institutional Context

While they consist of distinct student populations, the two universities served by this course, CWRU and CIM, share attributes that present the instructors of English 150 with similar challenges. First, as CWRU is a research university whose primary focus is on the sciences and engineering, CWRU's students are often vocationally focused and sometimes view writing and writing instruction as less important parts of their university or post-university lives. All CWRU students follow a general education curriculum termed the Seminar Approach to General Education and Scholarship (SAGES), a writing across the curriculum (WAC) program that integrates traditional composition pedagogy with themed courses spanning a wide range of disciplines and capstone courses in a student's major. CWRU students in English 150, therefore, take it as an elective, rather than a required composition course, meaning that it is sometimes secondary to their major or required coursework. Like the career-minded students of CWRU, the students at CIM, an international music conservatory, train in a rigorous and competitive program for positions in music performance and related fields. CIM students, therefore, like CWRU students, sometimes view proficiency in "writing" and "reading" as secondary to the myriad other skills they are expected to master during their post-secondary education. In English 150, therefore, instructors must navigate the teaching of writing with students whose vocational aspirations sometimes lack transparent links to their undergraduate writing experiences.

Beyond perceived lack of relevance, English 150 presents an additional challenge in that it serves L1 and L2 students at various levels of proficiency. The course, focused on academic and research writing, is designed to serve students who have already taken a composition course or who have AP credit in college writing; CIM students, unless excused by AP credit, will have taken an introduction to composition course (English 148), and students from CWRU will have taken at least one semester of writing instruction under the SAGES program. Even with a semester-long course as a prerequisite, however, students in English 150 have often had only limited exposure to academic English. Both CWRU and CIM enroll a significant proportion of international students for whom English is a second or even third language; ten percent of CWRU's undergraduate student body in the academic year 2014-2015 consisted of international students, while at CIM the proportion was twenty-five percent. In addition, students may take the course at any stage in their academic career; therefore, a typical ENG 150 class includes students who have been writing at a university level for some time next to students with a single semester of composition instruction. Our section of English 150 presented us with these two scenarios, as our class was evenly split between L1 and L2 writers and had a mixed population of second semester first-year students and more advanced writers.

This unique mixture of students offers great advantages for students and composition instructors, as well as challenges. The diversity of experience, academic background, and language proficiency in the English 150 classroom creates a dynamic range of perspectives beneficial to class discussions and to the cultivation of students' understanding of the material. Such wide variation in student writing levels and college experience, however, can make it challenging to provide students with consistent, intensive instruction and feedback on their work throughout the semester, even without the difficulties of instruction produced by language barriers. In a class of students who may have preconceived notions about the relevance of the course for their academic and professional futures, keeping a diverse set of students interested and invested in the course material can be a significant hurdle for instructors.

## Theoretical Rationale

Working to address the challenges presented by English 150 through collaborative teaching, we designed a course that would both offer resistant students greater investment in their writing processes and provide multilingual students with individualized instruction and extensive feedback. We focused on several shared elements of our personal teaching philosophies, namely: the conviction, most clearly articulated by Kathleen Blake Yancey (1998; Smith and Yancey), that self-reflection is an integral part of the writing classroom; a dedication to the importance of collaborative learning and peer review, particularly for multicultural students (Ferris and Hedgcock); and the belief that integrating gaming and other multiliteracies into writing instruction can afford a learning experience that promotes transfer and reflection, often more effectively than traditional teaching strategies (Ellington, Fowlie, and Gordon; Gee). To this end, we created a "gamified" course curriculum. By a gamified course, we mean a course design that draws on the cooperative and competitive aspects of games, augmenting more traditional pedagogy with the aim of making the practices of academic writing more accessible to students. At its heart, a game is a localized instance of "overt competition" (Ellington, Fowlie, and Gordon 1) with a set of rules designed to govern the interactions, choices and risks players may take. These rules support potential results and rewards, while the process of working toward those goals can inculcate valuable skills and habits and enable players to form significant relationships with others. We envisioned our gamified classroom as a means to interact more closely with our students in order to address their diverse needs directly, and as a space in which students could teach and learn from each other, thus developing their writing practices through collaboration with peers.

Gamifying a curriculum poses a number of challenges for both instructors and students, as traditional pedagogical methods and expectations are modified to create a more active and decentered classroom. As writing instructors, our aim in gamifying in this composition course was to foreground the course's pedagogical goals by placing those goals within the context of an overarching role-playing scenario. Our iteration of English 150, titled "Spies Like Us," used themes of espionage and government intelligence to actively engage students with the processes, genres, and rhetorical strategies involved in academic writing. We integrated game elements, course readings, and low-risk writing exercises with the higher-risk expository assignments to create a cohesive learning experience for our students.

Research on the use of games in pedagogy has indicated that games can create a more engaging, active learning environment. Since the 1960s, researchers have viewed games as effective tools to cultivate students' "powers of application, analysis, synthesis and evaluation" (Ellington, Fowlie, and Gordon 8). Games access multiple levels of cognition and, in doing so, cater to a broader range of learning styles than many traditional teaching approaches. The value of games as educational tools within primary and early childhood education is undisputed today; however, this view of games has not been widely embraced within post-secondary education until much more recently. With the acceptance of game theory as a science and the rise of contemporary work in new media, new literacy studies, digital rhetoric and multimodal composition, games are finally receiving much-deserved attention in post-secondary education.

Because much of the scholarship on games in the composition classroom is being performed by scholars of new media, new literacy studies, multimodal composition, and digital rhetoric, the focus of this research trends toward digital and video gaming and simulation (Alexander; Gee; Kress; Sabatino; Selfe and Hawisher). However, regardless of whether they are carried out in digital environments, games possess the ability to increase students' engagement and enjoyment in the classroom (Bunce, Herbert, and Collins 201). This point is especially poignant for a course such as English 150, given the diversity of students' language experiences, educational backgrounds, institutional identities, and levels of investment (Pillay and James). Through simulation, identity exploration, teamwork, continuous feedback, and intertextual reading and writing, games can promote students' acquisition and retention of the various literacy practices that we ask our students to navigate in composition courses (Alexander 55). These practices can include genre and audience awareness, multicultural literacy, collaborative writing, critical reflection, and problem solving (Sabatino 43), all of which are practices we focused on in this course.

The game portion of our course was composed of two distinct elements: an overarching role-playing scenario, in which the students were positioned as spies-in-training, and a series of targeted competitions, which we referred to as "training exercises" and designed to reinforce a particular lesson or practice. We linked the course thematically through readings on intelligence work in contemporary politics and popular culture. Using vocabulary from the government intelligence field, we compared the process and genres of academic writing to the work of spies, highlighting how both endeavors require careful attention to textual analysis, source evaluation, audience awareness, the development of sound arguments, and organized, clear communication. On the first day of class, we set up the scenario of class-as-spy-academy by situating the students as newly minted spies embarking on the process of training to become master intelligence operatives. First, we divided the students into three teams. We administered a diagnostic essay in the first week of class that asked students to reflect on their skills and background with academic writing. After reading and evaluating these essays, we created teams of students that offered diversity in language background, experience with academic writing, class level, and school affiliation. We then assigned an instructor as the team leader. Students participated in the training exercises as teams, competing in targeted activities each week of the semester. We also enacted the role-playing aspect by explicitly linking intelligence work and academic writing in the formal essay assignments. We positioned these sequenced assignments as "missions" for which the students were training. Within this frame, the summary and response essay became the "Brief," the review essay became an exercise in "Reconnaissance," and the final essay became a "White Paper." For each mission students received feedback on their individual essay drafts from their other team members in a peer review session and from their team leaders in one-on-one consultations.

To further enhance the role-playing experience of the classroom, we gave students a comprehensive "skills and statistics" game sheet, which borrowed from the language of intelligence. This handout broke down academic writing and the processes involved into easily identifiable areas with tangible vocabulary that students could learn and take forward in their academic careers. We laminated these "skill sheets" for easy editing with a wet-erase marker, and required students to track their progress (see appendix A). The sheet included five categories of "statistics" (decryption, analysis, performance, insight, and process), which were further divided into global and local writing "skills" (such as decoding, audience awareness, transitions, thesis statements, and revision). When students received five skill points in any of the larger statistics categories, they "leveled up" in that category. The points for each category never "maxed out," meaning that students could "level up" infinitely. Rather than having students become a "master" of a given category, we wanted to demonstrate to students that even the most polished and experienced writers continue to work on and improve the different aspects of their writing, even after they become "experts."

We also used points and skill sheets to foreground self-reflection. On the first day of class, we gave students a starting budget of points to assign to the categories in which they felt they were particularly adept. In other words, we asked them to self-assess their writing strengths, weaknesses, and initial goals. Over the course of the semester, we continuously used the skill sheets and points system to promote reflection and self-assessment. We did so in order to provide real weight to the points students earned over the course of the semester; rather than implementing points merely for fun or without a purpose, therefore, we used points as a means of facilitating conversation with students about their development as writers.

The skill point system gave us a method to transform grades and feedback into a system of positive reinforcement by approaching writing as a complex practice, rather than working backwards from beginning writers' notions of a "perfect" text. By experiencing the writing process broken down into transparent skills, students were able to evaluate and articulate their own strengths and challenges and track how their writing practices grew and evolved over the course of the semester. Students also earned skill points for their formal essays ("missions"), which were awarded in whatever category their instructor chose. Regardless of the grade the student received on the assignment, each essay earned four skill points. By awarding a standard number of skill points to each essay, the instructor was able to focus on what the student did well, even if the text needed significant improvement. This process also allowed a student to track her progress from assignment to assignment. For example, if by the third mission, a student had received many points in the analysis category but few in the performance category, then she could see that in her next mission she could benefit by spending a greater amount of time on local concerns and proofreading than in previous assignments.

Skill points were also an integral part of the training exercises, or team competitions. We designed each training exercise to focus on a particular writing practice or writing concern. As part of the Enriching Curricula Grant that made this class possible, we designed and printed a game board (see appendix B) that allowed us to flag which skills were being covered by a given exercise. This game board allowed each team to see their progress over the course of the semester by tracking movable game pieces along the board. The spy team that most successfully completed the exercise received bonus points for the specific skills emphasized in that day's activity, which also translated back to their individual skills sheets. At the end of the semester, the winning team received a small prize. We designed the skill points and training exercises to not only afford students a way to continuously reflect on their work and progress, but also give a friendly, competitive edge to the work of the course.

Key to the success of our gamified classroom was a continued focus on the collaboration and teamwork of both the instructors and students. Collaboration requires that students learn to adapt to new discourse communities and communicate across disciplines, languages, and cultures. When students become a cohesive group, what Kenneth Bruffee calls a new "transitional community," they "nest that transitional community in the considerably larger discourse community of the class as a whole" (46). Small groups, when focused on a particular goal and situated within a particular theme, can encourage students to work together to strengthen both their collective understanding of the course goals and materials and to assist each other in their own personal development as writers.

To foster solidarity within the small groups, we did as Kathleen Hunzer suggests and kept the groups stable throughout the semester. Having students work repeatedly in consistent groups "strengthen[s] the students' interpersonal skills as well as their trust in their peers" (Hunzer 73), which then allows them to build a greater sense of camaraderie (67) and accountability (68) than they would by completing a one-off group assignment. We used small group exercises and facilitated work with collaborative writing platforms such as Google Docs. Doing so allowed our students to gain valuable experience in productive peer-review and collaborative research and writing, which are important practices for students to develop, as writing done outside the academy is often collaborative (Bruffee xiii). We further reinforced the importance of collaboration throughout the course, using Gerald Graff and Cathy Birkenstein's *They Say/I Say: The Moves That Matter in Academic Writing* to discuss how successful academic writing is by nature a collaborative conversation (Bruffee 54), and also by highlighting the role that collaboration plays in the intelligence field.

In addition to the focus on collaboration, we designed this course with several different ways for the students to practice self-reflection throughout the semester. We strongly believe, as Kathleen Yancey has posited, that self-reflection is key both to the development of a successful writing practice, as "students begin to know their own processes" (Yancey 27), and to the transfer of writing practices from the composition classroom to students' writing within their respective disciplines. Taking "reflection" to mean both "a looking forward to goals we might attain, as well as a casting backward to see where we have been" (Yancey 6), we asked students to engage in this practice from the very first day of class, through not only the self-assignment of skill points, but also identifying areas for improvement and setting personal goals for the course. We used the skill sheets to promote continual reflection, and we met with students to discuss any modifications they wanted to make to these goals. In addition, we organized due dates and peer reviews to facilitate a pattern of reflection and revision. At the close of the semester, we assigned a brief individual reflection paper asking students to articulate their evolution as writers over the semester by identifying specific areas of improvement, posing questions about their own processes, and making plans for approaching writing in future courses.

## Critical Reflection

When we envisioned the overall structure of this gamified course, it was clear how the various game elements complemented each other, as well as the course outcomes. In practice, navigating these different elements sometimes felt unwieldy. Because we feel that several aspects of the game were particularly successful, we would retool our approach in a future iteration of this course to bring those elements to the forefront.

The most effective game element in this course was, by far, the skill sheets. The skill sheets allowed students to practice ongoing critical self-reflection, create strategic revision plans, and set clear goals for future assignments and courses. One CIM student was pleased when, at the end of the semester, she understood more clearly how to make her "opinion stronger" in argumentative writing, and how to express her thoughts in a more organized way. During a one-on-one conference at the end of the semester, she expressed excitement over being able to take these new abilities into other classes and to continue to improve in areas in which she felt less confident. The skill sheets were integral to her self-reflection and acquisition of the vocabulary of academic writing. While all of our students benefited from this tool, the skill sheets resonated most strongly with our L2 students. When we asked students at the beginning of the semester which aspects of their writing they wished to improve, a significant portion of our L2 students simply said "grammar." Over time, the self-assessment facilitated by the skill sheets allowed our students to take up the specific terminology of expository writing and articulate not only areas for further improvement, but also what they had learned, a practice that facilitates knowledge transfer from the composition classroom to a student's other courses (Yancey 56).

A major component of the success of the skill sheets was their utility in giving direction to team leaders' interactions with students during individual conferences. We paired the skill sheets with one-on-one meetings and individualized feedback in order to observe and facilitate progress towards each student's personal writing goals. Students met with their team leader/instructor to discuss a draft or outline of an essay assignment, or mission, the week before each was due. These sessions provided continuity for students by both focusing on their individual concerns and reinforcing the vocabulary and concepts discussed in class. This customized feedback enabled us to maximize the time we spent in individual meetings as the semester progressed, as we could prioritize the areas in which the student most needed improvement. One CIM student, for instance, struggled with selecting and using sources at the beginning of the course. When she met with her team leader, they began each session by evaluating her works cited page and her source integration. By the end of the semester, she was able to clearly articulate both how to evaluate sources and how to integrate those sources into her writing. By thus emphasizing the connections between students' work in the class and their individual writing performance, these meetings made clear to students how their investment in the course led to measurable improvements in their writing over the semester.

In addition to providing continuity and an opportunity to prioritize pressing issues, these individual conferences allowed students to see writing as a continual process of revision. These one-on-one sessions provided opportunities for students to take charge of their own improvement, as the conferences themselves would be entirely directed by the students' questions and skill sheets. We encouraged students to incorporate feedback they received in these sessions into their revised final drafts. Often, a student's final submission would transform significantly from its initial draft. One advanced CWRU student noted that the course requirements made it impossible to think of his writing as "something he could write in a few hours" and, for him, demonstrated the value of thoughtful revision. From our observations in these individual sessions, students made significant progress in identifying their specific challenges with writing, using error mapping, and becoming aware of their writing as a process over which they had control. Rather than approaching their missions as finished products that happened all at once, then, students focused on the progressive steps involved in writing fully formed drafts, a practice which demystified their writing and enabled them to heighten their strengths and focus on making improvements.

Students also responded readily to the collaborative aspects of this course. The students were generally excited at the opportunity to work with their fellow classmates, quickly forming strong relationships with the other members of their teams, which was evident in the playful team names that they chose based on common interests or inside jokes. One team, for example, composed of violinists, viola players and piano players named themselves "The Quintet"; another, dismayed at the arctic temperatures of January in Cleveland, named themselves "Zero Below"; and the last team named themselves after a musical meme they all enjoyed, calling themselves "Trololo." This sense of community deepened as students spent time working together on training exercises, in peer review, and in other in-class activities. We encouraged students to see each other as resources in the various team activities we created. This aspect of collaboration was most obvious in peer review, which we conducted for every formal assignment. In observing students during peer review, we found that they had built a communal knowledge bank and vocabulary through active participation in class discussions and training exercises. Further, our more advanced students quickly realized that they were responsible not only for their own learning and writing progress but also that they could bring their particular skills to bear in helping others, particularly their L2 teammates, succeed. Peer review quickly transformed from a day of silent reading and commenting into a day of discussion, teaching, and debate, in which students engaged their trusted team members in discussions about the best ways to approach pressing problems in their work.

The collaborative aspects of the course gave students the space to share insights, learn from one another, and build both competence and confidence in their work. In addition to the benefits of camaraderie in the classroom, placing students on teams where they could earn points and compete in training exercises allowed us to cover fundamental aspects of expository writing thoroughly while making the process of learning this material entertaining. Even our most experienced students benefited from a closer examination of the basic rhetorical strategies of reading, writing, and researching, particularly since these training exercises highlighted the relationship between the specific skill (such as "thesis statements") and how that "skill" manifested in their final drafts. For each of the ten training exercises, we designed targeted games that used active learning. Rather than having students sit through a library information session, for example, we assigned the three teams a library scavenger hunt. While the team leaders served as expert advisers, students were left to complete the task largely on their own, competing with other teams for bonus skill points in the stat categories of perception and analysis. As a result of this practice of active learning, students demonstrated significant improvements in the skills emphasized in a particular training exercise. These improvements, reinforced by the individualized feedback of our one-on-one meetings with students, were largely retained throughout the course.

While the course was successful in its use of skill sheets, individual conferences, and collaborative learning—all of which increased students' investment in their own writing processes and prompted self-reflection and knowledge transfer—we would modify other elements of the game in future courses. While our theme of academic-writers-as-spies worked on a theoretical level, providing students a framework for thinking about themselves as academic code breakers or intelligence analysts sometimes caused students to struggle with their lack of context for the course content. While we had hoped that readings on this dynamic yet niche topic would bridge the disparate backgrounds of our students and instructors, students' lack of prior knowledge was occasionally discouraging. Our international students especially expressed frustration, as their unfamiliarity with U.S. foreign policy and western history made grappling with many of the readings more challenging than we had anticipated. As the semester progressed, we adjusted some of our readings on spies and spying, as well as the essay topics we assigned, to more clearly relate to students' interests and experiences with music and technology. In future classes, it might be beneficial to choose course content about which students have greater prior knowledge; such a shift would allow students to focus their time and attention on the aims and outcomes of the course rather than feel that they need to master a whole new subject area in addition to writing skills.

Additionally, while the collaborative aspects of this course were successful in many ways, some of the more experienced students found the introductory nature of the course frustrating. This frustration resulted from disparities in prior writing experience and language proficiency among the students. One student said in their course evaluation, "For me this course was too easy in the sense that I did not feel challenged or motivated." In future iterations of this course, we would incorporate modifications for students who are at different places in their writing proficiency, such as offering "stretch goals" and/or extra credit assignments, as well as integrating advanced students' natural tendencies toward leadership roles within the teams. Such modifications would offer students opportunities for more responsibility and more challenging tasks. We anticipate that the opportunity for more challenging personal goals would lessen some of the frustration with collaborative work.

We found that collaborative instruction not only allowed us to model effective teamwork and rich class discussion, but also encouraged students to reach out to their peers as part of their writing processes. While this course demonstrated the benefits of collaborative teaching, we recognize that our institutional experience was unique and that team-teaching will not always be possible, for us or for our colleagues. Solo instructors who wish to incorporate games or collaborative learning models into their courses may choose to modify our approach to the gamified classroom by calling on students to take on greater leadership roles in the team structure. An instructor might assign small groups and use the initial personal assessments to appoint rotating student leaders to help oversee team work. This approach would not only offer students additional opportunities for engagement, perhaps lessening the frustration we observed in our students, but also would give students a chance to gain experience in team building and project management. Also, as a solo instructor would be overseeing all peer review, we would recommend a directed approach that asks students to complete concrete tasks in order to maximize class time and provide more precise feedback. A directed peer review would not only provide focused assistance to students by supplementing the individualized feedback of the instructor, but also help students further exercise their critical reading skills and their new vocabulary of reflection and response.

The practice of expository writing, as complex, critical, and necessarily collaborative, lends itself to active learning, group work, and game-based approaches to composition pedagogy. These approaches, however, need not be limited to traditional composition courses. The use of an overarching theme, targeted self-assessment, and team competitions can all effectively be modified for professional communication, technical writing, and other writing in the disciplines (WID) courses that engage with their own sets of genres, outcomes, research styles, and levels of student investment. Additionally, given the responses we received from our L2 students, the game elements could find a successful place in the ESL composition classroom. Despite the challenges that arose in our iteration of English 150: Spies Like Us and the changes we would make in the future, all three of us will absolutely continue to gamify our writing pedagogy. By gamifying writing instruction, instructors can create a space where students take ownership of their writing processes and articulate how the benefits of their hard work transfer beyond the composition classroom.

## Acknowledgments

We would like to thank the English Department of Case Western Reserve University for allowing the three of us to work collaboratively and the Baker-Nord Center for the Humanities for awarding us an Enriching Curricula Grant that provided funding for our course materials. We would also like to thank Kimberly Emmons, who provided guidance and formative feedback as we developed this class.

## Works Cited

Alexander, Jonathan. "Gaming, Student Literacies, and the Composition Classroom: Some Possibilities for Transformation." *CCC* 61.1 (2009): 35-63. Print.

Bruffee, Kenneth A. *Collaborative Learning: Higher Education, Interdependence, and the Authority of Knowledge.* Baltimore: Johns Hopkins UP, 1998. Print.

Bunce, Matthew, Marjorie Herbert, and J. Christopher Collins. "Taking Flight: Learning Differences Meet Gaming Literacies." Selfe and Hawisher 191-202.

Ellington, Henry, Joannie Fowlie, and Monica Gordon. *Using Games and Simulations in the Classroom.* London: Kogan Page, 1998. Print.

Ferris, Dana R., and John Hedgcock. *Teaching ESL Composition: Purpose, Process, and Practice.* Hoboken: Routledge, 2013.

Gee, James Paul. *Good Video Games and Good Learning.* New York: Peter Lang, 2013.

Graff, Gerald and Cathy Birkenstein. *They Say/I Say: The Moves That Matter in Academic Writing.* 3rd Edition. New York: W. W. Norton and Company, 2015.

Hunzer, Kathleen M. "Connecting Writing Process with Personality: Creating Long-Lasting Trust Circles in Writing Classes." *Collaborative Learning and Writing Es-*

says on *Using Small Groups in Teaching English and Composition*. Ed. Kathleen M. Hunzer. North Carolina: McFarland and Company, Inc., 2012. 66-74. Print.

Kress, Gunther. *Literacy in the New Media Age*. New York: Routledge, 2003. Print.

Pillay, Soma, and Reynold James. "Gaming Across Cultures: Experimenting with Alternate Pedagogies." *Education + Training* 55.1 (2013): 7-22. Print.

Sabatino, Lindsay. "Improving Writing Literacies through Digital Gaming Literacies: Facebook Gaming in the Composition Classroom." *Computers and Composition* 32 (2014): 41-53. Print.

Selfe, Cynthia L., and Gail E. Hawisher, eds. *Gaming Lives in the Twenty-First Century: Literate Connections*. New York: Palgrave Macmillan, 2007. Print.

Smith, Jane Bowman, and Kathleen Blake Yancey, eds. *Self-Assessment and Development in Writing: A Collaborative Inquiry*. Cresskill: Hampton Press, 2000. Print.

Yancey, Kathleen Blake. *Reflection in the Writing Classroom*. Logan: Utah State UP, 1998. Print.

## Appendix A: Skill Sheet

Skill Categories

Decryption
Score: _____
Ex: How well can I find what I need in a source? How well do I analyze and understand the things I read? Can I take what I learn and apply it to other topics or sources?

Analysis
Score: _____
Ex: How well can I recognize genres of writing? How do I know what sort of writing I'm being asked to do? What is the goal of this assignment or writing prompt?

Performance
Score: _____
What audience am I writing for, and how do I customize my information for them? How is my grammar? Is my writing easy to read and understand? Is my writing concise and clear?

Insight
Score: _____
What do I do well in writing? What do I need to work on? What sorts of errors to I tend to make? How does my writing process work, and how could I improve it?

Process
Score: _____
How well do I plan my writing? What parts make up a paper? How do I know how long my paper needs to be, and how much information will fit?

## Personal Training Goals

Writing Strength:

Writing Weakness:

Training Goal(s):

Skills
Decryption
Decoding          _____
Source Integration _____
Research          _____
Evaluation        _____

Analysis
Genre Identification   _____
Audience Identification _____
Organization      _____
Keywords          _____

Performance
Grammar           _____
Thesis Statements _____
Transitions       _____
Citations         _____

Insight
Strengths         _____
Weaknesses        _____
Self-Assessment   _____
Error Mapping     _____

Process
Planning          _____
Outlining         _____
Drafting          _____
Revision          _____

# Syllabus

## English 150: Expository Writing
## Spies Like Us: Breaking the Academic Code

*Course Description*

English 150 is an introduction to academic/expository writing. Throughout this course, through a variety of writing activities and assignments, you will gain experience in the kinds of academic writing you will need for your university career. Some of the topics we will cover include reading critically, exploring and organizing ideas, moving through stages of the writing process, considering your audience, using the conventions of academic writing, identifying and using appropriate sources, and developing and making arguments, often in response to the arguments of others.

In this section of ENGL 150, we will focus our attention on the theme of espionage and intelligence, especially as it might be related to higher education. Through the reading and writing assignments, we will explore how various aspects of this broad topic, including definitions of intelligence work, current events, and the various practices of espionage, such as encrypting information and filing reports, relate to an academic setting. Course readings on these topics will supplement selections from *They Say/I Say*, allowing us to discuss rhetorical and argumentative principles in action.

To allow you to become even more familiar with these skills and practices, this section of ENGL 150 will allow you as a class to use a role-playing game as a way to interact with the material and keep track of your goals and progress. Through teamwork, individual assignments, group Missions and points tracking, you will be able to see your writing practices grow and evolve over the course of the semester.

*Course Objectives*

By the end of the course, you should be able to:
- Identify and summarize the main points of a formal piece of writing
- Critically engage with academic texts
- Develop independent revision skills
- Write coherent, organized, argument-based prose
- Evaluate the credibility and usefulness of outside sources
- Appropriately integrate outside sources into your writing
- Plan a research project with a well-focused thesis/research question
- Engage in productive group work in an academic setting

*Texts to Purchase (available at bookstore)*

*Argo.* Dir. Ben Affleck. Perf. Ben Affleck, Bryan Cranston, Alan Arkin. Warner Bros., 2012. Film.

Booth, Wayne C, Gregory G. Colomb, and Joseph M. Williams. *The Craft of Research*. Chicago: U of Chicago P, 2008. Print.

Graff, Gerald, and Cathy Birkenstein. *They Say/I Say: The Moves That Matter in Academic Writing*. 2nd ed. New York: Norton, 2010. Print.

Mendez, Antonio. *Argo: How the CIA and Hollywood Pulled off the Most Audacious Rescue in History*. New York: Penguin, 2012. Print.

*Readings/Selections available on Blackboard*

Dargos, Manolha, and A.O. Scott. "Critic's Notebook: Confronting the Fact of Fiction and the Fiction of Fact." *New York Times Online* 22 Feb 2013. Web. <http://www.nytimes.com/2013/02/23/movies/awardsseason/the-history-in-lincoln-argo-and-zero-dark-thirty.html>.

Gannon, James. "Speak Ciphers." *Stealing Secrets, Telling Lies: How Spies and Codebreakers Helped Shaped the 20th Century*. Dulles: Brussey's Inc., 2001. 236-49. Print.

Glinsky, Albert. *Theremin: Ether Music and Espionage*. Chicago, IL: University of Illinois Press, 2000. Print.

Herman, Susan. "The USA PATRIOT Act and the Submajoritarian Fourth Amendment." *Harvard Civil Rights-Civil Liberties Law Review* 41 (2006): 67-132. Print.

Herszenhorn, David M., and Ellen Barry. "From Russia With Wig: American Spy Suspect Is Ejected." *New York Times Online* 14 May 2013. Web. 21 June 2017. <http://www.nytimes.com/2013/05/15/world/europe/russia-detains-american-saying-he-is-cia-agent.html>.

Jaeger, Paul T., John Carlo Bertot, and Charles R. McClure. "The Impact of the USA Patriot Act on Collection and Analysis of Personal Information Under the Foreign Intelligence Surveillance Act." *Government Information Quarterly* 20.3 (2003): 295-314. Web. <http://www.sciencedirect.com/science/article/pii/S0740624X03000571>.

King, Stephen. "What Writing Is." *On Writing: A Memoir of a Craft*. New York: Simon and Schuster, 2000. 103-7. Print.

Lamott, Anne. "Shitty First Drafts." *Language Awareness: Readings for College Writers*. Ed. Paul Eschholz, Alfred Rosa, and Virginia Clark. 9th ed. Boston: Bedford/St. Martin's, 2005. 93-96. Print.

Levitin, Daniel J. "Why Music Moves Us." *Nature* 464.8 (8 April 2010): 834-35. Print.

Lunsford, Andrea A. *The Everyday Writer*. 5th ed. New York: Bedford/St. Martin's, 2012. Print.

Lunsford, Andrea A., John J. Ruszkiewicz, and Keith Walters. *Everything's an Argument*. 6th ed. New York: Bedford/St. Martin's, 2012. Print.

Mell, Patricia. "Big Brother at the Door: Balancing National Security with Privacy under the USA Patriot Act." *Denver University Law Review* 80 (2002/3): 375. Web. <http://heinonline.org/HOL/LandingPage?collection=journals&handle=hein.journals/denlr80&div=19&id=&page=>.

Shane, Scott. "An Exotic Tool for Espionage: Moral Compass." *The New York Times Online*. 28 Jan 2006. Web. 21 June 2017. <http://www.nytimes.com/2006/01/28/politics/an-exotic-tool-for-espionage-moral-compass.html>.

United States Department of Justice. "What is the USA PATRIOT Act?" United States Department of Justice, n.d. Web. <https://www.justice.gov/archive/ll/highlights.htm>.

Various, "Do We Still Need the PATRIOT Act?" *New York Times Online*, September 7, 2011. Web. 21 June 2017. <https://www.nytimes.com/roomfordebate/2011/09/07/do-we-still-need-the-patriot-act>.

Warner, Michael. "Wanted: A Definition of Intelligence." *Covert and Overt: Recollecting and Connection Intelligence Service and Information Science*. Ed. Robert V. Williams and Ben-Ami Lipetz. Lanham: Scarecrow Press, 2005. 199-209. Print.

Wernicke, Sebastian. "Lies, Damned Lies, and Statistics (about TED Talks)." *TED*. Feb 2010. Web. 21 June 2017. <https://www.ted.com/talks/lies_damned_lies_and_statistics_about_tedtalks>.

*Assignments and Grading*

Your grade for the course will be determined by your completion of the following requirements (more detailed descriptions of the individual Missions are below):

| | |
|---|---|
| Participation (class discussions, training exercises, peer review, individual conferences) | 30% |
| Mission 1: The Brief | 10% |
| Mission 2: Synthesis | 10% |
| Mission 3: Reconnaissance | 10% |
| Mission 4: Research Analysis | 20% |
| Mission 5: Ethics White Paper | 10% |
| Revision of Mission of your choice | 10% |

Total: 100%

*Course Requirements*

Attendance and Participation: Your presence in class is required. Class participation, worth 30% of your final grade, is an extremely important element of this class. Your participation grade will be based on the following:

- Attendance and punctuality
- Preparation for class (coming with all materials and readings)
- Engagement in and contribution to class discussions, whether large-group, small-group, or in individual conferences
- Preparation for and constructive participation in peer review workshops, training exercises and individual conferences
- Completion of incidental in-class and out-of-class writing assignments (these will be graded on a check/check+/check– scale)

This is not a lecture class; it depends upon your participation, and if you are not present (and participating), the integrity of the course is undermined. For most classes, you will be asked to put away your laptops and phones. If you must miss a class, please talk to or email your team leader before class if at all possible, and be sure to speak to your teammates or team leader to find out what you missed. In addition, please be on time so that we can begin (and end) class in a timely manner.

*Class Organization*

The class will be divided into groups. These groups will be your spy teams for the semester, and you will compete for points in the training exercises (explained below). While all teams will win prizes for their continued participation in the course, the team with the most points at the end of the semester will win an additional gift certificate to the college bookstore. Your team will, more importantly, become your support system throughout the semester. As you master new skills, you will work with your team on in-class assignments and the ten training exercises scattered throughout the semester. Your team members will also read all of your papers and provide feedback during peer review sessions. Each team will have an instructor assigned to it; this instructor will serve as your team leader. She is your primary contact; she will work with you on specific group work and will be the person to whom you turn for questions about your assignments and who will provide feedback on your papers and progress in the course. All instructors are available to all students and have equal responsibility in the course, but your team leader will be the most familiar with your work and goals.

*Spy Training*

In addition to the standard letter grades received in the class, both formal writing assignments and in-class activities will allow you to chart your progress in a more tangible way. At the beginning of the course, you will receive your own personal statistics ("stat") sheet. This sheet reflects your growing proficiencies in the core skills for writing throughout your academic career. "Stats" represent broader categories of writing skills: Analysis, Decryption, Perception, Performance, Insight, and Process. At the beginning of the course, you will split 12 points between the six core stats, determining the areas of writing you identify as either strengths or weaknesses. No stat may have a zero.

> Ex: Michelle sets out to assess her abilities. She can give herself a two in each one, but that doesn't differentiate very much. She feels she's better in Analysis than she is in Process, so she drops Process to one and raises Analysis to three. She isn't sure how she feels about the rest of them yet, so she leaves them at average.

Her initial scores are, therefore, Analysis 3, Decryption 2, Perception 2, Performance 2, Insight 2, and Process 1.

After performing this self-assessment, you, in consultation with your team leader and the feedback on your diagnostic essay, will determine your individualized goals for the course.

To track your progress toward these goals, you will log your progress through the accumulation of stat points. Each of the stats contains four discrete "skills." The stat Decryption, for example, contains four writing skills: decoding (or critical reading), source integration, research (finding sources), and evaluation of sources. You can gain skill points from in-class assignments and team activities, as well as the formal weekly essay writing Missions. When working with the rest of your team, either in regular class discussions or in training exercises, you will earn skill points related to the particular writing concerns being addressed in that session. Team leaders may also distribute points at their discretion for participation, etc. Accumulating five skill points within a stat category allows you to "level up" in that area and add an additional stat point to that area.

At the end of the semester, you will meet with your team leader to review and reflect on both your progress on your goals and your mastery of the six different stat areas.

*Training Exercises*

In addition to informal opportunities for your team to gain points in everyday class discussions and activities, this course features ten formal "training exercises," team competitions that focus on the cultivation of targeted writing skills. The skills tested in these training exercises will be directly related to the paper ("Mission") for a given section of the course and will supplement our class discussions, so you should come prepared to participate.

*Individual Missions*

The formal writing assignments for this course (termed "Missions") are similarly tied to the six stats and twenty-four skills on which you will work over the course of the semester. These essays assess your individual mastery of the skills we've been working on in our in-class discussions and in our training exercises. Each Mission will build on the skills tested in previous Missions, leading to the two final Missions, the Research Analysis and the White Paper, which put all of the skills developed over the course into practice. You will earn four points for each essay, assigned by your team leader, in areas where you have demonstrated mastery. The Missions will proceed as follows:

> Mission 1: The Brief (Summary and Response Essay, 2-3 pp.)
> Mission 2: Synthesis (Compare/Contrast Essay, 2-3 pp.)
> Mission 3: Reconnaissance (Literature Review Essay, 2-3 pp.)
> Mission 4: Research Analysis (Research Paper, 6-8 pp.)
> Mission 5: Ethics White Paper (Persuasive Essay, 3-4 pp.)

You will also have the opportunity to revise one Mission for a higher grade in the last week of class.

*Individual Conferences*

Before each major essay assignment ("Mission"), you will sign up for individual 30-minute conferences with your team leader to discuss a complete first draft of your work. It is your responsibility to sign up with your team leader in advance. In individual conferences, we will work one-on-one on your draft of the upcoming assignment, focusing on your questions and concerns and preparing you to do final revisions for the draft of the paper that you will turn in for a grade. While your team leader will provide you with feedback on the strengths and weaknesses of your individual draft, you should come prepared with a set of questions and concerns that you would like to address in your individual meeting, in addition to a paper copy of your essay draft.

*Peer Review*

The week before final papers are due, you will participate in peer review with the members of your team. You should come prepared with printed copies of your completed essay drafts for review and with questions and concerns that you want to pose to your team members.

*Course Schedule*

| Section 1 – Decoding | |
|---|---|
| Week 1 | Class introduction, Diagnostic Essay, Team placement, Game overview |
| Week 2 | Prompt decoding<br>Read: Gannon, "Speak Ciphers"; Warner, "Wanted: A Definition of Intelligence"<br>Entering the conversation<br>Read: *They Say/I Say* Preface and Ch. 1<br>Training Exercise #1: Incorporating feedback/error patterning |
| Week 3 | Peer Review of Mission 1<br>Drafting<br>Read: Lamont, "Shitty First Drafts"<br>Writing as Encoding/Reading as Decoding<br>Read: King, "What is Writing?"; Levitin, "Why Music Moves Us" |
| Section 2 – Briefing | |
| Week 4 | Due: Mission 1 final draft<br>Responding Critically to Texts<br>Read: *They Say/I Say* Ch. 4-5; Dargos and Scott, "Confronting the Fact of Fiction and the Fiction of Fact"<br>*Argo*: the Book<br>Read: Mendez, *Argo* (selections)<br>*Argo*: the Movie<br>Prepare: Watch *Argo* before class |
| Week 5 | Peer Review of Mission 2<br>Outlining and Paper Structure<br>Training Exercise #2: Deconstruction (Outlining) |

| | |
|---|---|
| **Section 3 – Analyzing and Responding to Issues: The Patriot Act and Homeland Security** | |
| Week 6 | Due: Mission 2 final draft<br>Summary, Paraphrase, Quotation and Citations<br>Read: "From Russia, With Wig: American Spy Suspect Is Ejected"<br>Evaluating sources<br>Read: *Craft of Research*, Ch. 5; Department of Justice, "What is the USA PATRIOT Act?"<br>Training Exercise #3: Engaging with Sources<br>Read: Various, "Do We Still Need the PATRIOT Act?": "Introduction"; Posner, "There's still a need"; Rosen, "Too Much Power"; Sales, "A Vital Weapon"; Herman, "Too Many Needless Provisions"; Ahmadi, "Giving the U.S. a Bad Reputation" |
| Week 7 | Peer Review of Mission 3<br>Evaluating sources<br>Read: Herman, "The USA PATRIOT Act and the Submajoritarian Fourth Amendment";; Jagaer, Bertot and McClure, "The impact of the USA Patriot Act on collection and analysis of personal information under the Foreign Intelligence Surveillance Act"; Mell, "Big Brother at the Door: Balancing National Security with Privacy under the USA Patriot Act"<br>Training Exercise #4: Quote Integration Gameshow |
| **Section 4 – In the Field: Outfitting your Tool Belt** | |
| Week 8 | Due: Mission 3 Final Draft<br>Mid-term self-evaluations<br>Reading Triage<br>Read: Lunsford, *The Everyday Writer*, Ch. 12<br>Elements of Argument - Logos, Ethos, Pathos<br>Read: *Craft of Research*, Ch. 3<br>Library instructional session |
| Week 9 | Training Exercise #5: Library Scavenger Hunt<br>Argument & Style<br>Read: Lunsford, Ruszkiewicz, and Walters, *Everything's an Argument*, Ch. 13<br>Argument - Doing it Wrong: Fallacies<br>Read: Lunsford, *The Everyday Writer*, "Fallacies" |
| Week 10 | Peer Review of Mission 4<br>Argument – Thesis<br>Read: *They Say/I Say*, Ch. 7<br>Due: Bring in your thesis statement for workshopping<br>Training Exercise #6: Arguments in action |

| Week 11 | Due: Mission 4 |
| --- | --- |
| | Argument – Thesis |
| | Read: *They Say/I Say*, Ch. 7 |
| | Due: Bring in your thesis statement for workshopping |
| | |
| | Argument and Persuasion |
| | Read: "An Exotic Tool for Espionage: Moral Compass" |
| | Training Exercise #7: Paragraph sequencing |

## Section 5 – In the Field: Ethics and Persuasion

| Week 12 | Ethics, research and communication |
| --- | --- |
| | Watch: Wernicke, "Lies, damned lies, and statistics (about TED Talks)" |
| | Acknowledging alternate viewpoints |
| | Read: *Craft of Research*, Ch. 10; *They Say/I Say*, Ch. 6 |
| | Training Exercise #8: Audience |
| Week 13 | Peer Review of Mission 5 |
| | Rhetorical Analysis |
| | Read: Glinsky, *Theremin: Ether Music and Espionage* (selections) |
| | Training Exercise #9: Revision |

## Section 6 – Performance Review and Revision

| Week 14 | Due: Mission 5 final draft |
| --- | --- |
| | Revising your argument and organization |
| | Read: *Craft of Research*, Ch. 14 |
| | Revising sentence level concerns |
| Week 15 | Training Exercise #10: Team meetings/progress assessment/team awards |
| | Due: Revisions of one Mission of your choice |

# Where We Are: Latinx Compositions and Rhetorics

"Where We Are" highlights where we are as a field on matters current and compelling. In these invited contributions, we bring together a small group of scholars at the forefront of a particular issue or practice, who together issue a progress report of sorts in 800-1200 words. Throughout the included pieces, "HSI" is abbreviation for Hispanic-Serving Institution. *–Editor's Note*

## In Defense of Latinx

*Christine Garcia*

"Latinx" is an intersectional identity term meant to be used by gender fluid and gender nonconforming people, LGBTQIA persons, cisgender men and women, and those taking a political stance that ethnicity and gender exist on a spectrum and are not dichotomous. The term was conceived around 2004 and popularized on social media outlets, experienced a waning in usage for a few years, and has since reemerged, most noticeably around 2014, on forums helmed by and dedicated to AfroLatinx and indigenous-centered Spanish speaking people (Gamio). The conceptualization of the "x" is rooted in the decolonization of the terms Latina/Latino on two levels: first, confronting and challenging the gender binary, and second, rejecting the silencing and erasure of AfroLatinx and indigenous languages by standard Spanish, the language of the colonizer of much of Latin America and the Southwestern United States. The term "Latinx" has since entered mainstream use, and, as an emergent term, it continues to be defined and contested.

The introduction of the "x" in lieu of the gendered endings was more of a gradual shift rather than a sudden debut. The evolution of the term began with the common gendered endings of "a" or "o" (Latina/feminine and Latino/masculine), which moved into a collapsing of the two onto the end of the word signifying inclusion of both genders (Latina/o) with one gendered ending placed first based on author discretion. Next was the short lived "Latin@," economical because it integrated both gendered endings into one symbol, but nonfunctional online due to the use of "@" for tagging purposes on social media. "Latine" has occasionally been proposed as an easy to pronounce gender neutral term such as "presidente," yet this erasure is counter to the semantic goal of acknowledgment and inclusion that the "x" represents.

It is within the argument of connotation that much of the battle over the "x" is located. The traditional use of the gender assumptive "a" or "o" was used innocuously for much of recent history with the gendered assignment all but accepted as unproblematic. Trouble arose as Latinas and Latinx of Afro and indigenous roots challenged the default to the masculine in mixed gender situations as well as the either/or identification based on Euro-Hispanic roots of the terms. Around two decades ago, woke users of the Spanish language in the United States began the collapsing of the endings in a move that signaled both inclusiveness and efficiency. Feminine and masculine were combined into one word, typically written with a slash separating gendered endings (i.e., Latina/o), which challenged the default to the masculine yet did not account for the myopic dichotomy of genders. The most raucous debates regarding the collapsed "a/o" gendered endings that occurred—prior to the shift to "x—was whether the "a" or the "o" should appear first in the word. These debates over which gender ending would appear first were rhetorical in nature and situated in the connotative questions of preference and power. These challenges and changes to the gendered endings of "Latinx" reflect the evolution of U.S. Spanish speakers' initial acceptance of the masculine as default and eventual resistance against essentialization and erasure. The "x" adaptation contains within it the movement towards intersectionality and the acknowledgement that ethnicity and gender are interlocked identity constructs, which is a direct linguistic manifestation of what is happening socioculturally in our academic institutions and in our communities and families.

The move away from the usage of "a/o" to "x" marks an amelioration of "Latina/o" and its variants through the dismissal of the gender binary in a move that marks gender and ethnicity inclusion. Not all Latinx identify with Euro-Hispanic roots and not all Latinx identify as either female or male, and the "x" accounts for these important identity markers. This semantic shift is indicative of a larger sociocultural shift, one in which Spanish language users in the United States, many, but not all of whom are multilingual, are becoming more sensitive to the denotative power of words; specifically, users recognize that concretizing words with gender markers often creates false implications and incorrect representations of referents. While imperfect and not applicable to all Spanish-speaking peoples, the evolution of the term "Latina/o" into "Latinx" is the most functional contemporary label for many of us. The imperfectness of the term, especially this hotly debated shift to "x," is but one step in the continual decolonization of the Spanish language. Whether Latinx is a temporary buzzword, as some detractors claim, or the springboard for further acts of linguistic decolonization, the term is proof positive that language is alive, evolving, and is a tool and a reflection of our human-ness. And, for those still struggling to find the right articulation of the term, it is pronounced /laˈtiːnɛks/ or "Lah-teen-ecks."

**Works Cited**

Gamio, Arlene. *Latinx: A Brief Guidebook*. Princeton LGBTQ Center. 2016. Accessed 02 July 2017. <https://www.academia.edu/29657615/Latinx_A_Brief_Guidebook>.

# Chicanx/Latinx Rhetorics as Methodology for Writing Program Design at HSIs

*Aydé Enríquez-Loya and Kendall Leon*

Academia and English departments pose particular challenges and create contested spaces for students and faculty of color alike. As Chicanx[1] faculty in an English department, we find ourselves tasked with building a writing program at a kairotic time: our campus was recently designated a Hispanic-Serving Institution (HSI). Subsequently, we were hired as assistant professors in Chicanx/Latinx rhetoric—a position title we had never seen before, which speaks to an epistemological, ideological, and material shift in our field and our institution. We see this position as an act of identifying with a newly designated HSI campus, as well as an act of identification with students at this campus. We recognize this new position as an opportunity to centralize Chicanx/Latinx rhetorics in our work as scholars. For this forum, we connect what we know as Chicanx scholars with our work as teachers and administrators designing a writing program at an HSI campus. Establishing a reciprocal dialogue between Chicanx/Latinx rhetoric, which we define as rhetoric that focuses on decolonizing, reinventing and remembering, and writing program administration and design is an emergent, and important, research area.

One challenge within HSIs and their English departments has to do with the general impression that the growing Chicanx/Latinx population is Other, and that demographic changes are just now coming into fruition. As such, the imperative to make drastic changes in our classrooms and programs is perceived as sudden. Yet, Chicanx/Latinx students have been on our university campuses for a long time. The impression of suddenness may be exaggerated among English faculty since their departments have traditionally been unable to attract many Chicanx/Latinx students. Many institutional spaces were not designed for students of color. This is especially true in rhetoric and composition programs, perhaps even more so than literary studies, and even truer when we focus on composition programs and their administration. As more and more Chicanx/Latinx students enroll in postsecondary institutions, most programs have failed to acknowledge what this influx means in terms of building programs for students of color[2]. For example, what does it mean for Spanish heritage speaking students to major in English or take an English class? Are they learning English or learning to work with languages within bordered spaces? Samuel Huntington argues that Mexicans' resistance to assimilation makes them a threat to the United States (qtd. in Villanueva 39). Victor Villanueva explains that Mexicans are perceived to have unbreakable ties to Aztlán/Mexico, creating imaginary boundaries that make their full assimilation unattainable (38). These imaginary boundaries mark Mexicans and other Latinos as continually foreign (38).

Likewise, our Chicanx/Latinx theories and scholarship have been treated as foreign to writing program design and administration, as the Other in these spaces and therefore relegated to special topics in journals or as appendage to the real body of work in writing program administration and pedagogy. Villanueva reminds us that this is an imaginary border used to keep people (like us, like our students) out (38-41). On the other hand, we must also acknowledge that administrative and institutional theorizing has not been centralized in Chicanx/Latinx rhetorics.

To begin a discussion about Chicanx/Latinx rhetorics and writing program administration, we turn to the work of Gloria E. Anzaldúa, who provides a methodology for designing change, which can be extended to writing programs. In her essay "now let us shift," Anzaldúa outlines a path to *conocimiento*, a process of developing a critical and decolonized consciousness that moves from rupturing, to fragmentation, to connecting, assembling and rebuilding. As Iris Ruiz argues in *Reclaiming Composition for Chicanos/as and Other Ethnic Minorities*, when we look at histories of rhetoric and composition, we see that our work and ideas have often been placed as ruptures—as breaks from the center. We find this marginalization especially when we look at curricular design of writing programs. Most writing programs are designed based on canonical works and epistemologies associated primarily with white male Christian scholars (even in rhetoric and composition) and tend to present scholarship by people of color as specialized rhetorics, or as relevant only in relation to language variance. Centralizing Chicanx rhetoric in the design of writing programs allows us to shift our way of thinking as a whole and create new ways of understanding the field of rhetoric, of the role of our work as a department within increasingly diverse institutions, and of the potential that Chicanx/Latinx students bring into these spaces. As Anzaldúa demonstrates in her writing, centralizing experience is not just about the stories we tell, but the approach as well. Therefore, at our HSI we consider not just curricular topics we can include in our programs, but also the practices that reflect our Chicanx/Latinx beliefs and rhetoric, as well as learning outcomes and assessments that utilize our HSI identity as part of our design methodology.

For instance, Chicanx writers often interrogate borders and boundaries. Boundary disruptions and challenges to binaries can be approaches integrated within a course or within writing program learning outcomes[3]. From an administrative standpoint, Chicanx/Latinx writing programs and administrators can claim Chicanx/Latinx in a deliberate affiliative act that makes visible our commitment to purposefully disrupt what voices are allowed to be heard and to speak within our classrooms and departments, challenging all individuals to break molds and build alliances through shared knowledges and to create community within academic and localized spaces. Re-envisioning how we think of composition classrooms and programs as spaces that must be infused with diverse knowledges and rhetorical practices is especially pertinent at HSIs, as the number of these institutions grow along with population shifts (HACU, "HSI Fact Sheet"). We believe the future goal for our field should be to answer what it means to utilize and start from Chicanx/Latinx rhetoric as a design methodology. A design methodology is not just about integrating content into courses; it is about epistemologies, values, histories, goals, assessments that invent from Chicanx/Latinx at its very foundation. As we see it, we have a challenge as Chicanx/Latinx rhetoric and writing teachers and scholars to be able to take what we know and believe and move toward assembling the stories, theories, and lineages we share within our administrative spaces. This work must take place not only in our scholarship, but also in designing programs and institutions. As more institutions are recognized as HSIs, they must work to transform their programs and departments so that new students of color entering these spaces are not simply counted, noted, and filed. Instead, we argue for the use of Chicanx/Latinx rhetorics for the transformation of these spaces, especially in terms of program design. In particular, we suggest utilizing Chicanx/Latinx rhetorics as a methodology for program design. In doing so, we are moving beyond adding Chicanx rhetorics into stabile writing programs; instead, it is time to build writing programs with Chicanx/Latinx rhetorics at their core.

**Notes**

1. We use the term "Chicanx" when referring to ourselves and our identity. We use Chicanx/Latinx in all other instances for inclusivity.

2. According to a 2014 Pew Research Center Study, in 2014 35% of Latinos were enrolled in postsecondary education, which is 13% more than were enrolled in 1993. Despite the enrollment increase, though, Latinos are still behind other cultural groups in obtaining college degrees, with only 15% of Latinos between the ages of 25-29 holding bachelor's degrees (Krogstad). This speaks to the need for educators to build programs that connect with this student group.

3. This kind of border disruptive pedagogy is happening in the writing program at University of Texas at El Paso, which connects Latinx students with the surrounding community.

**Works Cited**

Anzaldúa, Gloria E. "now let us shift...the path of conocimiento...inner work, public acts." *this bridge we call home: radical visions for transformation*. Ed. Gloria E. Anzaldúa and Ana Louise Keating. New York: Routledge, 2002. 540-78. Print.

HACU Office of Policy Analysis and Information. "2017 HSI Fact Sheet." *Hispanic Association of Colleges and Universities*, March 2017. 26 July 2017. Web. <http://www.hacu.net/images/hacu/OPAI/2017_HSI_FactSheet.pdf>.

Krogstad, Jens Manuel. "5 Facts About Latinos and Education." *Pew Research Center*, 28 July 2016. 26 July 2017. Web. <http://www.pewresearch.org/fact-tank/2016/07/28/5-facts-about-latinos-and-education/>.

Ruiz, Iris. *Reclaiming Composition for Chicanos/as and Other Ethnic Minorities*. New York: Palgrave Macmillan, 2016. Print.

Villanueva, Victor. "Metonymic Borders and Our Sense of Nation." *Crossing Borders, Drawing Boundaries: The Rhetoric of Lines Across America*. Ed. Barbara Couture and Patti Wojahn. Logan: Utah State UP, 2016, 29-42. Print.

# Crafting a Composition Pedagogy with Latino Students in Mind

*E. Domínguez Barajas*

Adaptive writing instruction focusing on common language use is particularly important when working with Latino students, as their ethnic background is very often tied to a non-mainstream linguistic profile (i.e., many Latinos are either bilingual, monolingual in Spanish, or English monolingual in a non-standard vernacular) that sets them apart in the popular imagination and perception, if not in actuality. Existing and emerging research on this demographic indicates that Latinos' sociolinguistic profile is as impactful on their academic experience as is their socioeconomic and phenotypical profile.

It is imperative, however, to acknowledge that beyond sociolinguistic heritage—which is not the same as actual language spoken—there is little that all Latinos have in common. The various peoples of Latin-American ancestry in the U.S. not only do not all speak Spanish, but they also do not exclusively share one race, social class, national origin, religion, single history or culture, degree of educational attainment, political orientation or affiliation, or time of residency in the U.S. If there is one commonality for this ethnic group, it is that the term "Latino" indicates the legacy of Spanish and Portuguese colonialism on the various cultures of Latin America and how said legacy continues to manifest itself to the present day among U.S. populations tracing their heritage to Latin American countries.

Not withstanding such intra-ethnic diversity, the prominent linguistic dimension of Latino identity seems naturally to bring the matter of language use and personal identity to bear on pedagogical concerns, especially in rhetoric and composition (Mejía). How to adequately attend—and positively transform—writing instruction in response to the linguistic profiles and cultural perspectives of Latinos in the classroom is the aim of the scholarship referenced here. In fact, what arguably makes the following pedagogical approaches innovative is that they have moved beyond tolerance of non-standard features in students' written expression, often sidelined so that students can "master" standard forms, to centering them as legitimate expressive forms that carry their own rhetorical nuances and sociocognitive benefits.

Scholar-practitioners such as Isis Artze-Vega, Isabel Baca, and Aydé Enríquez-Loya are particularly cognizant of the linguistic and cultural aspects of the Latino experience, and they propose changing the writing curriculum accordingly (especially at officially designated HSIs, those institutions of higher learning where more than 25% of the student population is Latino) in order to ensure that the sociocultural and linguistic uniqueness of Latinos is fruitfully engaged instead of ignored, dismissed, or belittled. Acknowledging linguistic practices when implementing or recommending pedagogies for Latino students, these scholar-practitioners' curricular innovations achieve not only respect for linguistic diversity but also cultivation of multilingualism and multidialectism.

Isis Artze-Vega et al., for instance, advance the idea of bilingual composition classes in which an instructor who is unfamiliar with the student's home language or dialect will be, in Janet Bean et al.'s words, "in the interesting and fruitful position of having less knowledge and authority about the language being used than the student has" (qtd. in Artze-Vega et al. 103). The bilingual composition classroom that Artze-Vega et al. describe is what amounts to a dual-language environment where "students are invited to speak both languages . . . read texts in Spanish, English, and a combination of the two, and produce written texts in both languages" (103). The exciting and challenging idea of multilingual composition forwarded by Artze-Vega offers a practical response to the needs of the Latino populations they describe.

Isabel Baca similarly expands the composition curriculum in response to expanding Latino identities in liminal spaces such as the U.S.-Mexico border. In Baca's experience, the Latino students populating her classrooms range from those whose ancestors had the border redrawn around them to those who cross the border literally every day in order to attend school. The linguistic foundations, cultural frames of reference, and socio-educational expectations that Latinos embody prompt Baca to propose an innovative approach to writing instruction that, perhaps unsurprisingly, leads her to the same conclusion as that of Artze-Vega: namely, that idealized linguistic forms have to give way to actual linguistic practices in order to teach students productive writing practices. From her perspective, language ideologies that tout idealized standards of English and Spanish are not conducive to learning for many Latino students whose linguistic backgrounds do not align with those restrictive ideals. Among the nine guidelines offered by Baca for teaching writing to non-mainstream speakers of English are the use of individual conferencing, promoting extensive reading, giving credit for all of the stages of the writing process, allowing students to use their vernacular and to "code-switc[h] . . . in the classroom," and demonstrating "positive language attitudes" that convey to students the instructor's awareness of the student's degree of sophistication and a general willingness to collaborate with them instead of merely molding them (157).

At this year's College Composition and Communication Conference, Aydé Enríquez-Loya underscored the need for linguistic pedagogical adaptions for Latinos within an HSI framework. Enríquez-Loya's argument is that the sociocultural and linguistic focus that scholars based at HSIs promote is suitable, with adjustments, for all contexts where Latinos are taught to write at the college level ("Interrogating"). Enríquez-Loya's teaching praxis establishes an interdiscursive paradigm that blurs the line between literature and rhetoric, between sociocultural and political borders, and between societal and institutional demands. Approximating what Patricia Bizzell termed "hybrid academic discourses" as early as 1999, Enríquez-Loya promotes "decolonial storytelling strategies for fyc bilingual students" as a means for transforming writing instruction for students of color ("Interrogating"). In particular, she encourages the adoption of storytelling within composition classrooms to dismantle intra-disciplinary hierarchies and stale genre prescriptions ("Crossing" 158-60). Narratives, Enríquez-Loya considers, need to be privileged for Latinos, and personal narratives in particular must not be displaced by the conventions of academic discourse if writing instruction is to mitigate the alienation that thwarts Latino academic success.

What emerges as a priority for Latino composition and rhetorics from this limited overview is how to reconcile academic and vernacular discourses in order to minimize the social and linguistic alienation many Latino students experience in college. From this vantage point, hybrid discourses, an inevitable result of linguistic and cultural contact, are key to establishing culturally responsive writing pedagogies. This return to Bizzell's advocacy for hybrid discourses promises to be a fruitful way to develop innovative writing pedagogies that place sociolinguistic diversity at the center of Latino-oriented classrooms.

## Works Cited

Artze-Vega, Isis, et al. "*Más allá del inglés*: A Bilingual Approach to College Composition." Kirklighter et al. 99-117.

Baca, Isabel. "It Is All in the Attitude—The Language Attitude." Kirklighter et al. 145-68.

Bean, Janet, et al. "Should We Invite Students to Write in Home Languages? Complicating the Yes/No Debate." *Composition Studies* 31.1 (2003): 25-42. Print.

Bizzell, Patricia. "Hybrid Academic Discourses: What, Why, How?" *Composition Studies* 27.2 (1999): 7-22. Print.

Enríquez-Loya, Aydé. "Crossing Borders and Building Alliances: Border Discourse within Literatures and Rhetorics of Color." Diss. Texas A&M U, 2012. Print.

---. "Interrogating Ghosts in the Writing Classroom: Decolonial Storytelling Strategies for FYC Bilingual Students." Conference on College Composition and Communication, Portland, OR, 18 March 2017. Lecture.

Kirklighter, Cristina, et al., eds. *Teaching Writing with Latino/a Students: Lessons learned at Hispanic Serving Institutions*. Albany: SUNY, 2007. Print.

Mejía, Jaime Armin. "Latina and Latino Rhetorical Issues." *Rhetoric, the Polis, and the Global Village: Selected Papers from the 1998 Thirtieth Anniversary Rhetoric Society of America Conference*. Ed. C. Jan Swearingen and Dave Pruett. Mahwah: Lawrence Erlbaum Associates, 1999. 15-17. Print.

# Latinx and Latin American Community Literacy Practices *en Confianza*

Steven Alvarez

I conduct collaborative community literacy research with Latinx and Latin American immigrant communities using participant-action methodology. In my research, I have focused on ethnographic case studies of homework mentors, librarians, teachers, students, and parents as they collectively navigate school systems with the help of after-school programs. I draw upon a decade of research in New York City, Kentucky, and Arizona to detail how schools and teachers can learn about these valuable community literacies. From these portraits, I explore what lessons we can draw from them that could impact how we teach writing in school in ways that respect the dignity of students' families and homes. I hesitate to write that I enter into community literacy research with clear questions because ultimately I'm not striving for answers, but for praxis, or theoretically informed practice subject to continual revision as I grow as a learner, educator, and writer. The situation of my humanizing research agenda and teaching engagement is clear: I am participating in the literacy practices I write about, and my closeness to these communities indicates the depths of respect and direct contact I invest into community literacies and what the communities invest in me. The focus on community puts the local knowledge and experiences of Latinx and Latin American immigrant students and families in the forefront. Over the past fifteen years, there have been more ethnographic collaborations that examine Latinx and Latin American literacies in academic and non-academic spaces, research that intersects questions of race, gender, sexuality, migration, and class. In the coming decades, I predict more qualitative research that turns to the grassroots literacy practices of Latinxs across the nation emerging from scholars across composition and rhetoric, education, and applied linguistics. These studies will point to the dynamic literacy practices of Latinx communities, but I urge future scholars to ground their ethnographies explicitly in trust, respect, and sustainability *en confianza*.

The most important point impacting literacy research going forward is the importance of K-university writing teachers expanding their knowledge of the literacy practices of Latinx and Latin American students by engaging with students' communities, learning from their expertise with the trust of *confianza*. *Confianza* translates literally as "confidence," but in practice *confianza* means reciprocating a relationship where individuals feel cared for (Bartlett and García). The sense of *confianza* is a feeling that translates between Latinxs and Latin Americans, as it means the same in Spanish across regions. *Confi-*

*anza* is humanizing process centered on local communities, which involves exchanging mutual respect, critical reflection, caring and group participation. *Confianza* is dialogical trust, acceptance and confirmation between researchers and communities.

In my articles and books, I expand on this notion of *confianza* and learning about students and their communities, as well as how a stance open to students' complete linguistic repertoires, in turn, impacts the students' and their families' literacies and their networks of bilingual support. Angela Valenzuela argues that the "cared-for individual responds by demonstrating a willingness to reveal her/his essential self, the reciprocal relation" (21). These caring qualities truly create not only a sense of validation and support *en confianza*, but also a sense of trust, resulting in open dialogues about schools and community. Not surprisingly, establishing *confianza* takes time but is vital for opening channels for collaboration with community literacy research and after-school programs, especially those engaging with Latinx and Latin American students.

Why is this notion of *confianza* so vital for working with Latinx and Latin American students and their families? For Latinx students, research shows that *confianza* between non-familial adults and youth has positive impacts on the academic outcomes of children and adolescents in immigrant families (Louie; Smith). I remind myself constantly about my duty as an educator to mentor and establish *confianza* with Latinx students at all levels, to build community by investing in a human connection, and to be cognizant of the obstacles thrown at Latinx students. As a mentor, I see the importance of *confianza* connecting Latinx students to one another, and also to faculty and opportunities for professional development.

The same, of course, goes for future educators who learn about themselves by learning ethnography and engaging communities respectfully. With teachers conducting fieldwork in the communities, the opportunity is ripe to collaborate with students as co-researchers, with close ties to communities that warrant attention of schools and educators. Student ethnographers in the field collect data to write about, do inquiry into their own communities, and learn from the practices of where they belong, or, rather, to find out where they belong and to uncover the strands of meaning in contexts they know intimately. Ethnographic methods to study learning document language and literacy practices. The ethnographer, thus, mediates between audiences, brokers representations with subjective experiences while being attuned to the conventions of different genres. To this I add the importance of ethical responsibility to be truthful while building *confianza* both with the community so as to gain the insider perspective and with one's audience. Building rapport with individuals involved in qualitative research is fundamental to being an ethnographer. *Confianza* is earned rapport, and rapport as I deem it in my community literacy research is about trust that comes in the form of bidirectional learning that disrupts hierarchized power inequalities. *Confianza* also requires literacy researchers and teachers to be participants in public communication practices and to learn from student writers. The hands-on practice with communities and humanizing research that serves future literacy teachers is also what I advocate. With deepened community experience, composition instructors can prepare for future interactions and grow as educators by developing pedagogical praxis emergent from qualitative research findings. Future teachers learn through community participation during fieldwork the funds of knowledge of students and their communities and coordinate classroom practices that embrace and extend care for students' strengths. Honoring plurality in classrooms is a worthy goal of ethnographic composition pedagogy.

## Works Cited

Bartlett, Leslie, and Ofelia García. *Additive Schooling in Subtractive Times: Bilingual Education and Dominican Youth in the Heights.* Nashville: Vanderbilt UP, 2011. Print.

Louie, Vivian. *Keeping the Immigrant Bargain: The Costs and Rewards of Success in America.* New York: Russell Sage Foundation, 2012. Print.

Smith, Robert Courtney. *Mexican New York: Transnational Lives of New Immigrants.* Berkeley: U of California P, 2006. Print.

Valenzuela, Angela. *Subtractive Schooling: U.S.-Mexican Youth and the Politics of Caring.* Albany: SUNY P, 1999. Print.

# Identity, Decolonialism, and Digital Archives

*Cruz Medina*

In April, I was the keynote speaker at the University of Texas at El Paso's Spring Symposium, an annual event hosted by Frontera Rétorica, the graduate student chapter of Rhetoric Society of America. In my talk, "Decolonizing Digital Platforms," I cited a 2017 Hispanic Pew Research report that provided exigency for my call to decolonize digital habits of mind in the context of the U.S./Mexico border. The Pew Report found that 54% of Latinxs felt confident about their place in the U.S. under the new presidential administration (Hugo Lopez and Rohal). These findings suggest disparities among Latinx in the U.S. in the levels of critical awareness about issues of race, class, citizenship, and language. Many Latinx rhetoric and composition scholars resist and counteract these disparities through a spectrum of emerging research foci, such as the decolonial potential of theory and practices for the field (Baca, *Mestiz@*; Ruiz and Sánchez), digital rhetoric and writing (Cedillo; Gonzales; Medina and Pimentel), feminist filmmaking methodologies (Hidalgo), critical race theory (Martinez; Sanchez and Branson) as well as issues that have traditionally been associated with Latinx research like immigrant rights and activism (Arellano; Ribero); multilingual literacy (Alvarez); service-learning (Baca, *Service*) and culturally relevant pedagogy (Mejía; Serna). In this spectrum of emerging and established research, Latinx scholars engage in historiography, theoretical articulation, and analysis of local practices, contributing to a growing body of knowledge that resists dominant narratives that delegitimize through deficit rhetoric and logic of the colonial imaginary.

My book *Reclaiming Poch@ Pop* looks at the popular culture producers who self-identify as pocha/o and resist anti-Latinx legislation in California and Arizona rooted in colonial paradigms. In my book, I cite a 2012 Hispanic Pew Research study that found about half of Latinx had no preference when it came to identifying as "Hispanic" or "Latino" (Taylor, Hugo Lopez, Martínez and Velasco). This report served to highlight how many Latinx do not recognize the need for rhetorical sovereignty (King) and provide context for the skeletons of colonialism that came out of our collective familial closets during the lead up and aftermath of the presidential election.

In Iris Ruiz and Raúl Sánchez's edited collection, *Decolonizing Rhetoric and Composition Studies: New Latinx Keywords for Theory and Pedagogy*, contributors articulate how familiar terms within and beyond the Latinx community can be critically re-read against colonial narratives. Decolonial theory provides a generative, intersectional method for bringing to light historically significant knowledge that has been ignored by history. Following indigenous scholar

Angela Haas' work on wampum belts as technology, there is a great deal of potential for examining existing multimodal and digital practices from Latinx rhetorical traditions that contribute to a fuller discussion of technology with regard to people of color who "hack and yack" about issues other than the digital divide and access. Octavio Pimentel and I are currently co-editing a collection for Computer and Composition Digital Press called *Racial Shorthand: Coded Discrimination Contested in Social Media*, wherein contributors critique mischaracterizations of people of color in online media and offer examples of multimodal productions that draw on the rhetorical traditions of these misrepresented communities.

In July, I was elected co-chair of the NCTE/CCCC Latinx caucus and I feel hopeful about the important scholarship coming from members of the caucus, which is evidenced by the NCTE Latinx Caucus Publications Google Doc. I first circulated the Google Doc in 2014[1] to create a collaborative archive for members to consult when embarking on new projects and to raise awareness of shared research interests. Currently, the doc includes more than 160 works, the vast majority of which have been published in the last ten years, from more than 30 caucus members whose professional levels range from graduate students to full professors. With current concerns regarding cuts to National Endowment for the Humanities, plans to erect border walls, and attacks on professors speaking publically on issues of race, ethnicity, gender, sexuality and disability, we are in a moment when more Latinx resist the neoliberal passivity of "wait and see" by participating in professional leadership positions, serving on the boards of new and established publications, and collaborating with one another to build and curate a growing body of knowledge about our communities from within our communities.

## Notes

1. To access the Latinx Caucus Works Cited from July 14, 2017, visit https://docs.google.com/document/d/1MekJxC1cb4qoPzJvuFsEqV1tcjwov4XXVzkhY_4COZQ/edit?usp=sharing.

## Works Cited

Alvarez, Steven. "Translanguaging *Tareas*: Emergent Bilingual Youth Language Brokering Homework in Immigrant Families." *Language Arts* 91.5 (2014): 326-39. Print.

Arellano, Sonia. "A Maker Project: Writing about Material Culture." *Blog Carnival 8*. Digital Rhetoric Collaborative. 24 March 2016. Web. 1 August 2017. <http://www.digitalrhetoriccollaborative.org/2016/03/24/a-maker-project-writing-about-material-culture/>.

Baca, Damián. *Mestiz@ Scripts, Digital Migrations, and the Territories of Writing*. New York: Palgrave Macmillan, 2008. Print.

Baca, Isabel, ed. *Service-Learning and Writing: Paving the Way for Literacy(ies)through Community Engagement.* Leiden, The Netherlands and Boston: BRILL, 2012. Print.

Cedillo, Christina V. "Diversity, Technology, and Composition: Honoring Students' Multimodal Home Places." *Present Tense: A Journal of Rhetoric and Society* 6.2. 5 (2017): np. Web. <http://www.presenttensejournal.org/volume-6/diversity-technology-and-composition-honoring-students-multimodal-home-places/>.

Gonzales, Laura. "Multimodality, Translingualism, and Rhetorical Genre Studies." *Composition Forum* 31 (2015): np. Web. <http://compositionforum.com/issue/31/multimodality.php>.

Haas, Angela. "Wampum as Hypertext: An American Indian Intellectual Tradition of Multimedia Theory and Practice." *Studies in American Indian Literatures* 19.4 (2007): 77-100. Print.

Hidalgo, Alexandra. *Cámara Retórica: A Feminist Filmmaking Methodology for Rhetoric and Composition.* Logan: Computers and Composition Digital P/Utah State UP, 2017. Print.

Hugo Lopez, Mark, and Molly Rohal. *Latinos and the New Trump Administration: Growing Share Say Situation of U.S. Hispanics is Worsening.* Pew Research Center, 23 February 2017. Web. 6 July 2017. <http://www.pewhispanic.org/2017/02/23/latinos-and-the-new-trump-administration/>.

King, Lisa. "Sovereignty, Rhetorical Sovereignty, and Representation: Key Words for Teaching Indigenous Texts." *Survivance, Sovereignty, and Story: Teaching American Indian Rhetorics.* Ed. Lisa King, Rose Gubele, and Joyce Rain Anderson. Boulder: Colorado UP, 2015. 17-34. Print.

Martinez, Aja Y. "Critical Race Theory: Its Origins, History, and Importance to the Discourses and Rhetorics of Race." *Frame: Journal of Literary Studies* 27. 2 (2014): 9-27. Print.

Medina, Cruz. *Reclaiming Poch@ Pop: Examining the Rhetoric of Cultural Deficiency.* New York: Palgrave Macmillan, 2015. Print.

Medina, Cruz, and Octavio Pimentel, eds. *Racial Shorthand: Coded Discrimination Contested in Social Media.* Logan: Computers and Composition Digital Press, forthcoming.

Mejia, Jaime Armin. "Bridging Rhetoric and Composition Studies with Chicano and Chicana Studies: A Turn to Critical Pedagogy." *Latino/a Discourses: On Language, Identity & Literacy Education.* Ed. Michelle H Kells, Valerie M. Balester, and Victor Villanueva. Portsmouth: Boynton/Cook, 2004. 40-56. Print.

Ribero, Ana Milena. "'In Lak'Ech (You Are My Other Me):' Mestizaje as a Rhetorical Tool that Achieves Identification and Consubstantiality." *Arizona Journal of Interdisciplinary Studies* 2 (2013): 22-41. Print.

Ruiz, Iris, and Raúl Sánchez, eds. *Decolonizing Rhetoric and Composition Studies: New Latinx Keywords for Theory and Pedagogy.* New York: Palgrave Macmillan: 2016. Print.

Sanchez, James Chase, and Tyler Branson. "The Role of Composition Programs in De-Normalizing Whiteness in the University: Programmatic Approaches to Racial Pedagogies." *Writing Program Administration* 39.2 (2016): 47-52. Print.

Serna, Elias. "The Eagle Meets the Seagull: The Critical, Kairotic and Public Rhetoric of Raza Studies Now in Los Angeles." *Reflections: A Journal of Public Rhetoric, Civic Writing, and Service Learning* 12.3 (2013): 80-93. Print.

Taylor, Paul, Mark Hugo Lopez, Jessica Martínez, and Gabriel Velasco. *When Labels Don't Fit: Hispanics and Their Views of Identity.* Pew Research Center. 4 April 2012. Web. 1 August 2017. < http://www.pewhispanic.org/2012/04/04/when-labels-dont-fit-hispanics-and-their-views-of-identity/>.

# Decolonial Options and Writing Studies

*Iris Ruiz and Damián Baca*

Decolonial praxis in writing studies (WS) is not altogether new for Latinxs. For many of us, the commitment to decolonial thinking, writing, and teaching might be traced to the groundbreaking work of late indigenous Chicanx feminist Gloria Anzaldúa. Like Anzaldúa, we have spent a considerable amount of time resisting patterns of thought that arose in the context of European colonialism. For Latinxs and other scholars of color, the effects of colonialism are most damaging, yet least understood, in WS. The critical project of decoloniality inspires new conceptual formulations to account for colonial knowledge practices still limiting the study of written language and to enact anti-colonial resistance and transformation. The matter of how decolonial concepts might fit within existing frameworks and imaginaries of the field gives rise to a range of potentials and obstacles for practitioners, and we address a few here.

One of the main problems with WS is its own colonial unconscious. Studies of written language still theorize and teach writing as an alphabetic technology that emerged in Western Europe and spread throughout the world from ancient Greece to imperial Rome to enlightenment Germany, to eighteenth-century Anglo-North America by way of Western global expansion. Two centuries later, in the twentieth century, while Eurocentric ontologies remained dominant, we witnessed a "moment when . . . decolonial skepticism, and the creative thought of figures such as the Caribbean-Algerian Frantz Fanon and the Chicana Gloria Anzaldúa ... animate[d] new forms of theorizing based on the scandal in the face of the continuity of dehumanizing practices and ideas" associated with limited Eurocentric theories and knowledge and meaning-making practices (Maldonado-Torres 4). Along with this decolonial skepticism, the "imperative of epistemic decolonization, and in fact, of a consistent decolonization of human reality was also born" (14).

Anzaldúa's work in particular helps us critique and ultimately supersede the field's hierarchy of knowledge adapted from colonial histories. Similarly, our attempt to formulate alternatives involves efforts to dismantle cultural hierarchies still enforced by colonialism. Furthermore, decolonizing WS involves rethinking and revising the field's teleological macro-narratives of human progress, with whitened, Europeanized fourth-century Greeks cemented as the field's intellectual cradle.

We apply the theories of Anzaldúa, Enrique Dussel, Linda Tuiwai Smith, Walter Mignolo and others outside the field to analyze how colonized populations are subjected not only to exploitation of their own resources but also to a hegemony of Eurocentric histories, theories, and pedagogies. Such critique allows us to understand the dialectical relationship between historical domination and the pervasive alienation that scholars of color continue to experience in higher education. It also allows us to think through Anglo- and Eurocentric structures of representation that continue to dominate the field's governing gazes. Since the 2008 publication of *Mestiz@ Scripts, Digital Migrations, and the Territories of Writing* (Baca), scholars in the field have turned greater focus on non-Hellenocentric, non-Eurocentric, non-Anglocentric, decolonial modes of knowing and representation with attention to Indigenous, Latinx, and Latin American writing practices (Baca and Villanueva; Cushman; Olson and De los Santos; C. Ramírez; D. Ramírez; Ruiz, Ruiz and Sánchez; Thieme and Makmillan).

Taken together, these studies have the potential to inspire an eventual paradigm shift in the field. While Thomas Kuhn likely never thought that his notion of scientific paradigm shifts would be positively appropriated by Latinxs, he surely never imagined Latinxs when he developed his theory to explain how one might look at the same information in new ways. Following from Kuhn's concept of paradigm shift, epistemological and ideological shifts emerge from "knowing better and doing better" (Angelou). A familiar historical example is how worldviews adapted from a geocentric model of the solar system to a heliocentric model. With this shift in understanding came a new school of thought open to varied interpretations of the earth's place within the universe. Decolonial theory can facilitate such shifts in understanding to imagine writing otherwise in WS, writing no longer limited by Eurocentric foundations.

While not on the same scale as the scientific paradigm shift, an epistemological rupture can be connected to WS in the 1970s, when students of color gained more visibility, and studies diverged from structuralist approaches to texts and textual production and manifested in an ideological and epistemological paradigm shift inextricably tied to the rise of composition studies (Bizzell). Today many are experiencing another shift in that Latinxs in WS are revising the ways we conceive of texts, memory, history, identity, artistic production, nutrition, writing and rhetoric. Anzaldúa and critical third world feminist traditions prepared us for this shift in the 1980s, and have opened the door for people of color to conceive of writing ourselves and our knowledge differently on and beyond the page. As Latinx scholars with an indigenous/decolonial consciousness, our psyches resemble a bordertown of subject positions, as articulated by Anzaldúa:

> The struggle is inner: Chicano, indio, American Indian, mojado, mexicano, immigrant Latino, Anglo in power, working class Anglo, Black, Asian—our psyches resemble the bordertowns and are popu-

lated by the same people. The struggle has always been inner, and is played out in outer terrains. Awareness of our situation must come before inner changes, which in turn come before changes in society. Nothing happens in the "real" world unless it first happens in the images in our heads. (87)

Latinx scholars are struggling to reclaim erased histories. And while Latinx suffer from the cultural amnesia produced by formal schooling, we persist through the halls of the ivory tower with one eye closed, always searching for decolonial options, decolonial possibilities. It is no longer sufficient to think from the canon of Western philosophy; to do so is to reproduce the epistemic ethnocentrism that makes difficult, if not impossible, any philosophy of inclusion. The limit of Western philosophy is the border where colonial differences emerge, making visible the plurality of cultural histories that Western thought hides and suppresses (Mignolo 66).

We've gone from the sixteenth-century characterization of "people without writing" to the eighteenth and nineteenth century characterization of "people without history," to the twentieth century characterization of "people without development" to the early twenty-first century of "people without democracy." Today, colonial legacies continue to essentialize, demonize, criminalize, detain, deport, imprison . . . but we are speaking back. As Chicana/Indigena/Mexicana/Latinx scholars, our decolonial border consciousness is like a rough-edged mental schism; it jaggedly slides back and forth through identities, experiences, traumas, languages, and histories, hitting bricks and pikes between transitions. Our decolonial imperative, our contribution to WS, is to create and recreate the tools, perspectives, and practices most effective in helping to heal from the colonial wounds of Western history, and to create global realities no longer determined by imperial, Eurocentric horizons.

## Works Cited

Angelou, Maya. Interview by Oprah Winfrey. "Oprah Talks to Maya Angelou." *O, The Oprah Magazine*, December 2011. Web. 4 Aug. 2017. <http://www.oprah.com/oprahs-lifeclass/the-powerful-lesson-maya-angelou-taught-oprah-video>.

Anzaldúa, Gloria. *Borderlands/La Frontera: The New Mestiza*. San Francisco: Aunt Lute, 1987. Print.

Baca, Damián. *Mestiz@ Scripts, Digital Migrations, and the Territories of Writing*. New York: Palgrave Macmillan, 2008. Print.

Baca, Damián, and Victor Villanueva, eds. *Rhetorics of the Americas: 3114 BCE to 2012 CE*. New York: Palgrave Macmillan, 2010. Print.

Bizzell, Patricia. *Academic Discourse and Critical Consciousness*. Pittsburgh: U of Pittsburgh P, 1992. Print.

Cushman, Ellen. *The Cherokee Syllabary: Writing the People's Perseverance*. Normal: U of Oklahoma P, 2012. Print.

Dussel, Enrique. *Filosofía de la Liberación*. México: Fondo de Cultura Económica, 2011. Print.

Maldonado-Torres, Nelson. "Thinking through the Decolonial Turn: Post-continental Interventions in Theory, Philosophy, and Critique—An Introduction." *Transmodernity: Journal of Peripheral Cultural Production of the Luso-Hispanic World* 1.2 (2011): 1-15. Print.

Mignolo, Walter. "The Geopolitics of Knowledge and the Colonial Difference." *South Atlantic Quarterly* 101.1 (2002): 57-96. Print.

Olson, Christa, and René De los Santos. "La Idea de la Retórica Americana/The Idea of American Rhetoric." *Rhetoric Society Quarterly* 45.3 (2015): 193-8. Print.

Ramírez, Cristina. *Occupying Our Space: The Mestiza Rhetorics of Mexican Women Journalists and Activists, 1875–1942*. Tucson: U of Arizona P, 2015. Print.

Ramírez, Dora. *Medical Imagery and Fragmentation: Modernism, Scientific Discourse, and the Mexican/Indigenous Body, 1870–1940s*. Lanham: Lexington Books, 2017. Print.

Ruiz, Iris. *Reclaiming Composition for Chicano/as and other Ethnic Minorities*. New York: Palgrave Macmillan, 2016. Print.

Ruiz, Iris, and Sánchez, Raúl, eds. *Decolonizing Rhetoric and Composition: New Latinx Keywords for Rhetoric and Composition*. New York: Palgrave Macmillan, 2016. Print.

Thieme, Katja, and Shurli Makmillan. "A Principled Uncertainty: Writing Studies Methods in Contexts of Indigeneity." *CCC* 68.3 (2017): 466-93. Print.

Tuiwai Smith, Linda. *Decolonizing Methodologies: Research and Indigenous Peoples*. London: Zed Books, 2012. Print.

# Problematizing *Mestizaje*

Eric Rodriguez and Everardo J. Cuevas

or maybe
> what I hear when i'm here is the sound of us not dying or disappearing,
> just eating and talking and laughing and driving,
>> remembering who we are

—Malea Powell (2011)

As Chicanx graduate students early in our careers, we are reflective about naming and acknowledging our disciplinary expectations in this home we sometimes call "composition and rhetoric," among other names. As we grow as scholars and members of settler-colonial institutions (our institutional home, Michigan State University, built on Nkwejong, is often labeled the *pioneer* land-grant), we listen for the expectations of our disciplinary and lived communities. Surrounded by intersectional feminism and academic pushes for decoloniality, in a (more) diverse (than most) rhetoric and composition program in a predominantly white institution, we listen to those who have come before us as we unpack our own identities and how they relate to academia.

As Chicanxs, we know we bring mestizaje to the table, or "the process of interracial and/or intercultural mixing . . . in the Americas, particularly in those areas colonized by the Spanish and the Portuguese" (Martínez-Echazábal 21). It is through our understandings of mestizaje, reflective of the settler-colonial politics that still affect our shared realities, that we theorize the state of Latinx comp/rhet. Like Tim Dougherty, we too listen to Onondaga Clan Mother Frieda Jacques and engage in the labor of "learn(ing) our own people's story" in the hopes of offering another "path to excavating important stories that can help to someday eradicate my—our—collective ignorance" (Dougherty 7). To begin, we look back to look forward with a short analysis of a powerful myth from the wake of the Mexican Revolution: Vasconcelos' Raza Cosmica.

As rector for Mexico's National University and Secretary of Public Education, Jose Vasconcelos is historicized as a driving force in the Mexican nationalist agenda that was expressed throughout Mexico, in an art and philosophy era known as Mexicanismo. Mexicanismo is a popular philosophy among Mexican muralists, artists and makers of the early- and mid-twentieth century and has informed generations of Mexicanos' sense of identity. As a philosopher, Vasconcelos is also known for his essay "La Raza Cosmica," which outlines an argument for the validity and creation of a mestizo race. Arguing that mestizaje emerged from colonialism, which allowed the "four races" of the world to finally mix, he sees the resulting mestizo as more human. As Vasconcelos puts it, "The white race has brought the world to a state in which all human types and cultures will be able to fuse with each other" (405).

A driving force in Mexico's nationalist agenda, this understanding of mestizaje fueled Mexicanismo and a view of Mexican identity that could all at once *claim* Indigenous[1] rights to settled land and *erase* specific understandings of Indigeneity and relations to land before colonization. One way Mexicanismo did this was through art, philosophy and literature that attempted to cement an Aztec/Nahuatl origin for all Mexicanxs into popular culture. This myth, still prevalent in Mexican aesthetic expressions of identity, resulted in systemic erasure of many different Indigenous identities and peoples. As inheritors of this history and myth, we accept the messy complex stories brought to light as we also dream forward in less colonial ways.[2]

When asked to identify "where we are" as a discipline, we are asked to engage in the process of positioning ourselves. Anishinaabe researcher Kathleen Absolon writes, "I begin by locating myself because positionality, storying, and re-storying ourselves came first" (13). In order to engage in this process, our relationship to Indigeneity through our mestizaje must be problematized. The act of composing, among the most vulnerable performances academic spaces require of students, cannot be separated from the self. As Chicanx scholars in rhetoric and writing studies, we must be aware of the ways in which Chicanismo and Indigeneity are not connected, and of our responsibility for the knowledges and stories we carry.

Mestizaje, in a sense, has been used to create a sense of nationalistic pride that is colonial in its erasure of Indigenous epistemologies and ontologies. The cultural practices we as Chicanxs engage in, while not uniform, are often extensions of Indigenous practices that go unnamed, disrespected and unrecognized. At times, it is necessary to delink our sense of Chicanismo and Indigeneity to model a practice of decoloniality. The practice of epistemic delinking "from the falsely universalized notions of rhetoric that have accompanied Western Modernity's spread across this hemisphere" has been theorized and applied in *Decolonizing Rhetoric and Composition Studies: New Latinx Keywords for Theory and Pedagogy* (Ruiz and Sanchez xiv). In the collection, Gabriela Raquel Ríos theorizes the implications of mestizaje in contemporary Chicanx and Indigenous studies. With Ríos, we agree that our field needs to "disavow [Mestizaje's] universalizing, racist, and reductive tendencies" so as to not "reify the logics of cultural and biological purity" (Ríos 121). We also agree with Santos Ramos and Angélica De Jesús when they argue that "it's essential for us to at least try and know something about how our various [Xicano] cultures are positioned in relation to one another" (3) as we begin to unpack our academic relations. We are problematizing our sense of mestizaje to disrupt the erasure of Indigenous epistemologies and ontologies. We should continue to work on understanding Indigeneity separate from mestizaje, denouncing some of the more toxic aspects of Chicanismo, such as problematic claims to land, practices, and knowledges that were not ours to begin with.

For Chicanx and Latinx scholars, we posit that the rhetorical choices we make in our scholarship and in our teaching should reflect the type of thinking we advocate when calling for a simultaneous delinking and rejoining of mestizaje. To embrace our messy, problematic stories is one way to practice decoloniality. Rather than trying to compose the mestizx through blood quantum, for instance, we should begin by examining our stories as they exist, our traditions, our words, our names, our foods—our rhetorical practices—and beyond simply acknowledging their Indigenous origins, re-membering and re-learning how to honor them. Alongside this notion, if anxious to start unpacking these relations because of not knowing "where to start," we acknowledge the difficulty of wading through colonial erasure as one of our challenges. Like Two-Spirit (non-citizen) Cherokee writer Qwo-Li Driskill challenging queer studies to "include a consciousness about the ongoing colonial reality in which all of us living in settler-colonial states are entrenched" (23), we suggest that self-educating about local Indigenous histories and supporting local struggles for Indigenous sovereignty on the lands we currently call home and the universities where we work is another way to begin to work through the fog of colonial erasure. We offer this short essay as a place to start the delinking process in the same way that we have begun to unpack our understandings of mestizaje by (un)learning from the people who came before us.

## Notes

1. We intentionally capitalize "Indigenous" following Shawn Wilson's choice in *Research is Ceremony*. Wilson uses the word as an adjective "relating to Indigenous people and peoples" (15). We capitalize to honor the peoples depicted by the word, while understanding there are many reasons to capitalize or not.

2. Here we draw from arguments posited by the Cultural Rhetorics Theory Lab in "Our Story Begins Here: Constellating Cultural Rhetorics" when thinking about the importance of listening to complex or even painful stories.

## Works Cited

Absolon, Kathleen. *Kaandossiwin: How We Come to Know*. Nova Scotia: Fernwood Publishing Company, 2012. Print.

The Cultural Rhetorics Theory Lab. "Our Story Begins Here: Constellating Cultural Rhetorics." *Enculturation: A Journal of Rhetoric, Writing, and Culture*, 25 Oct. 2014. Web. 21 Aug. 2017. <http://enculturation.net/our-story-begins-here>.

Dougherty, Timothy. "Knowing (Y)Our Story: Practicing Decolonial Rhetorical History." *Enculturation: A Journal of Rhetoric, Writing, and Culture*, 20 April 2016. Web. 12 July 2017. <http://enculturation.net/knowing-your-story>.

Driskill, Qwo-Li. *Asegi Stories: Cherokee Queer and Two-Spirit Memory*. Tucson: U of Arizona P, 2016. Print.

Martínez-Echazábal, Lourdes. "Mestizaje and the Discourse of National/Cultural Identity in Latin America, 1845-1959." *Latin American Perspective* 25.100 (1998): 21-42. Print.

Powell, Malea. "Real Indians." *Sovereign Erotics: A Collection of Two-Spirit Literature*. Ed. Qwo-Li Driskill, Daniel Heath Justice, Deborah Miranda, and Lisa Tatonetti. Tuscon: U of Arizona P, 2011. 57-58. Print.

Ramos, Santos F., and Angélica De Jesús. "Xicano Indigeneity & State Violence: A Visual/Textual Dialogue." *Present Tense: A Journal of Rhetoric in Society*, 2015. Web. 10 August 2017. <www.presenttensejournal.org/volume-5/xicano-indigeneity-state-violence-a-visualtextual-dialogue/>.

Ríos, Gabriela Raquel. "Mestizaje." *Decolonizing Rhetoric and Composition Studies: New Latinx Keywords for Theory and Pedagogy*. Ed. Iris D. Ruiz and Raúl Sánchez. New York: Palgrave Macmillan, 2016. 109-24. Print.

Ruiz, Iris D., and Raúl Sanchez. "Introduction." *Decolonizing Rhetoric and Composition Studies: New Latinx Keywords for Theory and Pedagogy*. Ed. Iris D. Ruiz and Raúl Sánchez. New York: Palgrave Macmillan, 2016. xiii-xx. Print.

Vasconcelos, Jose. "The Cosmic Race." *Modern Art in Africa, Asia, and Latin America: An Introduction to Global Modernisms*. Ed. Elaine O'Brien, Everlyn Nicodemus, Melissa Chiu, Benjamin Genocchio, Mary K. Coffey, and Roberto Tejada. Hoboken: Blackwell Publishing, 2015. 402-12. Print.

Wilson, Shawn. *Research Is Ceremony: Indigenous Research Methods*. Nova Scotia: Fernwood Publishing, 2009. Print.

# Speaking from and about Brown Bodies: A Personal and Political Story of Sharing Identities

*Nicole Gonzales Howell*

When I began studying the rhetorics of social activist Dolores Huerta, I was only vaguely familiar with her story. I knew she had worked closely with Cesar Chavez advocating for better working conditions for farm workers in California's Central Valley. With this limited knowledge, I felt drawn to her. I quickly discovered we shared so much. I, like Huerta, grew up in the Central Valley of California. I, like Huerta, was never a farm laborer but am very close to many who were. I, like Huerta, am Chicana and a mother. I, like Huerta, fight for authority and credibility in a field from a body that, to many, does not exude either.

Through my dissertation research analyzing the rhetorical strategies Huerta utilized to construct her ethos, I found that Huerta's most highly recognizable embodied identities—her gender, ethnic and racial identity—as well as her social class significantly impacted how she crafted her connections to her varied audiences. Huerta was often received and perceived as a mother-woman-Chicana before she was seen as the Vice President of the United Farm Workers Union or the chief negotiator for farm laborer rights.

This finding does not disrupt our understanding of composition and/or composition studies. In fact, it is in keeping with many theories of composition and rhetoric. It does, however, emphasize the importance of intersectionality. Kimberlee Crenshaw first coined the term, which calls attention to the challenges of negotiating multiple oppressions. I learned this word many years ago and felt I understood the theory, the meaning, and the implications. But one day, it was no longer just a theory. It was, indeed is, so much more.

Huerta's life, her story, her ways of being, and her rhetorical strategies pushed me toward meta-awareness of how my own identities messed with my academic research methods, messed with my learning, messed with my teaching, writing, and growing. My research was no longer just about Huerta. My work "about her" became work about me and people like me. Like her.

> As a Latina, I have a vested interest in understanding how my body influences my ethos, my credibility, my trustworthiness. My relationship to power.

> As a Chicana and mother, I have a vested interest in how my motherly ethos affects my authority.

As a monolingual Latina, I have a vested interest in how the lack of a shared language with those that I share a heritage affects my credibility.

In other words, in researching Huerta, my intersectional identities and ethos became heightened alongside hers.

Both of my parents were farm workers. I grew up hearing stories of their hard childhoods and the backbreaking labor they worked so hard to keep us from enduring. I appreciate my parents for making certain we didn't have to do the same. But that distancing from their roots and hardships came at a big cost for me, and my sisters, too. Because my parents worked so hard to get away from their impoverished beginnings—my dad, a college graduate, and my mother, a small business owner—we ended up in white upper-middle-class neighborhoods, which meant that most of our community spoke "clear" and "unaccented" English and practiced white middle-class traditions.

We were never taught
Spanish. Never had a quinceañera.
Never made tortillas.
Instead we learned "proper" English.
We attended high performing schools, and we tried not to get too tan.

Although born decades earlier, Huerta's beginnings—much like mine—were forged in a middle-class home. Huerta's mother, Alicia Fernandez, was a small business owner. She owned a 70-room hotel that often housed migrant farmworkers at affordable rates. Huerta completed high school and earned her provisional teaching credential from the University of Pacific's Delta College. In her early career Huerta was a schoolteacher. It was after seeing many of the school children—often the children of farm workers—show up to school without shoes on their feet and without food in their bellies that she was moved to action. She began community organizing. Huerta was the inaugural vice president of the United Farm Workers union, and, at the time of this writing, she continues to champion social justice at age 87. Hers is a story of embodied sacrifice, of unrelenting service to others, and of breaking through boundaries and limitations often attributed to identity.

But, again, this isn't the only story here worth telling. The story often left untold when researchers examine subjects with whom they share so much, especially researchers and/or subjects who embody oppressed identities, is that the work is deeply political and personal.

I find it difficult to position Huerta and myself within a culture that tends to privilege rationality and objectivity and that often does not support the passionate and subjective people we both are and represent. For so many of us Huerta broke barriers, but critics and allies alike would often question her rationality. She's been called a "dragon lady," positioned as someone to fear, charged with being irrational. Delicate, fragile, contingent is the authority of a woman of color. Thus, I felt my heart in my throat when during my research, I encountered Huerta's use of the disparaging term "wetbacks" to describe undocumented Mexican nationals in the U.S. I chose to avoid any analysis. In academia, steeped in canonical study and highbrow ways, I am her protector. She fought for equality from a compromised body. We continue to fight for change in institutions that think we are deficient because of our writing, our thinking, our inability to quack like ducks.

And now my multiple oppressions are showing.

Huerta's intersectionality, her complex and varied identities, provided channels for both connection and distance to and from her audiences. My intersectionality offers channels for connection and division to and from my audiences.

This is a story of two Chicanas who built credibility one piece at a time from whatever resources were accessible. We are two Chicanas who built authority from bodies that carry with them many cultural symbols that place us in the margins. But our bodies are central to our lived realities; they are not actually "marginalized" or "othered." They are not "somewhere out there" because they are ours.

Yet, this story is but a fragment of a much larger project investigating the challenges of doing scholarly work with figures of study who are traditionally marginalized and who directly affect the scholar both as researcher and as part of the community/identities being studied. Due to my own disciplining I would like to offer some "new" finding because that's what "good" academics do; that's what we need. But I offer you no conclusion, no solutions, no resolutions, and no interventions. Instead, I offer a story because our stories matter, and when surveying "where we are," I see that we still need more stories that are by and about Latinx communities. We need to speak frankly and in familiar styles that demonstrate the power that comes from our stories. Indeed, our stories are not somewhere in the margins. They are stories of power and authority. Stories of a will to survive in unfriendly territories. And stories that are central to all of us.

## Works Cited

Crenshaw, Kimberle. "Mapping the Margins: Intersectionality, Identity Politics, and Violence Against Women of Color." *Stanford Law Review*. 43.6 (1991): 1241-99. Print.

# Book Reviews

**Decolonizing Rhetoric and Composition Studies: New Latinx Keywords for Theory and Pedagogy**, edited by Iris D. Ruiz and Raúl Sánchez. New York: Palgrave Macmillan, 2016. 195 pp.

*Reviewed by J. Paul Padilla, University of Arizona*

*Decolonizing Rhetoric and Composition Studies: New Latinx Keywords for Theory and Pedagogy* represents a movement among some twenty-first century Latinx scholars to claim and reclaim rhetoric and writing from colonialism. As a whole, *Decolonizing Rhetoric and Composition Studies* distinguishes itself because of its conceptualization and application of the decolonial, which until now, with some exceptions, has been limited to indigenous studies in rhetoric and composition. The concepts of decolonization, decoloniality, and epistemic delinking serve as the lens through which Latinx scholars analyze rhetoric and writing from theoretical, pedagogical, and research perspectives and attempt to epistemically delink language "from the falsely universalized notions of rhetoric that have accompanied Western Modernity's spread across this hemisphere" (xiv).

The Latinx culture itself inspires and influences the conceptual framework and application of the decolonial in this collection. Editors Iris D. Ruiz and Raúl Sánchez intended to bring the field "closer to issues that are relevant to Latinx's experiences" (xiv). Latinx scholars in *Decolonizing Rhetoric and Composition Studies*, argue Ruiz and Sánchez, follow "the process of recreating, redefining, and reviving" (xvi) that characterizes the work of rhetoric and writing scholars Victor Villanueva and Damián Baca, particularly in their edited collection *Rhetorics of the Americas* (xiv). To my mind, this process harkens back further to Villanueva's scholarship on memory and racism, Ellen Cushman's scholarship on the rhetorician as an agent of social change, and Scott Richard Lyons's scholarship on the formation of publics for publicly oriented writing classrooms.

In what follows, I evaluate *Decolonizing Rhetoric and Composition Studies* through the authors' conceptualization and application of the decolonial, description of the significance of racism to epistemic delinking and decoloniality, questions about the role of Latinx in the decolonial, and articulation of the problem the decolonial may pose to the field—a problem about which bell hooks wrote more than twenty years ago.

Decolonization, decoloniality, and epistemic delinking are interrelated concepts attributed to Walter Mignolo, the Argentine semiotician influenced by the Peruvian sociologist Aníbal Quijano, both pillars in the field of decolonial studies. To understand and implement epistemic delinking, the distinction between decolonization and decoloniality must be understood. In Mignolo's *The Darker Side of Western Modernity*, he describes decolonization as "a complex scenario of struggles" (82, qtd. in Sánchez) during which the elites—namely, European colonizers and their descendants—sought to govern themselves and expel "the imperial administration from the territory" (82, qtd. in Sánchez). Decoloniality, in contrast, addresses the aftermath of the elites' self-governance, an "imperialism without colonies" (82) that bred epistemic colonialism: *coloniality* (Ruiz and Sánchez xvi). Decoloniality, for Sánchez, represents the response to two rhetorical spheres: "the crooked rhetoric that naturalizes 'modernity' as a universal global process and point of arrival" (82), and coloniality that creates and continues the epistemic subordination of certain people and areas (82). Despite political independence, the elites rely on the colonial matrix of power (82), "the ongoing (and thoroughgoing) system of epistemological, ideological, economic, and cultural hegemony that was established, developed, and maintained through European expansion across the globe" (82).

Epistemic delinking entails thinking of language, writing, and discourse beyond the influences of colonialism and coloniality. Latinx scholars focus on different facets of epistemic delinking in their work. In "Poch@," for example, Cruz Medina defines Mignolo's decolonial act of delinking in terms of its ability "'to change the terms and not just the content of the conversation,' thereby changing the content more profoundly" (95). Steve Alvarez, in "Literacy," draws on Mignolo's definition of delinking, offered in "Delinking," as "a 'decolonial epistemic shift leading to ... pluriversality as a universal project'" (20, qtd. in Alvarez) that examines the political-economic dynamic and informs strategies to disrupt the power imbalance resulting from the colonial matrix of power (20). In advocating for delinking through translingualism, Alvarez identifies the liberating potential for language-based social justice in rhetoric and composition studies because "(d)elinking entails the ability to re-read the world and the opportunity to re-write it" (27).

Epistemic delinking through re-appropriation concentrates on overarching objectives to address hegemonies. These objectives may contemplate smaller populations within the Latinx community, such as Cruz Medina's argument for the epistemic delinking of the pejorative term "pocho"—roughly, "cultural traitor" or "white-washed" —by reimaging pocho as "Poch@," a decolonial trope that would function "as a positive term, even a term of resistance" (94) for Latinx blogger groups in academia, and perhaps beyond. These objectives may apply to larger populations with national and international implications, as demonstrated in "Citizenship" by Ana Milena Ribero and "Illegal" by Amanda Espinosa-Aguilar. Ribero argues for the decolonization of U.S. citizenship in order to delink undocumented immigrants and others from exclusion and segregation created by the illusion of homogeneity among citizens (42). Espinosa-Aguilar argues that the concepts "immigrant" and "citizen" reflect the problem of linguicism—language that creates, promotes, and reproduces inequalities in power structures (159), planting fear into voters, which is often "tied to the distribution of limited resources" (155), to garner support for anti-immigration legislation. But, as productive as the re-appropriation of concepts like "immigrant" and "citizen" can be, the re-appropriation of pejorative terms, I fear, presents a different dynamic and, thus, a different problem of linguicism where, despite re-appropriation, pejorative terms like *pocho* continue to reinforce hegemonies.

In "History," Jose Cortez also builds on Mignolo's work to identify the ideological forces of colonialism in Latin America as evidenced in the relationship between alphabetic technology, including writing, and cultural identity at the core of political sovereignty (51). Language in rhetoric and writing becomes a central concern politically, epistemologically, and ontologically. For Latinx in the U.S., the analysis of language in rhetoric and writing calls for a confrontation with a core element of colonialism and coloniality: racism.

Iris D. Ruiz, in "Race," and Gabriela Raquel Rios's "*Mestizaje*" provide important perspectives on racism critical to decoloniality and epistemic de-linking. Racism, Ruiz argues, as an operation of race, is a social instrument of domination that constructs classifications and hierarchies through discourse. Examining definitions of race from Michel Foucault, James Berlin, and Linda Brodkey, Ruiz argues that racism "serves current power structures, affects material realities unequally across racial groups, and distorts the real-life experiences of humans who belong to races with long histories of oppression" (14). W.E.B. DuBois, Ruiz notes, describes the troubling complexities of race: race is not a concept, but a group of contradictions—contradictory trends, tendencies, forces, and facts—that ultimately "kills people" (14).

Rios questions the re-appropriation of racial tropes and the exclusion of essential cultural perspectives on those tropes and decoloniality. Rios concentrates on *mestizaje*, a category of racial configurations in Mexico and other countries that signifies the mixture of Spaniard and Indigenous blood and cultural worth. Chicanx and others have re-appropriated *mestizaje* as a trope to communicate its intellectual traditions. But this re-appropriation "often unwittingly reifie[s] the racial dynamics through which *mestizaje* functions, both epistemologically and ontologically" (109) and promotes "the logics of cultural and biological purity" (121). The romanticizing and fetishizing of Indigenous cultural practices, including writing; the erasure of indigenous futurity; and the pure/mixed fallacy (121)—these three tendencies associated with *mestizaje* trap Indigenous cultures in time and vitiate Indigenous rhetorical practices, rhetorical agency, and writing (121). Rios argues that a decolonial approach to *mestizaje* should disavow the trope entirely or "its universalizing, racist, and reductive tendencies" (121). Rios' decolonial approach exposes disparities in the focus and purpose of decolonization. Rios argues that Latin American Studies approaches decolonization as discursive, epistemological, and future orientated while Indigenous Studies approaches decolonization as an issue of sovereignty primarily, which emphasizes settler colonialism and the dismantling of colonialism (113).

Through these perspectives, Ruiz and Rios underscore a salient point about the decolonial, which, for some readers, also underlies a criticism of the collection: decolonization, decoloniality, and epistemic delinking are not exclusive to Latinx. Moreover, *Decolonizing Rhetoric and Composition Studies* focuses almost entirely on the Latinx community in the U.S., yet the term "Latinx" is not explicitly defined. The absence of a definition may raise confusion among readers unfamiliar with the complex nationalities, cultures, and communities that cannot be so easily conflated.

The pages of *Decolonizing Rhetoric and Composition Studies* capture Latinx scholars grappling with hegemonic rhetoric and writing from public, political, and private forums that couple Americana with Latinx, the Ivory Tower with kitchen tables, the classroom with publics, History with silences. As Villanueva puts it in the forward to the volume, "Colonialism remains, despite the post- and the de-. It's a knotty problem. In the pages that follow attempts are made to lay out the problems so that we might begin to untie the knots" (viii). Indeed, the scholars who contribute to the collection imagine the decolonial as the means to shape theory, pedagogy, and research and to challenge notions of colonialism and coloniality in rhetoric and writing. These scholars imagine liberating potential of the decolonial, captured best by Alvarez who claims that epistemic delinking creates "the ability to re-read the world and the opportunity to re-write it" (27).

Epistemic delinking, decolonization, and decoloniality require grappling with the core of colonialism and coloniality, racism. Grappling with racism may require grappling with ourselves. "In short," Ruiz writes, "the field has not addressed racism in all of its complexities" (5). Ruiz calls for us "to talk about race, as it is still the 'absent presence'" in the field (5), a phrase borrowed from Catherine Prendergast. Addressing pedagogical theory in the classroom, bell hooks wrote of the significance of grappling with racism in 1994, alongside her then-Oberlin College colleague Chandra Mohanty: "We had not realized how much faculty would need to unlearn racism to learn about colonization and decolonization . . . " (38). Our knotty problem. Grappling with our problem would reveal the challenges in re-reading and re-writing the world—the risks of entanglement that we would have to accept to free knots, our own and others, and the choice inherent to the decolonial option that we would have to face: to engage or to ignore.

*Tucson, Arizona*

**Works Cited**

Baca, Damián, and Victor Villanueva. *Rhetorics of the Americas: 3114 BCE to 2012 CE*. New York: Palgrave, 2010. Print.

Cushman, Ellen. "The Rhetorician as an Agent of Social Change." *CCC* 47.1 (1996): 7-28. Print.

DuBois, W. E. B. *Dusk of Dawn*. 1940. Oxford: Oxford UP, 2007. Print.

hooks, bell. *Teaching to Transgress: Education as the Practice of Freedom*. New York: Routledge, 1994. Print.

Lyons, Scott Richard. "Rhetorical Sovereignty: What Do American Indians Want from Writing?" *CCC* 51.3 (2000): 447-68. Print.

Mignolo, Walter D. *The Darker Side of Western Modernity: Global Futures, Decolonial Options*. Durham: Duke UP, 2011. Print.

---. "Delinking: The Rhetoric of Modernity, the Logic of Coloniality, and the Grammar of De-Coloniality." *Cultural Studies* 21.2-3 (2007): 449-514. Print.

Prendergast, Catherine. "Race: The Absent Presence in Composition Studies." *CCC* 50.1 (1998): 36-53. Print.

Villanueva, Victor. "'Memoria' Is a Friend of Ours: On the Discourse of Color." *College English* 67.1 (2004): 9-19. Print.

**Cross-Border Networks in Writing Studies,** by Derek Mueller, Andrea Williams, Louise Wetherbee Phelps, and Jennifer Clary-Lemon. Anderson: Parlor P; Edmonton: Inkshed, 2017. 196 pp.

*Reviewed by Chen Chen, North Carolina State University*

*Cross-Border Networks in Writing Studies* examines the disciplinarity of Canadian writing studies using a "networked methodological approach" (6). Tracing the scholarly, social, and professional networks of the field from both distant and close perspectives, the authors explore the development of the Canadian branch of writing studies and its relationships with the U.S. discipline. This book contributes to our understanding of the challenges faced by Canadian writing studies in terms of both legitimizing its disciplinary identity and sustaining its disciplinary networks. Also, others can adapt its methodological approach to study a variety of disciplinary networks.

A major inspiration for a networked view of the discipline comes from Randall Collins's *The Sociology of Philosophies,* which argues that intellectual activities are essentially networked ideas produced and enhanced through social engagements among scholars by way of "interactive rituals" both in writing and in face-to-face communication such as conferences, lectures, or workshops (qtd. in Mueller, Williams, Wetherbee Phelps, and Clary-Lemon 82). This view proves productive for the authors when they begin to investigate the characteristics of Canadian writing studies, including the history, development, disciplinary identity, and shape of its social networks. Canadian writing studies is still an emergent field because there are very few writing programs or departments in Canadian universities, both at the undergraduate and graduate levels. Many Canadian writing scholars have been trained in graduate programs in the U.S. before either working in Canada or staying in the U.S.; they have also been primarily publishing in U.S. journals. These institutional and national constraints and educational and professional experiences have led to many border-crossing activities—including mentorships, publications, and professionalization activities—and to the construction of complex disciplinary networks.

The authors argue that these unique border-crossing characteristics of scholarly activities call for a unique networked methodological approach to examine the history and development of Canadian writing studies. Informed by network studies, the authors have carried out a networked "series of operations" through related and coordinated interdependent methodologies (7), each distinctively presented in chapters two through five, and involving methods ranging from a qualitative survey and geographical data mapping, to qualitative interviews, genre analysis, and instrumental case study. This methodological approach represents the principles of "networks" borrowed from Clay Spinuzzi, who describes them as "heterogeneous, multiply linked, transformative, and black-boxed" (8). Because the relationships and associations between participants traced here are heterogeneous and constantly shifting, research findings are often evolving as participants relocate for professional reasons (changing jobs, moving from graduate school to professorship), thus impacting their professional networks. The studies represented in this collection are linked in that results from one study inform the design of another, and one study may provide a magnified view of smaller parts of another. The networked phenomena constituted by people, texts, narratives, identifications, institutions, and locations are not stagnant; these phenomena are transformed as they circulate through the case studies, pointing to variations of interdependency between Canadian and U.S. writing studies. In this research process, certain complex black-boxed qualities, such as assumptions about participants' national identifications, get unpacked, revealing the historical development of scholarly activities that constitute and maintain these identifications (9). Finally, the authors add a fifth principle focused on "deliberate, purposeful considerations of scale (distance versus close) and aperture (wide versus narrow)," that illustrates in more detail transformations of the networked phenomena (9).

In chapter two, Derek Mueller takes the most distant approach to map the professional networks of Canadian writing scholars, including the geographic reach of their self-identification, engagement with professional organizations, conferences, listservs and publishing, and the locations associated with their professional activities. Distant methods produce an innovative view of disciplinarity that expands the traditional scholarship defining Canadian writing studies in the "context of teaching, writing, and research" (Clary-Lemon 99) by noticing its "time-sensitive patterns and emerging shapes" in the process of disciplinary formation (23). Visualized networks in these maps demonstrate that a scholar's career can be both "emplaced and distributed" as illustrated by a map showing the networks of one scholar, Dale Jacobs, both diachronically throughout his career across the national border and synchronically connecting with other members of the field through mentorship (43).

Informed by Mueller's survey results, in chapter three Andrea Williams examines more closely the scholarly and professional identities of Canadian writing studies scholars through in depth interviews about their interpersonal relationships built in broader professional contexts such as academic conferences and intra- and inter-institutional contexts. Williams argues that scholarly communities established and sustained in these contexts serve an important role in supporting the evolving identities of individual scholars, both new and experienced. For example, institutional hubs such as the Carleton group at Carleton University—the home of one of the few Canadian doctoral programs in writing studies (PhD in Applied Linguistics and Discourse Studies) and founded by Professor Emeritus Aviva Freedman—have produced many Canadian writing studies scholars through direct mentorship. Investigation into scholarly communities also reveals that other factors such as funding mechanisms and disciplinary structures in Canadian academia impact the evolving identities of scholars and the discipline because Canadian scholars often struggle with disciplinary marginalization and invisibility in their own institutions and/or nationally.

Due to this marginalization and invisibility, individual scholars and the rare writing programs suffer the lack of "presence" measured by peer recognition (84), which is usually acknowledged through conventional publications, not in the context of the dynamic, competitive environment that characterizes the Canadian disciplinary landscape. Therefore, chapter four and five focus on specific cases at the individual and programmatic levels respectively, where presence can be achieved through cross-border, interdependent activities and relationships. In chapter four, Louise Wetherbee Phelps examines how four scholars' unconventional genres of publication contribute to the dynamic Canadian disciplinary networks even though they may not fit the model of the traditionally recognized disciplinary-based research. She argues that such genres should be considered scholarly disciplinary work. In chapter five, Jennifer Clary-Lemon's case study of the only Canadian independent writing department at University of Winnipeg illustrates cross-border interdependent disciplinary relationships both diachronically and synchronically. In this case, departmental development is informed by models and scholarship from American writing studies but also influences both Canadian and U.S. writing studies by offering details on curriculum design that would be applicable in both countries. These case studies also illustrate the collaborative and recursive interdependent relationships between Canadian and U.S. branches of writing studies.

The concluding chapter offers suggestions to strengthen Canadian writing studies and its disciplinary networks. One is to build alliances among Canadian institutional hubs such as Carleton University and University of Toronto, which focus on research and teaching respectively (150), to help secure more research funding for writing studies north of the U.S. border. Opening institutional networks will also enhance the social networks of scholars built both through scholarly publications and through scholarly activities such as conferences and cross-institutional mentorship. However, the authors do note the challenges of sustaining Canadian writing studies publications, as most Canadian scholars have been publishing primarily in American journals. Furthermore, the book also suggests inquiries into other networked disciplinary activities. One example is to trace the development of a specific idea in Canadian writing scholarship through disciplinary networks. Finally, the authors argue that more graduate programs need to be established in Canada to train writing scholars and writing teachers, which would continue to expand its disciplinary networks.

Traditionally, scholarship on the disciplinarity of rhetoric and composition has focused on the historical and professional development of the discipline, its epistemological shifts as reflected in the production of scholarship, and the history and the work of writing program administration. Only recently have we begun to venture into other ways to write our discipline. For example, in Bruce McComiskey's edited collection of the microhistories of rhetoric and composition authors bring into focus the previously neglected stories and accounts in the discipline that have contributed to our disciplinary development and challenged the dominant narratives of disciplinarity. Additionally, Jeremy Tirrell and Derek Mueller have both adopted distant methods to map the discipline's publications. This book presents yet another example of networked disciplinarity that focuses on the interrelations among scholars across geographical and institutional boundaries. Especially impressive are the authors' extensive "multi-scale/multi-scopic" (165) efforts to trace the expansive networks through the social and professional experiences of members in the field. They transform the ways we define disciplinarity and disciplinary work, informing research such as my own work on networked activities at CCCC and WPA-L, and accounting for the varied lived experiences of scholars and the constant shifting of the heterogeneous disciplinary networks. As rhetoric and composition continues to expand beyond the confines of the United States, which is already exemplified in scholarship on international writing research and exchanges at scholarly sites such as Writing Research Across Borders conferences, this methodological approach will be useful in studying various forms of disciplinary work and disciplinary networks.

*Raleigh, North Carolina*

**Works Cited**

Clary-Lemon, Jennifer. "Shifting Tradition: Writing Research in Canada." *American Review of Canadian Studies* 39.2 (2009): 94–111. Print.

Collins, Randall. *The Sociology of Philosophies: A Global Theory of Intellectual Change.* Cambridge: Belknap, 1998. Print.

McComiskey, Bruce, ed. *Microhistories of Composition.* Logan: Utah SUP, 2016. Print.

Mueller, Derek. "Grasping Rhetoric and Composition by Its Long Tail: What Graphs Can Tell Us about the Field's Changing Shape." *CCC* 64.1 (2012): 195-223. Print.

Spinuzzi, Clay. *Network: Theorizing Knowledge Work in Telecommunications.* Cambridge: Cambridge UP, 2008. Print.

Tirrell, Jeremy. "A Geographical History of Online Rhetoric and Composition Journals." *Kairos: A Journal of Rhetoric, Technology, and Pedagogy* 16.3 (2012): np. www.kairos.technorhetoric.net/16.3/topoi/tirrell/. Accessed 8 July 2017.

**The Meaningful Writing Project: Learning, Teaching, and Writing in Higher Education**, by Michele Eodice, Anne Ellen Geller, and Neal Lerner. Logan: Utah State UP, 2016. 176 pp.

*Reviewed by Rick Fisher, University of Wyoming*

In my various past and present roles teaching service-learning courses, supporting an institutional transition to new writing-across-the curriculum course outcomes, and directing a writing center, I have always been interested to know more about "what matters" in writing assignments and instruction. Thus I was eager to read Michele Eodice, Anne Ellen Geller, and Neal Lerner's *The Meaningful Writing Project: Learning, Teaching, and Writing in Higher Education*.

As the title suggests, the book sets out to answer the question, "What does it mean for writing to be meaningful?" Based on results of a four-year study conducted across the authors' home institutions—University of Oklahoma, St. John's University, and Northeastern University—and including senior student survey responses (707) and interviews (27) as well as faculty surveys (160) and interviews (60), the book explores "meaningful" writing assignments primarily from a student-centered learning standpoint. It contributes to ongoing conversations in composition studies by providing new evidence to support arguments for best practices in composition, by challenging emerging notions of transfer, and by arguing for the importance of "expansive" learning opportunities (cf. Engle et al.) in the undergraduate curriculum. While other readers may find many different sections of this book compelling, I am drawn to the book's claim that meaningful writing is often related to an instructor's balance between choice and restriction, to its brief comparison of the authors' results to National Survey of Student Engagement (NSSE) data, and to the fascinating, small set of student participants who completed the survey primarily to say that they had never completed a meaningful writing project. As I think about how to engage colleagues across the curriculum in discussions about the kinds of writing projects they assign, these moments in the text seem likely to promote rich discussion.

The first chapter of the book situates this text among other book-length explorations of student writing (including books by Anne Beaufort; Lee Ann Carroll; Anne Herrington and Marcia Curtis; Nancy Sommers and Laura Saltz; Marilyn Sternglass; Rebecca Nowacek; and Dan Melzer), adding new breadth to the types of institutions and students represented in these previous works. An important goal of their project is to push back against a "narrative of crisis" (5) that frames college students as largely unprepared for college and for the dim employment prospects beyond. Eodice, Geller, and Lerner view that narrative as inadequately acknowledging the knowledge, experiences, and meanings that students bring to texts they create. Like Juan Guerra, Elizabeth Moje et al., and Kevin Roozen, the authors prefer to explore the richness—rather than the deficits—of students' prior experiences. The authors acknowledge the methodological complexities of their approach, which includes cross-institutional IRB processes, low participant response rates (just 7.4% for the survey of seniors), and poor inter-rater reliability. Despite these problems, their description of data collection and analysis is valuable reading for anyone considering the prospect of multi-site qualitative research. Ultimately, their grounded theory approach to analyzing the data guides Eodice, Geller, and Lerner to identify *agency, engagement,* and *learning for transfer* as key terms that drive much of the book's structure.

As the book shifts towards key findings, chapter two addresses the various ways that agency is reflected in student descriptions of meaningful writing projects, claiming that "agency, from the perspective of students participating in our research, consists of opportunities to pursue matters they are passionate about and/or to write something relevant to a professional aspiration or future pursuit" (35). Further, their analysis suggests that such opportunities are related to instructors and the task itself; other agential actors identified through the analysis include peers, the community, content, and the students' imagined future tasks and selves. I found it especially interesting to learn that the researchers found a co-occurrence of terms like "allowed" and "forced" in student responses. In other words, many instructors identified as assigning meaningful writing projects were characterized by participants as effectively blending freedom of choice with required components. This interpretation suggests that students view agency not as total autonomy but rather as embedded in social relationships, sometimes including the instructor as guide.

As chapter three moves away from *agency* toward the category of *engagement*, there are points of overlap between categories that make me wish for a tighter frame of analysis. Partially compensating for this categorical looseness, though, is the authors' decision to include case studies in most chapters. These engaging and illustrative sections reveal the complexity and depth of the responses. For example, the case study at the end of chapter two describes a student whose most meaningful writing project was a business ethics paper written mostly in a twenty hour all night session for an instructor the student did not like. Examples like this one draw attention to the ways that students' actions may not always match teachers' hopes and intentions. Yet, in a comment that echoes a broader conclusion of their work, the authors close this chapter with the caution that, "like empowerment, agency is not something we can (or should) bestow upon students. At best, we can build optimal conditions for agency to emerge" (53).

In chapter three, as the authors describe how *engagement* serves as a process that leads into meaningful writing projects, a strength of analysis is the careful identification of engagement as a social, rather than as only internal process. Critiquing definitions of engagement anchored in individualistic terms, the chapter focuses on the engagement that students described with "instructors and peers, with future selves, and with nonhuman entities" (56) and argues that meaningful writing projects serve as a point of convergence among student, teacher, and content.

Though this chapter is somewhat less tight than the previous chapter as it tries to unite numerous codes under its broad concept of *engagement*, the authors include statistical analysis that further contrasts meaningful writing projects with students' other writing experiences in college. Importantly, their comparison of NSSE data with a subset of their student survey responses allows Eodice, Geller, and Lerner to show that meaningful writing projects were statistically more likely to make use of composing and teaching practices that the field of composition "has put forth as ideal" (71)—practices such as informal writing, real or hypothetical audiences for writing projects, and peer review and feedback during various stages of the process. Writing program administrators might find this comparative section valuable in justifying resource and staffing goals—like faculty workloads and class sizes (see 72-73)—that are sometimes seen as extravagant or unnecessary by upper administrators. Additionally, I can envision using the graphs about writing practices, writing types, and instructor practices mentioned in meaningful writing projects (70-72) to promote dialogue among teachers across the curriculum about their approaches to writing projects.

In connecting meaningful writing and *learning for transfer*, chapter four contributes some of the book's most interesting theoretical work. Carefully acknowledging the contemporary difficulty of defining and assessing transfer, this chapter promotes a shift in focus from *teaching* for transfer toward *learning* for transfer. For the authors, this shift encourages a more "generative, reciprocal arrangement" (97) that entrusts students with responsibility for an authorial role in their learning. Additionally, the researchers' analysis suggests that students found writing meaningful when they were able to practice or learn something that allowed them to stretch existing knowledge or skill into new spaces—often in agentive or engaged ways that allowed students the freedom to transfer a part of themselves into their writing projects. This finding contrasts with deficit-oriented conceptions of *teaching* for transfer, according to the authors, in that "an orientation toward teaching for transfer may limit our understanding of what students actually do transfer in learning and writing" (94). I suspect many readers may find this chapter to be an important contribution to the contemporary dialogue about transfer in composition and in learning more generally.

Focusing on *faculty* surveys and interviews, chapter five helps triangulate the claims of previous chapters. Though the researchers had initially expected students to refer to relatively few instructors of meaningful writing projects, they instead discovered nearly 500 unique faculty members named in the 700 student survey responses. While the primary contribution of this chapter is depth (in that the faculty responses substantially reinforce student views), it also discusses *explicitness* as an additional characteristic of meaningful writing experiences; teachers who were identified as assigning meaningful writing "were easily able to articulate the ways writing worked in their classes, the importance they saw for disciplinary writing, and the challenges and triumphs they faced repeatedly in their work with students" (128). Though this finding may seem unsurprising, it provides another opportunity to challenge faculty across the disciplines to explain the genre expectations of their writing assignments, and perhaps even more importantly, to unpack for students why they are asking them to do what they are doing.

In the closing chapter, this book offers some takeaway suggestions. Here the authors are careful to avoid over-extending the implications of their work and focus instead on reinforcing their major claim that meaningful writing is, ultimately, a student-centered determination:

> What seems key to is us that faculty . . . set assignment parameters with enough student choice and enough encouragement of student agency that students may *choose* to take up the invitation, and, if allowed and further encouraged, will bring the power of personal connection, future relevance, and deep immersion to what they're thinking, writing, and researching. (133)

While this conclusion is not an earth-shattering one (for example, it echoes Vincent Tinto's distinction between student retention and student persistence), the authors' effort to center students' views of meaningful writing, rather than teachers', is an important one. As I mentioned in the opening, I found one of the most interesting results of the study to be a group of 28 students who, rather than ignoring the study's survey request, took time to explain that they had had no meaningful writing project in their undergraduate experience. While the authors suggest that these responses may thus indicate "absence of agency" (43), the responses also demonstrate the kinds of experiences that *could have been* meaningful for these students. Rather than leaving me feeling pessimistic about lost opportunity, this part of the book—and indeed the larger project overall—encourages me to rethink my own teaching and my approaches to engaging colleagues in discussions about what matters most in the writing projects we invite our students to participate in.

*Laramie, Wyoming*

## Works Cited

Beaufort, Anne. *College Writing and Beyond: A New Framework for University Writing Instruction*. Logan: Utah State UP, 2007. Print.

Carroll, Lee Ann. *Rehearsing New Roles: How College Students Develop as Writers*. Urbana: SIUP, 2002. Print.

Engle, Randi A., et al. "How Does Expansive Framing Promote Transfer? Several Proposed Explanations and a Research Agenda for Investigating Them." *Educational Psychologist* 47.3 (2012): 215-31. Print.

Guerra, Juan C. *Language, Culture, Identity, and Citizenship in College Classrooms and Communities*. New York: Routledge, 2015. Print.

Herrington, Anne, and Marcia Curtis. *Persons in Process: Four Stories of Writing and Personal Development in College*. Urbana: NCTE, 2000. Print.

Melzer, Dan. *Assignments Across the Curriculum: A National Study of College Writing*. Logan: Utah SUP, 2014. Print.

Moje, Elizabeth Birr, et al. "Working Toward Third Space in Content Area Literacy: An Examination of Everyday Funds of Knowledge and Discourse." *Reading Research Quarterly* 39. 1 (2004): 38-70. Print.

Nowacek, Rebecca. *Agents of Integration: Understanding Transfer as a Rhetorical Act*. Urbana: SIUP, 2011. Print.

Roozen, Kevin. "'Fan Fic-ing' English Studies: A Case Study Exploring the Interplay of Vernacular Literatures and Disciplinary Engagement." *Research in the Teaching of English* 44.2 (2009): 99-132. Print.

---. "Tracing Trajectories of Practice: Repurposing in One Student's Developing Disciplinary Writing Processes." *Written Communication*, 27. 3 (2010): 318-54. Print.

Sommers, Nancy, and Laura Saltz. "The Novice as Expert: Writing the Freshman Year." *CCC* 56.1 (2004): 389-411. Print.

Sternglass, Marilyn S. *Time to Know Them: A Longitudinal Study of Writing and Learning at the College Level*. Mahwah: Lawrence Erlbaum, 1997. Print.

Tinto, Vincent. "From Retention to Persistence." *Inside Higher Ed*. 26 Sept. 2016. Web. 13 July 17. <www.insidehighered.com/views/2016/09/26/how-improve-student-persistence-and-completion-essay>.

*From Boys to Men: Rhetorics of Emergent American Masculinity*, by Leigh Ann Jones. Urbana: NCTE, 2016. 147 pp.

*Reviewed by Timothy Ballingall, Texas Christian University*

Despite much research and scholarship over the past two decades in the interdisciplinary field of masculinity studies, rhetoric and composition scholars have been slow to examine the ways in which language and symbol use invite participation in the social construction of masculinity and what possibilities open up for the teaching of writing as a result. Addressing this need, Leigh Ann Jones's *From Boys to Men: Rhetorics of Emergent American Masculinity* presents three historical case studies and a composition course design that explore the rhetorics of male youth organizations. Drawing on gender theory, nationalism studies, and constitutive rhetoric, Jones argues that mainstream male-dominated organizations in twentieth-century American society have presented boys as a metonym for Americans and crafted the transformation from boyhood to manhood in such a way that stabilizes hegemonic American manhood. Jones points to organizations whose members are in their formative years because rhetoric about the "process of moving from boy to man . . . is perhaps the most fundamental element of representations of masculinity in the United States" (2). Indeed, rhetoric about *becoming* a man can often be more revealing than rhetoric about *being* a man. Some methodological problems notwithstanding, Jones' book makes a groundbreaking contribution to the field of gendered rhetorics and extends constitutive rhetoric in an important new direction.

Building on the scholarship of Robert Connors, Luke Winslow, James V. Catano, and Lindsay Green McManus, Jones argues persuasively in chapter one for the study of masculine rhetorics, particularly through the lenses of Kenneth Burke's pentad and Maurice Charland's constitutive rhetoric. Linguistic, symbolic, and embodied acts that perform (and thus, construct) masculinity not only encourage feelings of group identification but also constitute what Michael Billig calls "banal nationalism," which he defines as "not a flag . . . being consciously waved with fervent passion; it is the flag hanging unnoticed on the public building" (qtd. in Jones 16). The masculine rhetorics used by the subjects of Jones's case studies—the Boy Scouts of America (BSA) in the early years of the twentieth century, the Sigma Chi (SC) fraternity in the 1960s and 1980s, and the U.S. army between 2001 and 2006—used identity appeals and embodied acts to hail boys and teenagers into a liminal state between boyhood and manhood. This transformative state is used "as an attempt to reconcile the ambiguities that arise in the process of constituting male identity" (5). While Jones offers minimal explanation for choosing the particular organizations and texts that are subjects of her case studies, it is clear these organizations often promoted an image of American manhood as straight, white, Christian, and middleclass, despite varying degrees of racial, religious, and economic diversity in their memberships.

Amidst vast cultural and demographic shifts in turn-of-the-century American society, Jones argues in chapter two—perhaps the most cohesive of the three case studies—that the BSA rhetorically reinforced American hegemonic masculinity in both textual and visual ways. Jones defines hegemonic masculinity, in accordance with gender theorist R. W. Connell, as a way of doing gender that privileges men and maintains their power over women and over those who embody alternative masculinities (21). Founded in 1910 by William D. Boyce, the BSA shored up white masculinity by presenting scouting as comprehensive citizenship training for developing boys. Influenced by the British boy scouts, formed two years prior, and by President Theodore Roosevelt, the BSA emphasized physical conditioning, character building, and militarism. To support her claims, Jones consults the BSA oath, the organization's motto ("Be Prepared"), scout law, scout uniforms, badge-earning rituals, and the 1908 scouting handbook, *Scouting for Boys*, which tells the origin myth of Boyce getting lost in a fog during a visit to London when a British boy scout suddenly appears, calmly helps Boyce find his destination, and then, just as suddenly, disappears. Jones highlights the ambiguities in the early years of the BSA, particularly a debate in scouting magazines about whether scouts should be taught to use firearms (52-54).

Jones then turns our attention to fraternities. Chapter three examines the rhetoric of becoming and exclusivity embodied in the SC house at Columbia University, focusing specifically on the fraternity's handbook, *The Norman Shield*. This handbook describes the importance of—but not the details of—an initiation ritual and emphasizes ideals or "god terms" such as brotherhood, tradition, merit, and democracy. Much like BSA's handbook, *The Norman Shield* tells the story of SC's origins: In 1854, six members of Miami University's Delta Kappa Epsilon broke with that fraternity over a disagreement of principles and formed SC. Because of the parallels between the forming of SC and the American Revolution, writes Jones, "Sigma Chi . . . is a scene of firmly held principles that echo the deepest-held principles of American national identity" (78). To see these principles in conflict with racial and gender equality, Jones highlights significant debates in the fraternity's history, specifically the 1960s when civil rights supporters criticized SC in the campus newspaper for being racially discriminatory in its membership, and the 1980s when a student group advocated desegregating Greek life by gender. Members of the student group argued that single-sex fraternities created what we would call today a "rape culture" and SC countered with vague ideals about tradition.

Although in many ways the chapter was richly compelling, I felt its analysis would have been stronger had Jones used the editions of *The Norman Shield* contemporaneous with the controversies in the 1960s and 1980s, rather than using a more recent edition of this text.

The final case study presented in chapter four is of the U.S. army's "Army of One" campaign, which, Jones writes, relied primarily on before-and-after images of new recruits (i.e., directionless high school graduates) and experienced soldiers, embodying American manhood, to present the army experience as transformative. Jones extensively analyzes the visual and textual rhetoric of two brochures produced by this campaign to highlight its appeal to individualism and self-actualization (90-100). While somewhat persuasive during peacetime, the "Army of One" messaging became increasingly problematic during the ramp up to the U.S. invasion of Iraq. The army attempted to mitigate the individualism of the campaign with a rewriting of the "Soldier's Creed," which Jones analyzes closely, to include references to more wartime camaraderie and the addition of four lines called the "Warrior Ethos Statement" (100-4). Ultimately, the "Army of One" campaign failed to produce strong widespread identification and, Jones suggests, Americans came to see soldiers' individuality less in terms of self-actualization and life-meaning and more in the context of nightly news reports about casualties in Iraq and Afghanistan (108-9).

In chapter five, Jones relocates the reader away from a London fog, the fraternity house, and the battlefield and into the writing classroom where she advocates writing teachers explore with students the function and appeal of organizations like the BSA, fraternities, and the US army. When exploring these issues with students, Jones writes, "the most useful pedagogical approach we can take is to engage students in an understanding of why such organizations, myths, recruiting tactics, and creeds appeal to so many of us and how they fit into a historical context" (112). The remainder of chapter five comprises an overview of a course Jones teaches titled "The Rhetoric of Emergent Masculinity in American Youth Organizations." Jones provides the theoretical lens, readings, learning goals, means of assessment, and a condensed sample syllabus of this upper-division course, and likewise suggests how the syllabus might be modified for graduate student and fyw audiences.

The book concludes by suggesting avenues for further research on masculinity, nationalism, and constitutive rhetoric. Specifically, more work should be conducted on other male youth organizations like the YMCA, the Civil Air Patrol, and so on, as well as organizations whose male memberships are aging. Such research, she argues, should answer questions such as "how do organizations like the Freemasons, the Knights of Columbus, the Veterans of Foreign Wars, and other[s] . . . negotiate members' aging as a part of masculine identity?" (123). Finally, Jones suggests that subsequent research ought to focus on organizations that target men who identify with alternative and non-hegemonic masculinities and on the ways in which women and girls respond to, and resist, male youth organization rhetorics.

As a graduate instructor who has been teaching an intermediate composition course themed around masculinity studies for a couple of years, I can appreciate the interdisciplinary approach and Trump-era timeliness of *From Boys to Men*. Engaging college students about how they are positioned and shaped by the rhetorics of masculinity can lead to productive, meaningful discussions and writing. Students can engage specifically with the rhetorics of fraternities, for example, and generally with those of the "residue of at least a century and a half of dominant white masculinity in this country . . . [which has] always asserted itself most strongly as a response to fear," as Jones said in her Studies in Writing and Rhetoric interview, recorded one week after the 2016 presidential election ("SWR Interview"). Despite Jones's emphasis on student gains—which I find to be a strength of the book—I was disappointed with the lack of discussion of student work, or a substantive explanation of how Jones has modified her syllabus (117-19) for different levels, or how it might be modified for different institutional contexts. Nevertheless, the book's limitations and strengths speak to the dual need for, and the promise of, more historical case studies of masculine rhetorics and more explorations of masculinity/ies in readings, classroom discussions, writing assignments, and pedagogical strategies.

Overall, this book demonstrates the persuasiveness and pervasiveness of rhetorics that constitute boys and young men as hegemonic men-to-be. Masculinity and national identity are often imbricated in rhetorics we and our students observe in big events, such as presidential campaigns, and banal rituals like wearing Greek letters. Jones attunes us to the rhetorical power of emergent masculinity and the need to examine it alongside our students. I primarily recommend *From Boys to Men* to any writing teacher who incorporates gender analysis into their course design, and secondarily to writing teachers using Burkean or constitutive rhetoric. Ultimately, Jones offers writing and rhetoric teachers historical context for many masculine rhetorics of identification that persist today in the lives of our students and cause for using the classroom as a space to facilitate intervention in those rhetorics.

*Fort Worth, Texas*

## Works Cited

Billig, Michael. *Banal Nationalism*. London: Sage, 1995. Print.
Catano, James V. *Ragged Dicks: Masculinity, Steel, and the Rhetoric of the Self-Made Man*. Carbondale: SIUP, 2001. Print.

Charland, Maurice. "Constitutive Rhetoric: The Case of the *Peuple Québécois.*" *Quarterly Journal of Speech* 73.2 (1987): 133-50. Print.
Connell, R. W. *Masculinities*. 2nd ed. Berkeley: U of California P, 2005. Print.
Connors, Robert J. "Teaching and Learning as a Man." *College English* 58.2 (1996): 137-57. Print.
McManus, Lindsay Green. *Performing Masculinity: Control, Manhood, and the Rhetoric of Effeminacy*. Diss. U of South Carolina, 2007. Ann Arbor: UMI. *Google Book Search*. Web. 23 Sept. 2015.
"SWR Interview with Leigh Ann Jones." Interview by Vincent Portillo. *Conference on College Composition and Communication*. National Council of Teachers of English, 17 Jan. 2017. Web. 19 July 2017.
Winslow, Luke. "Style and Struggle: The Rhetoric of Masculinity." Diss. U of Texas at Austin, 2009. U of Texas Libraries. Web. 23 Sept. 2015.

**Ambient Rhetoric: The Attunements of Rhetorical Being**, by Thomas Rickert. Pittsburgh: U Pittsburgh P, 2013. 334 pp.

*Reviewed by Mark Christopher Lane, Wayne State University*

If the intent is to "attune" its readers to the necessity of retheorizing or rethinking aspects of rhetorical theory, then Thomas Rickert's *Ambient Rhetoric: The Attunement of Rhetorical Being* is profoundly successful. If, however, Rickert intended his book to transcend the boundaries of a space in which theory simply *takes place* to a place which allows for an examination of what those theories might look like in action, then, as the author admits, much work remains to be done. For it seems that Rickert's call to action is ultimately this very (re)attunement itself: rhetorical theory's grounding in humanism, its support of the subject/object paradigm, prevents exploration of the human/world relationship as reciprocal, and as the world in which rhetorical theory exists continues to change, becoming a progressively complex ecological web of networked-weddedness, "we need conceptions of rhetoric that keep pace with these transformations" (33). In other words, his reworking of what rhetoric is requires "some action" because "rhetoric from an ambient perspective can no longer be situated solely in human subjective performance" (29). However, Rickert's action seems to imply more than just intellectual engagement with or epistemological restructuring of traditional notions of rhetoric, as he questions the ways in which an attunement to ambience would change the ways we write and compose, the concerns or interests we have as teachers, writers, and rhetoricians, while foregoing a discussion of what those changes might look like in practice. The negation of an answer to these and other questions essentially categorizes the book as a highly insightful and minutely detailed block on which to build: "Ambient rhetoric . . . is less an answer in itself than an invitation to disclose anew, to build further, and so begin to dwell" (37). Dwelling, in the sense that Martin Heidegger uses that term, is a crucial component of Rickert's thoroughly researched scholarly work that presents rhetoric as a concept with an ontological, a priori weddedness to the material world. The author seeks to convince us of our inherent enmeshment with our surroundings, claiming that who we are, how we invent—and pointedly—how we engage each other rhetorically can no longer be considered a product of human subjects acting on objects, but rather a result of ambient osmosis, a blending of place, people, and materiality: "The boundaries between brain and body, self and world, language and thought, beginning and end, are permeable" (100). Indeed, Rickert makes an almost impenetrable argument as to why rhetoric needs to be rethought from an ambient perspective and provides conclusions as to the future of what such rethinking will bear, while leaving the practical application of his theories in the hands of his readers.

Engaging with scholarly work by Julia Kristeva, Jacques Derrida, and Gregory Ulmer, Rickert begins with a reconceptualization of the Greek terms *chora* and *kairos*, seeking not to abandon their traditional interpretations, but rather to expand on them and further their complexity. Working with Plato's understanding of *chora* in the *Timaeus*, Rickert argues that the *chora* cannot be relegated to the Aristotelian theory of place, or interval—also frequently referred to as a receptacle—in which we find the genesis of invention, because it also refers to mobility, a certain kind of navigation "a movement, a going beyond boundaries and returning, that nevertheless cannot give a specific place to invention" (72). Plato's idea of a vibrant and generative universe informs Rickert's theory of ambience in that the world becomes more than just a background for human inhabitation; the world is a suffusion of everything that exists in a coadaptive space, which ultimately contributes to invention. In other words, *choric* movement relates to the navigation of thought, Platonic form, body, place, and space, toward a locus of creation. Likewise, traditional conceptions of *kairos* need to be reconsidered. *Kairos*, for Rickert, is more than just an opportune time or place for rhetorical activity; *kairos* itself is capable of *willing* invention. In perhaps his most lucid and compelling example of a culmination of the *choric* and *kairotic*, Rickert describes the rhetoric of Keyser Soze in the film *The Usual Suspects* (1995). When Soze—believed to be a patsy named Verbal—is interrogated by detective Kujan, Soze makes use of Kujan's questions and the room itself in order to weave a tale of such persuasion that it convinces the interrogator of its own validity, thus, "[demonstrating] that the environment is always situating us in arrangements that simultaneously unleash some possibilities and foreclose on others," concluding that "ambient environs generate various affordances that invent us in kairotic moments" (96). The interrogation room provides Soze with the necessary tools to complete his story, willing the story into creation in a way specific to that context, representing the rhetor's necessary *choric* navigation of a *kairotic* moment in an ambient space. The example of Soze and Kujan is perhaps the most illuminating in regard to the potentiality of a practical application of Rickert's theories in the field, a topic I will return to later.

Upon laying the foundation for his argument, the origins of which are situated in antiquity, Rickert further develops his position through a heavily Heideggerian "lattice-work" that complicates contemporary understandings of being, dwelling, and language insofar as they relate to rhetorical theory, further contributing to a view shared by Heidegger and Kenneth Burke that suggests meaning "inhere[s] in the world" (182). In what becomes a fairly even divide, the book first introduces and persuades the reader that ambience creates a coadaptive space in which meaning, ideas, and action become reciprocal, before culminating in a lengthy conclusion which argues that a simple rethinking is not complete without "taking the necessary next step of acknowledging that rhetoric's work is distributed and ecological" (221). Furthermore, "nonhuman elements and forces are always in play as part of human doing," and the "accomplishments of rhetorical practice are entwined with (re)organizations of the world" (221). All of which seems fairly straightforward, though getting there is less than simple: if we accept and embrace the idea that rhetoric should be viewed from an ambient perspective, one derived from a blending of the actors and that which is acted upon in a kind of synthetic reciprocity, then the result is one of ecological ontology as opposed to a static epistemology. Plasticity is a term Rickert often invokes, and it seems to perfectly encapsulate the call to action which he promotes. We must be adaptive in our conceptualizations of rhetorical theory, lending exigence to materiality, resulting in an ever-evolving ecological practice that has more to do with being than with knowledge.

Although for all the reasons explained, *Ambient Rhetoric: The Attunement of Rhetorical Being* is well worth the read—the innovative and insightful ideas challenge perceptions of an academic discipline—I'm still left wondering what a practical application of his theories, from a methodological, pedagogical perspective, might look like, particularly in regard to the composition classroom. Indeed, as first-year-writing programs continue to be an academic mainstay in undergraduate education, rethinking our pedagogical approach from an ambient perspective offers potential solutions for mitigating student resistance and affecting positive engagement in discussions of difference, such as race, gender, and equality. Students who consider the composition course simply a means by which they learn to write correctly are often resistant to discussions of these issues because they view the classroom as a neutral site in which they learn the mechanics of writing, not interact with difficult sociocultural issues. Pedagogy often fails to overcome this resistance due to the prescriptiveness from which it originates; much of our methodology, our pre-course planning, remains static as we move into disparate classrooms with their own unique and individual needs. In other words, it is difficult to overcome student resistance if we, as teachers, rely too heavily on prescriptive pedagogies that seek to import critical awareness of diverse, sociological issues because they do not allow for adaptation in the moment. This suggests that critical pedagogies must become adaptive, and perhaps this adaptation should stem from an ambient perspective, which would allow pedagogy to become its own kind of ecology that responds to its immediate context and promotes plasticity in the moment. From this perspective, a composition classroom is much like the interrogation room in *The Usual Suspects*: each room allows for opportunities while foreclosing on others, and if we, as teachers, create our pedagogy using only the available means, developing the content as we teach, we strengthen our ability to engage our students in the act of composing because we join with them in an act of collaborative invention.

If Keyser Soze can spin his way out of juridical indictment utilizing the nonhuman and human elements of the room in which he is situated, what might that mean, what effects might that kind of *choratic* navigation have in the *kairotic* moment of teaching? Although Rickert's work does not answer this question, future scholarship should explore the answer.

*Detroit, Michigan*

## Work Cited

*The Usual Suspects*. Directed by Bryan Singer, performances by Kevin Spacey, Gabriel Byrne, Chazz Palminteri, Stephen Baldwin, and Benecio del Toro, Polygram, 1995.

**Reclaiming Accountability: Improving Writing Programs through Accreditation and Large-Scale Assessments,** edited by Wendy Sharer, Tracy Ann Morse, Michelle F. Eble, and William P. Banks. Logan: Utah SUP, 2016. 335 pp.

*Reviewed by Maggie Collins, Saint Xavier University*

Higher education's interest in standardized assessment and big data has continuously increased since the mid- to late-twentieth century. With writing programs currently responding to national and higher learning institutions' "current desire for more comparability of results across college campuses," Wendy Sharer, Tracy Ann Morse, Michelle F. Eble, and William P. Banks assembled *Reclaiming Accountability: Improving Writing Programs through Accreditation and Large-Scale Assessments* to encourage writing scholars to take advantage of the opportunities accreditation and assessment present (25). Following the intellectual tradition of assessment scholars such as Chris Gallagher, Bob Broad et al., and Edward White, Irvin Peckham, and Norbert Elliot, this collection is successful because it fills a gap within assessment research, beginning the needed conversation about writing programs' productive and rewarding approaches to assessment and accreditation opportunities. Highlighting collaboration between accrediting entities, writing instructors, and WPAs, the collection offers an important twist on assessment narratives, inspiring change in how such work is managed and how writing programs evaluate their students.

Each of the three sections focuses on how assessment and accreditation can support writing programs and enhance writing studies scholarship. Part one contains three chapters that consider the benefits and limitations of large-scale assessment from the perspectives of the accreditors, writing instructors, and WPAs. In the first article—Cindy Moore, Peggy O'Neill, and Angela Crow's "Assessing for Learning in an Age of Comparability: Remembering the Importance of Context"—the authors argue that comparability is sought across all college campuses, which has inspired companies to capitalize on transparency by making big data programs, and that writing professionals should be involved in the process of deciding goals of their assessment and how companies collect data. Susan Miller-Cochran and Rochelle Rodrigo as well as Shirley K. Rose extend this discussion in their respective chapters, "QEP Evaluation as Opportunity: Teaching and Learning through the Accreditation Process" and "Understanding Accreditation's History and Role in Higher Education: How it Matters to College Writing Programs." They inform readers about popular assessment methods, like Quality Enhancement Plan (QEP), complicate their use, and then share how accrediting institutions have influenced higher education and why it is important to work with these entities to improve student learning.

Following this section, parts two and three include case studies that employ various methods to approach accreditation and large-scale assessment. Part two furthers the possible outcomes of assessment by providing "a toolkit of methods" for enhancing curricula and adding cost-effective programmatic support (65). Consisting of seven articles, this toolkit overviews topics including QEP reaccreditation, general studies assessment, curricular standardization, programmatic assessment at two-year colleges, accountability and expertise, writing mentors, and ePortfolios. Several writers address programmatic assessment, problematize "top-down" standardization, and involve faculty in assessment through dynamic criteria mapping. Here, the authors continue the conversation started in *Organic Writing Assessment: Dynamic Criteria Mapping in Action* (Broad, Adler-Kassner, Alford, Detweiler, Estrem, and Harrington) by narrowly examining large-scale assessments and dynamic criteria mapping while also introducing methods to readers for their localized contexts. This is shown in David Weed, Tulora Roeckers, and Melanie Burdick's "Making Peace with a 'Regrettable Necessity': Composition Instructors Negotiate Curricular Standardization," in which they assert that assessment and standardization as "'top-down' mandates are likely to be more harmful than helpful because they disregard all local needs and considerations," making assessment less reliable and valid (109). Using dynamic criteria mapping to acknowledge everyone's voices and identify themes in participant responses, their study revealed that instructors liked having a standardized curriculum.

Part two emphasizes the idea that successful assessment occurs because of faculty involvement in the process, as Malkiel Choseed's "A Tool for Program Building: Programmatic Assessment and the English Department at Onondaga Community College" argues. Using authentic programmatic assessment, Choseed discovered that instructors were concerned about how assessment could lead to programmatic change that would affect their workload and create surveillance of their teaching methods; however, he concluded by noting that all faculty "need to take control of the assessment process" so that it reflects the localized context, an important feature of assessment discussed at length in *Very Like a Whale: The Assessment of Writing Programs* (White, Norbert, and Peckham, 137).

The final part of this collection presents additional case studies focusing on faculty mandates that may result from accreditation mandates. The five chapters center around writing across the curriculum and how writing demonstrates disciplinary knowledge. Because writing (and accreditation) occurs across campus, the authors of these chapters found they needed to collaborate with faculty in other fields. For example, "'Everybody Writes': Accreditation-Based

Assessment as Professional Development at a Research Intensive University," by Linda Adler-Kassner and Lorna Gonzalez, recounts a faculty workshop that began a conversation about writing across disciplines. This exercise showed faculty what terms like *thesis* could mean to other fields, clarifying the need for all faculty to address writing in their classrooms and thereby provide students with the disciplinary knowledge required to succeed.

Disciplinary specialties also open networks to improve assessment, as Maggie Debelius argues in "A Funny Thing Happened on the Way to Assessment: Lessons from a Threshold-Based Approach." To make disciplinary knowledge visible, Debelius utilized threshold concepts to create a "flexible and organic assessment approach" (265). Her approach sought to leverage instances of top-down accreditation to analyze student learning as well as remove accountability regarding assessment from accrediting associations by "hightlight[ing] inquiry driven by scholarly expertise" through threshold concept theory (273). This approach shifts the focus from writing-to-test to writing-to-demonstrate-disciplinary-knowledge, signaling how faculty development opportunities can increase writing knowledge across the disciplines and improve its visibility among campuses.

As a result of case studies, *Reclaiming Accountability* shines through its use of detailed examples: there are multiple reports, survey examples, data points, budgets, rubrics, and workshop heuristics that help readers examine their approaches to assessment and accreditation. Readers can then adapt these examples to fit their local contexts or use them as inspiration to articulate their own needs. This information is important as little scholarship of this kind has been published. However, in some of the chapters, like those by Karen Nulton and Rebecca Ingalls as well as Jim Henry, I desired more quantitative data so that I could see to what degree student writing or faculty practices improved following the studies. This information would have helped me, as someone new to assessment, discover which methods could create data that would be useful during conversations with internal and external writing program stakeholders.

This criticism acknowledged, the book helped me recognize my role in assessment, even though I am not heavily involved in writing assessment as an adjunct instructor. The collection highlighted my importance in this process, showing that—to improve student learning—assessment must be a program-wide venture, not a practice solely for WPAs or accreditation bodies. With a strong emphasis on collaboration, *Reclaiming Accountability* fills a gap in assessment research, providing possible methods to use accreditation for institutional or programmatic revision, as well as raises new questions about what best practices will look like when working with the recent trend of comparability. *Reclaiming Accountability,* then, begins a conversation surrounding assessment that all writing scholars should be involved in.

*Chicago, Illinois*

## Works Cited

Broad, Bob, Linda Adler-Kassner, Barry Alford, Jane Detweiler, Heidi Estrem, and Susanmarie Harrington. *Organic Writing Assessment: Dynamic Criteria Mapping in Action.* Logan: Utah SUP, 2009. Print.

Gallagher, Chris. *Reclaiming Assessment: A Better Alternative to the Accountability Agenda.* Portsmouth: Heinemann, 2007. Print.

White, Edward, Norbert Elliot, and Irvin Peckham. *Very Like a Whale: The Assessment of Writing Programs.* Logan: Utah SUP, 2015. Print.

***Women, Writing, and Prison: Activists, Scholars, and Writers Speak Out,*** edited by Tobi Jacobi and Ann Folwell Stanford. Lanham: Rowman and Littlefield, 2014. 250 pp.

*Reviewed by Annie Osburn, University of Wyoming*

When we discuss the problems of materiality in the classroom, we often ask about the outside forces that impede students' lives and how those forces impact their writing. With writing workshops in women's prisons, however, the impeding force is inherently "inside." The walls of the classroom are the same walls that keep the women—the incarcerated—bound to rules designed to undermine what we traditionally ask writers to value: that is, the processes of discovering one's own voice, of recognizing and challenging cultural codes, of expressing one's self to an audience and of making one's self heard. Conversely, these values pose a threat to the control prisons exert over the bodies and minds of the incarcerated, which prisons try to undermine them at all costs. As a former criminal defense attorney, my interactions with the incarcerated did little to subvert that system of control. While I encouraged my clients to write to me and develop their stories, I had a specific agenda: I needed the facts that would work in their favor at trial or feed into a plea bargain. I did not ask them what they wanted to write. I did not ask them to challenge the system that incarcerated them. In fact, I strongly encouraged them against it. But now, as an MFA student designing curricula for prison writing workshops, I strive to understand the issues of materiality in carceral spaces that shape and limit writerly opportunities. What is the value of writing for women in prison? How can we create a public space for exploring tensions between communities and discourses in lockdown? How can we create ethical prison writing programs that foremost benefit writers? For me as a reader, Tobi Jacobi and Ann Folwell Stanford's edited collection *Women, Writing, and Prison: Activists, Scholars, and Writers Speak Out* is successful because it develops a flexible framework educators can use to answer these tough questions.

While several collections of incarcerated women's writing have been published to acclaim, including Gayle Bell Chevigny's *Doing Time*, Jeff Evans' *Undoing Time*, Wally Lamb's *Couldn't Keep It to Myself*, and Jodie Lawston and Ashley Lucas's *Razor Wire Women*, this collection focuses on teaching writing in women's prisons and jails. Jacobi, a professor of composition and literacy studies at Colorado State University, and Folwell Stanford, a professor of interdisciplinary and literary studies at DePaul University, have many years of experience teaching in traditional and not-so-traditional classrooms. As Stanford writes in the introduction, they set out to achieve three goals with this collection: to draw attention to the writing of incarcerated women; to challenge public stereotypes through the interplay of writing by incarcerated women and workshop facilitators; and finally to "interrogat[e] romantic notions of the writing teacher [. . .] as transformative agent or savior" (3).

The collection's contributors largely succeed in these aims. Essays, letters, memoirs and poems from currently and formerly incarcerated women focus on the transformative act of writing in the confines of prison, poignantly representing incarcerated writers as individuals of value. Jacobi and Folwell Stanford supplement participants' contributions with essays by program facilitators that detail different approaches to prison writing workshops, whether such programs are delivered in person or through correspondence. Most of the facilitators' essays acknowledge the divide between the white, heterosexual, middle class academics who tend to organize these workshops and the incarcerated women participating in them, who are far more likely to be of color, queer, and from working- and poverty-class backgrounds. On top of recognizing the concrete division between incarcerated and free, the facilitators who contribute to the collection universally find that acknowledging race, sexual orientation, and class divides is vital to ensuring workshops are spaces for participants to explore and make public their own voices—not the voices of authority figures running the prison or even the prison writing program.

The collection is divided into three sections: Writing and Reclaiming Self, Bridging Communities: Writing Programs and Social Practice, and Writing, Resistance, and the Material Realities of U.S. Prisons and Jails. Though there is significant interplay among these sections, it is instructive to view them as separate entities. The first focuses on the identification and reclamation of voice while incarcerated. As Stanford discusses in her introduction, a majority of incarcerated women have a history of mental illness, and at least half have suffered abuse (6). Each of these struggles can have a silencing effect on the incarcerated, but in concert, the silence such women experience is deafening. Writing allows incarcerated women to reclaim their voices and reconnect with a world outside of prison walls. Contributors Jessica Hill, Nancy Birkla, and Shelley Goldman find different connections between the words and art of their childhood to the writing that saw them through their imprisonments, revealing and then solidifying their identities as writers outside of their incarceration. The innate power of words is further established in Dionna Griffin's powerful recollection of her sentencing in "'This Ain't No Holiday Inn, Griffin': Finding Freedom on the Blank Page," where she ruminates on how the word "guilty" transformed her life. She found herself powerless both inside the beautiful Art Deco courthouse of her sentencing and in the dank stale county jail—until, that is, she could secure legal pads, pencils, and stamps to carry her writing to the outside world. Words incarcerated her, but words also set her free.

Section two shifts the focus from individual voice to the creation of space for that voice, providing frameworks for facilitators to develop and evaluate writing workshops. In "'Good Intentions Aside': The Ethics of Reciprocity in a University-Jail Women's Writing Workshop Collaboration," Sadie Reynolds, founder of the Inside Out Writing Project and formerly incarcerated herself, recommends not building a program based on the idea that the participants are in any way deficient or in need of rehabilitation or charity. Instead, she argues that a program built on solidarity between facilitators and incarcerated women will benefit all, pushing facilitators to struggle against the system and not just acquiesce inside its walls. In a different vein, educators Tom Kerr, in "Incorporeal Transformations: Audience and Women Writing in Prison," and Wendy W. Hinshaw and Kathie Klarreich, in "Writing Exchanges: Composing Across Prison and University Classrooms," detail the tensions and benefits of connecting incarcerated women with an outside audience of undergraduate and graduate students. There is a slight strain between Reynolds's essay and the latter two pieces, which highlight the benefits college students receive from participating in these programs. Reynolds would likely categorize these benefits as being of little use to the incarcerated participants and therefore a poor focus for facilitators, much as she would find distasteful the concessions that must often be made in the name of access to prison writing programs (103-104). However, student benefits may be a necessary selling point to the educational institutions involved.

While incarcerated women's voices appear throughout the facilitators' essays, oftentimes commenting on the nature of the workshop or writing exchange, for me one weakness of this section is the absence of incarcerated participants' responses to and evaluations of workshop formats and structures. The letters and thoughts on the matter in "Writing Exchanges" and "Incorporeal Transformations," no matter how faithfully executed, are all offered by facilitators alone. An extended reflection from an incarcerated woman on the workshop experience would be a valuable addition for the next edition of this collection, or future ones like it.

In the final section, contributors explore the political and social impact of writers' voices coming out of prison workshops. Incarcerated writers face immediate and potentially permanently damaging retributions for their words, yet despite risks, they continue writing. Boudicca Burning, who helped other women draft legal claims while incarcerated, uses her piece, "I am Antarctica: I Shriek, I Accuse, I Write," to juxtapose the power her words have as a jailhouse law clerk with the powerlessness she felt after being forced to lie to her family about the treatment she received in prison. Further, one of the most memorable pieces in the collection, Velmarine O. Szabo's "'You Just Threatened My Life': Struggling to Write and Remember in Prison," interweaves memoir from her childhood with a description of the retaliation she faced in prison because of her self-expression. The horrifying abuse Szabo suffered as a child is echoed in the attempts a guard makes to punish her for expressing herself through writing. In each case, the accuser distorts the truth to justify the subsequent abuse, but in neither is justification for such punishment anything but erroneous and unimaginable.

Again, three questions echo throughout the collection: what is the inherent value of writing, how can facilitators find ethical ways to support prison writing efforts, and how can those efforts engender agency for women in prison? As contributors grapple to answer these questions, they provide essential lessons for anyone interested in supporting writers in prison. While prison workshops will never transform institutional walls into writing utopias, Jacobi and Folwell Stanford's collection demonstrates that important work and incredible writing can thrive in even the most difficult spaces.

*Laramie, Wyoming*

## Works Cited

Chevigny, Gayle Bell, ed. *Doing Time: 25 Years of Prison Writing*. New York: Arcade, 1999. Print.

Evans, Jeff, ed. *Undoing Time: American Prisoners in Their Own Words*. Boston: Northeastern UP, 2001. Print.

Lamb, Wally, and the Women of the York Correctional Facility, eds. *Couldn't Keep it to Myself: Testimonies from Our Imprisoned Sisters*. New York: Regan Books, 2004. Print.

Lawston, Jodie, and Ashley Lucas, eds. *Razor Wire Women: Prisoners, Activists, Scholars, and Artists*. Albany: SUNY Press, 2011. Print.

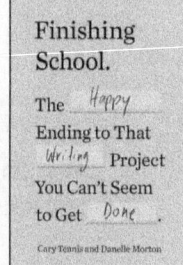

**Joe Fassler, editor**
## LIGHT THE DARK
### Writers on Creativity, Inspiration, and the Artistic Process
From forty-six renowned authors such as Stephen King, Junot Díaz, Elizabeth Gilbert, and Neil Gaiman, a stunning guide to finding creative inspiration and how it can illuminate your life, your work, and your art.
Penguin • 352 pp. • 978-0-14-313084-0 • $17.00

**Pamela Des Barres**
## LET IT BLEED
### How to Write a Rockin' Memoir
Des Barres guides women through the art of memoir writing by developing writing exercises to better understand themselves. Just as intimate as her in-person workshops, this book includes some of her own stories, as well as those of women she's taught.
TarcherPerigee • 304 pp. • 978-0-399-17420-9 • $18.00

**Cary Tennis and Danelle Morton**
## FINISHING SCHOOL
### The Happy Ending to That Writing Project You Can't Seem to Get Done
Tennis and Morton help writers overcome emotional roadblocks and share the proven techniques of their writing program, which eschews group critiquing sessions, breaks down daunting tasks into manageable pieces, and rediscovers the original passion behind the work.
TarcherPerigee • 272 pp. • 978-0-399-18470-3 • $16.00

**Alice Mattison**
## THE KITE AND THE STRING
### How to Write with Spontaneity and Control—and Live to Tell the Tale
A targeted and insightful guide to writing fiction and memoir without falling into common traps. Also includes tips for navigating the writing life: protecting writing time, preserving solitude, finding trusted readers, and setting the right goals for publication.
Penguin • 256 pp. • 978-0-14-311163-4 • $16.00

**A. O. Scott**
## BETTER LIVING THROUGH CRITICISM
### How to Think About Art, Pleasure, Beauty, and Truth
Drawing on his own work as well as the long tradition of criticism from Aristotle to Susan Sontag, the *New York Times* film critic shows how critical thinking informs artistic creation, civil action, and interpersonal life.
Penguin • 304 pp. • 978-0-14-310997-6 • $17.00

**David Orr**
## YOU, TOO, COULD WRITE A POEM
An anthology of reviews and essays from the past fifteen years by the *New York Times* poetry columnist. From Louise Glück to public figures, Orr brings an impeccable ear and a wealth of technical knowledge to elucidate what makes a poem or poet great—or not.
Penguin • 400 pp. • 978-0-14-312819-9 • $18.00

**PENGUIN PUBLISHING GROUP**     *www.penguin.com/academic*

# Contributors

**Cydney Alexis** is assistant professor of English and director of the writing center at Kansas State University. Her research focuses on the material culture of writing, including goods and practices that support writers in both their writing identity development and in their trade.

**Steven Alvarez** is assistant professor of English and coordinator of first-year writing at St. John's University. He specializes in literacy studies and bilingual education with a focus on Mexican immigrant communities. He is the author of *Community Literacies en Confianza: Learning From Bilingual After-School Programs* (NCTE, 2017) and the forthcoming *Brokering Tareas: Mexican Immigrant Families Translanguaging Homework Literacies* (SUNY).

**Damián Baca** is associate professor and director of the Rhetoric, Composition, and the Teaching of English graduate program at the University of Arizona. He is author of *Mestiz@ Scripts, Digital Migrations, and the Territories of Writing* and lead editor of *Rhetorics of the Americas: 3114BCE to 2012CE*, works that examine Latinx and Indigenous responses to Eurocentricism.

**Timothy Ballingall** is a PhD candidate in rhetoric and composition at Texas Christian University. He has taught undergraduate courses in writing, rhetoric, and gender studies. His research interests include women's and gendered rhetorics, rhetorical history, and the undergraduate writing major. His dissertation explores women's advice columns in the interwar years.

**Elías Domínguez Barajas** is an associate professor of English and the director of the Program in Rhetoric and Composition at the University of Arkansas. He teaches courses in composition pedagogy, ethnography of communication, discourse studies, and Latino/a literature. His research explores the relationships between discursive, cultural, and educational factors impacting language-minority populations.

**Janine Butler** received her PhD in rhetoric, writing, and professional communication from East Carolina University in 2017. She is assistant professor at Rochester Institute of Technology. Her research focuses on embodiment, multimodality, accessibility, and Deaf Studies and disability studies.

**Chen Chen** is a doctoral candidate in communication, rhetoric, and digital media at North Carolina State University. Her dissertation investigates how informal communication practices at the annual convention of CCCC and on the WPA listserv shape the disciplinary networks of rhetoric and composition.

**Everardo J. Cuevas** is a PhD student working, learning and dreaming on Nkwejong in the department of Writing, Rhetoric and American Cultures at Michigan State University. A qpoc community organizer, he is interested in cultural rhetorics methodologies and practices of community building.

**Maggie Collins** is adjunct instructor at Saint Xavier University, and she earned her MA in writing, rhetoric, and discourse at DePaul University. Her research interests are assessment and contingent labor through political economic lenses.

**Bethany Davila** is assistant professor in the rhetoric and writing program at the University of New Mexico and the co-coordinator of the stretch and studio composition program. Her research focuses on perceptions of written standardness, patterned connections between writing and identity, and rhetorical and discursive constructions of nonstandardness.

**Cristyn L. Elder** is assistant professor of rhetoric and composition at the University of New Mexico. She co-founded WPA-GO and *Present Tense: A Journal of Rhetoric in Society* and serves on the Executive Board of the Council of Writing Program Administrators. She researches WPA and WAC practices that support marginalized students.

**Aydé Enríquez-Loya** earned her PhD from Texas A&M University in 2012. She is assistant professor of rhetoric and composition, with a specialization in Chicanx/Latinx Rhetoric, in the English department at California State University, Chico. She teaches courses in technical writing, rhetorical and decolonial theory, composition, and Chicanx literature and rhetoric.

**Rick Fisher** is a doctoral student in literacy education and an assistant lecturer in the Department of English at the University of Wyoming. He teaches first-year composition and technical writing courses, and has coordinated the university's writing center and communication across the curriculum courses. His research explores the (re)creation of disciplinary literacies.

**Christine Garcia** is assistant professor of rhetoric and composition in the English Department at Eastern Connecticut State University. Her work focuses on Chicanx and Latinx rhetorics and writing across communities pedagogy and praxis.

**Nicole Gonzales Howell** was selected as one of the Gerardo Marin Dissertation Fellows at the University of San Francisco in 2014. She received her PhD in composition and cultural rhetoric from Syracuse University in 2016 and is currently assistant professor at the University of San Francisco.

**Kristine Johnson** is assistant professor of English at Calvin College, where she directs the Written Rhetoric Program. She teaches courses in writing, linguistics, and composition pedagogy, and she enjoys collaborating with undergraduate researchers. Her work has been published in several edited collections and journals, including *College Composition and Communication* and *Writing Program Administration*.

**Carrie Byars Kilfoil** is assistant professor of English at the University of Indianapolis, where she teaches composition and linguistics. Her work on language diversity and composition teacher training has appeared in *Rhetoric Review* and the edited collection *Integrating Content and Language in Higher Education: From Theory to Practice*.

**Kristin E. Kondrlik** is assistant professor of English at West Chester University of Pennsylvania. Her research examines the intersections of medical writing and ethos in long nineteenth-century print culture. She has published articles in *Poroi: Project on the Rhetoric of Inquiry* and the *College English Association Forum*.

**Mark Christopher Lane** is a PhD candidate in the English program at Wayne State University. His interests within the field of rhetoric and composition include multimodal strategies and composition pedagogy, material or embodied rhetoric, and affect theory as a means by which to view student reactions to the academic environment.

**Kendall Leon** is assistant professor of rhetoric and composition, with a specialization in Chicanx/Latinx/@ Rhetoric, in the English department at California State University, Chico. She teaches courses on rhetorical theory, professional writing, literacy studies, and composition.

**Michelle Lyons-McFarland** received her PhD in English literature from Case Western Reserve University in 2017. Her dissertation, "Literary Objects in Eighteenth-Century British Literature," focuses on how objects in literature transfer cultural understanding from authors to readers. Her research interests include eighteenth-century British literature, game-based pedagogy, and material culture.

**Cruz Medina** is assistant professor of rhetoric and composition at Santa Clara University, where he is a Bannan Institute Scholar on Racial and Ethnic Justice. This July, he was elected co-chair of the NCTE/CCCC Latinx Caucus and awarded the M. Ruth Marino Chair from the Bread Loaf School of English program.

**Sara Newman** is a professor of English at Kent State University. Her research addresses issues in medical and disability rhetoric, and, most recently, autism and the writing process. Publications include *Aristotle and Style*, *Writing Disability: A Critical History*, and articles in journals such as *Rhetorica* and *The Journal of Business and Technical Communication*.

**Annie Osburn** is an MFA candidate in fiction at the University of Wyoming and a podcast producer with Wyoming Public Media. She has worked as a lawyer, wilderness guide, housekeeper, and nanny.

**J. Paul Padilla** is a doctoral student in the Rhetoric, Composition, and the Teaching of English program at the University of Arizona. Mr. Padilla earned a Juris Doctor degree from the University of Wisconsin Law School. His creative writing has been published by National Public Radio and *Reed Magazine*, among other venues.

**Eric Rodriguez**, from Orange County, California, is currently a PhD student at Michigan State University in the Department of Writing, Rhetoric, and American Culture. He is interested in Chicanx rhetoric, community-based knowledge, and the classroom as a site of direct action.

**Iris Ruiz** is a lecturer with continuing appointment at University of California, Merced. She is also a Chicanx Studies Lecturer at California State University, Stanislaus. She serves as co-chair for the NCTE/CCCC. She has published a monograph titled *Reclaiming Composition for Chicano/as and other Ethnic Minorities: A Critical History and Pedagogy* (2016), and is co-editor and author of *Decolonizing Rhetoric and Composition Studies: New Latinx Keywords for Theory and Pedagogy* (2016).

**Carol Severino**, professor of rhetoric at the University of Iowa, directs the writing center and the Writing Fellows Program and teaches the tutor education courses associated with each. She also teaches travel writing, the focus of her creative writing, and second language research, the focus of her scholarship.

**Jessica E. Slentz** is assistant professor of writing at Ithaca College. Her work examines digital rhetoric and embodied experience in hybrid spaces of virtual and physical activity, from museums to writing classrooms. She has previously published in *Enculturation: A Journal of Rhetoric, Writing, and Culture* and *Community Literacy Journal*.

**Elizabeth Tomlinson** is associate teaching professor in the Department of Marketing at West Virginia University. She teaches business communication courses, and serves as a faculty associate for the Teaching and Learning Commons. Her current research interests include digital audiences, business communication, and writing processes of autistic writers.

**Michelle Tremmel**, PhD, is senior lecturer in the Department of English at Iowa State University. She teaches first-year composition and writing methods for pre-service English teachers, and mentors teaching assistants. Her publications include articles in the *Journal of Teaching Writing* and *Teaching English in the Two-Year College*.

# HELP STUDENTS CITE ANY SOURCE EASILY.

146 pp.
Paper ISBN: 978-1-60329-262-7
List price: $15.00

LARGE-PRINT EDITION
146 pp.
Paper ISBN: 978-1-60329-263-4
List price: $20.00

*Also available in e-book formats.*

"This is the most succinct and sensible revision to MLA documentation style in my long career."
—Andrea A. Lunsford, Stanford University

## Teach Students How to Master MLA Style

*MLA Handbook*, 8th ed.

Shorter and redesigned for writers at all levels, this groundbreaking new edition of the *MLA Handbook* recommends one universal set of guidelines, which writers can apply to any type of source.

The new *MLA Handbook* contains

- Visual aids
- Lots of examples
- Expert tips
- Classroom tools

## Discover Free Teaching Resources Online

style.mla.org

The only authorized Web site on MLA style, the new *MLA Style Center* is the free online companion to the *MLA Handbook*. No registration or site license is required.

- Guidelines on formatting research papers
- Ask the MLA
- Sample research papers
- Writing tips
- Lesson plans

**Modern Language Association** **MLA**

style.mla.org • www.mla.org

# JOIN THE MODERN LANGUAGE ASSOCIATION AND

## CONNECT
with colleagues

## LEARN
from leading thinkers

## GROW
your career

photograph courtesy of Jared Tennant Photography

Are you looking for an easy way to stay current with trends in the field, get professional development opportunities, and make new connections?

The Modern Language Association is the largest group of scholars in the humanities. The MLA is *your* community.

Join the MLA, and you'll join a unique group of thinkers who will welcome and inspire you.

Plus you'll get a wide array of exclusive member benefits, including

- member discounts on MLA Annual Convention registration
- early access to convention registration
- a free subscription to *PMLA*
- a free copy of the *MLA Handbook*, on request
- 30% off discount on all MLA titles
- and much more!

## JOIN NOW AND GET 20% OFF!

Use promo code **MLA20NOW**, and you'll receive 20% off the regular membership rates! This promo code is available only to new members through 31 December 2017.

## JOIN US IN NEW YORK CITY!

The 2018 MLA Annual Convention takes place in New York City from 4 to 7 January 2018. Become a member now and join us in NYC at the lowest possible rates!

## IT'S EASY TO JOIN!

- www.mla.org
- membership@mla.org
- 646 576-5151

@mlanews  @mlaconvention

# PARLOR PRESS
## EQUIPMENT FOR LIVING

## New, in Living Color!

*Type Matters: The Rhetoricity of Letterforms* edited by Christopher Scott Wyatt and Dànielle Nicole DeVoss

*Rhetoric and Experience Architecture* edited by Liza Potts and Michael J. Salvo

## New Releases

*The Framework for Success in Postsecondary Writing: Scholarship and Applications* edited by Nicholas N. Behm, Sherry Rankins-Robertson, and Duane Roen

*Cross-Border Networks in Writing Studies* edited by Derek Mueller, Andrea Williams, Louise Wetherbee Phelps, and Jennifer Clary-Lemon

*Labored: The State(ment) and Future of Work in Composition* edited by Randall McClure, Dayna V. Goldstein, and Michael A. Pemberton

*A Critical Look at Institutional Mission: A Guide for Writing Program Administrators* edited by Joseph Janangelo

## Congratulations to These Recent Award Winners!

*Antiracist Writing Assessment Ecologies: Teaching and Assessing Writing for a Socially Just Future* by Asao Inoue, **Best Book Award, CCCC, Best Book, Council of Writing Program Administrators (2017)**

*The WPA Outcomes Statement—A Decade Later*
 Edited by Nicholas N. Behm, Gregory R. Glau, Deborah H. Holdstein, Duane Roen, and Edward M. White, **Best Book Award, Council of Writing Program Adminstrators (July, 2015)**

www.parlorpress.com

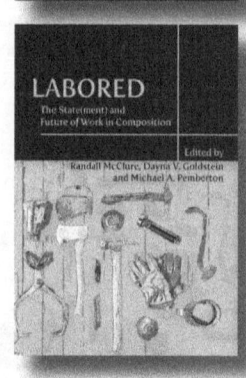

www.ingramcontent.com/pod-product-compliance
Lightning Source LLC
Chambersburg PA
CBHW031315160426
43196CB00007B/539